DATE DUE

#47-0108 Peel Off Pressure Sensitive

William E. Studwell

The Americana Song Reader

*Pre-publication
REVIEWS,
COMMENTARIES,
EVALUATIONS . . .*

" **T**he Americana Song Reader is a delightful addition to any library. This series of essays will entertain you while providing you with background information on everything from 'Pop Goes the Weasel' to 'The Anvil Chorus' from Verdi's *Il Trovatore*. Each informative essay is presented with a grain of humor, tempting us to read straight through this reference book. A librarian's delight!"

Linda Hartig, PhD
*Music Librarian,
University of Wisconsin*

" **T**he Americana Song Reader is, as are all of William Studwell's books, a joy to read and very informative. The stories behind so many well-known tunes will be a delight to both the well-trained musician or music lover and to the person who remembers a simple song from their childhood. The book is filled with songs to jog the memory and is a wonderful starting point if the reader wants to do further research on the subject. It is also peppered with Studwell's unique sense of humor, and having known him for a while now, this book is very much like having a conversation with him. This is a book you will refer to often."

Mark Baldin
*Musician, Radio Host,
WLKB Radio, Indiana*

"The breadth of William Studwell's *The Americana Song Reader* is truly remarkable. There are dancing and marching songs, rural and western songs, uplifting, lively tunes, and those that elicit a more introspective mood or even bring tears. There are children's songs, circus songs, drinking songs, and college songs. But what ties all of them together is the impact all have had on American daily life. These are the words and tunes with which Americans are generally familiar. They permeate our life together as a nation. Appearing in everything from sporting events to children's cartoons, these are the songs that we recognize, hum along with, and tap our feet to.

As readily identifiable as most of these pieces are to our ears, we often have no idea of who wrote them or when they first appeared. Studwell takes care of that. Composer and publication facts are part of every entry. The work is, after all, reference in character. But this book reads like few other reference works. Studwell delivers the basic information in a style that is both clever and entertaining. This is one reference book you won't want to put down."

Lawrence R. Rast, Jr., MDiv
Assistant Professor of Historical Theology, Concordia Theological Seminary, Ft. Wayne, Indiana

"In his dual role of educator and raconteur, William Studwell has approached the songs of our lives with a deft and spritely blend of scholarship and avuncular commentary, research, and wit.

In Bill Studwell's sure hands, *The Americana Song Reader* becomes a geneology of songs, tracing the roots of our most beloved and memorable tunes to their far-off original sources, often–just as in tracing a family tree–coming up with remarkable connections: such as the one between Milton Berle, the Lone Ranger, and Franz Liszt, or the one between the Viennese Waltz, Emperor Maximilian of Mexico, and modern American circuses, or the one linking Johannes Brahms, Rudy Vallee, and the University of Maine's football fight song (as well as the Gershwin brothers' contribution to UCLA's gridiron gladiators).

The Americana Song Reader is lively, informative, and often delightfully surprising."

Leo N. Miletich
Author of Broadways
Award-Winning Musicals
and Dan Stuart's Fistic Carnival

"William Studwell's new book, *The Americana Song Reader*, fills a perhaps surprisingly empty niche in the literature. Earlier similar collections such as those of Browne and Krythe, though broader in treatment, are narrower in focus and selection. Ewen's *American Popular Songs* includes far more entries, but also provides far briefer treatments. Indexes such as those of Stecheson and the Song Dex series of course provide virtually no historical information at all. The closest in nature to the present book is perhaps Fuld's *World Famous Music*, but it is not limited to songs of American connection and is more concerned in general with bibliographic issues rather than antiquarian ones. Studwell's book provides a pleasing cross between the reference source and the layman's guide. Both laymen and musicians should find it simply an 'interesting read' to dip into at random or read straight through, while reference librarians will welcome its usefulness for those multifarious questions that crop up and for which there has previously been no handy and reliable guide. In all, Studwell has provided a book that will serve the pleasure of the reader and the use of the librarian."

Sion M. Honea, PhD
Special Collections Librarian,
Sibley Music Library,
Rochester, New York

"William Studwell has written another in his series of excellent song readers. The over 130 pieces of music include excerpts from longer works as well as songs. All are a familiar part of the American popular culture landscape.

Mr. Studwell's earlier song readers have covered quite a bit of ground (popular songs, national and religious songs, Christmas carols, and rock and roll songs). This volume includes those songs not covered in previous volumes. Together these five volumes present a panoramic view of popular American music (not forgetting music borrowed from other countries).

Some of the musical pieces are familiar tunes from the classics: 'The Ride of the Valkyries,' 'The Sorcerer's Apprentice,' 'Barcarolle' (Offenbach), and the 'Toreador

More pre-publication
REVIEWS, COMMENTARIES, EVALUATIONS . . .

Song.' All are familiar to most Americans from their use in cartoons, television, film, or other popular media. Gounod's 'Funeral March of a Marionette,' for example, served as the distinctive theme of Alfred Hitchcock's television show.

Naturally, American music is not neglected either, and interesting sidelights on many familiar songs come to light. The 'Hootchy Kootchy Dance' was penned by Sol Bloom, who would later become a U.S. Congressman. I had long known the melody for the well-known state song 'Beautiful Ohio' had been composed by Mary Earl. Mr. Studwell points out that Mary Earl is actually the pseudonym of Robert A. King.

Other American classic songs contained in this reader include 'Jim Crack Corn,' 'Jesse James,' 'Home on the Range,' and 'Clementine.' Any lover of American popular songs will find much to delight.

This book displays Mr. Studwell's scholarship, love of music, and his fine sense of humor. This work is recommended for anyone (and any library) with an interest in American popular music or culture. Mr. Studwell's five volumes of song readers are essential sources for information on the most popular music in America."

Bruce R. Schueneman, MLS, MS

*Head of Collection Development,
Texas A&M University, Kingsville*

The Harrington Park Press
An Imprint of The Haworth Press, Inc.

The Americana Song Reader

HAWORTH Popular Culture
Frank W. Hoffmann, PhD and B. Lee Cooper, PhD
Senior Editors

New, Recent, and Forthcoming Titles:

Arts & Entertainment Fads by Frank W. Hoffmann and William G. Bailey

Sports & Recreation Fads by Frank W. Hoffmann and William G. Bailey

Mind & Society Fads by Frank W. Hoffmann and William G. Bailey

Fashion & Merchandising Fads by Frank W. Hoffmann and William G. Bailey

Chocolate Fads, Folklore, and Fantasies: 1000+ Chunks of Chocolate Information by Linda K. Fuller

The Popular Song Reader: A Sampler of Well-Known Twentieth Century Songs by William Studwell

Great Awakenings: Popular Religion and Popular Culture by Marshall W. Fishwick

The Christmas Carol Reader by William Studwell

Media-Mediated Relationships: Straight and Gay, Mainstream and Alternative Perspectives by Linda K. Fuller

The National and Religious Song Reader: Patriotic, Traditional, and Sacred Songs from Around the World by William E. Studwell

Rock Music in American Popular Culture: Rock 'n' Roll Resources by B. Lee Cooper and Wayne S. Haney

Rock Music in American Popular Culture II: More Rock 'n' Roll Resources by B. Lee Cooper and Wayne S. Haney

The Americana Song Reader by William E. Studwell

Images of Elvis Presley in American Culture, 1977-1997: The Mystery Terrain by George Plasketes

The Americana
Song Reader

William E. Studwell

Harrington Park Press
An Imprint of The Haworth Press, Inc.
New York • London

782.42
St-94a

Published by

Harrington Park Press, an imprint of The Haworth Press, Inc., 10 Alice Street, Binghamton, NY 13904-1580

Library of Congress Cataloging-in-Publication Data

Studwell, William E. (William Emmett), 1936–
   The Americana song reader / William E. Studwell.
      p.   cm.
   Includes index.
   ISBN 1-56023-899-2 (pbk. : alk. paper)
   1. Songs–United States–History and criticism. I. Title.
ML3551.S78   1997
782.42′0973–dc20

                                                    96-41539
                                                    CIP

CONTENTS

SONGS FOR SPECIAL PERSONS AND OCCASIONS

ABOUT THE AUTHOR

William E. Studwell, MA, MSLS, is Professor and Principal Cataloger at the University Libraries of Northern Illinois University in DeKalb. The author of *The Christmas Carol Reader*, Mr. Studwell is the author of eight other books on music, including reference books on popular songs, state songs, ballet, and opera. He has also written three books on cataloging and about 280 articles in library science and music. A nationally known expert on carols, college fight songs, and Library of Congress subject headings, he has made almost 260 radio, television, and print appearances in national, regional, and local media. Mr. Studwell is the editor of *Music Reference Services Quarterly.*

Introduction

Since its inception as colonies of Europe almost four centuries ago, the United States has relied on the creativity and hard work of both immigrants and persons born in the new land. The political system, economic system, and culture of the United States have been built with a mix of native ingenuity and the new ideas and practices of those arriving from abroad. This was true when the first Virginia colonists came ashore around the beginning of the seventeenth century, and is still true as we approach the twenty-first century and a new millennium.

The music of the United States, like the rest of American culture, is a combination of songs and other works from outside the country, Europe and various other places, and songs and other works written within the borders of the country, often influenced by foreign artistry or modes such as those from Asia or Africa. Whether the music comes from New York City, Chicago, New Orleans, Hollywood, some remote rural area of the South or West, or from Vienna, Paris, or Latin America, all music having some sort of impact on the lives of everyday Americans is truly part of Americana. No matter what the cultural source, or the ways the music has become known to the general populace of the United States (via classical concerts, popular songs, films, animated cartoons, radio, television, the theater, churches, clubs, social gatherings, etc.), such music is a sizable element of American life. Even if an individual knows nothing about the work and its composer, or even if the work's title is totally unknown, such music often remains strong in the consciousness of Americans. One does not need to have specific knowledge to enjoy and be emotionally and intellectually affected by the musical gems of our culture.

Gathered in this volume are over 130 essays about various pieces of music, mostly songs and excerpts from longer works, which have in a variety of ways enhanced and enlivened the everyday and special occasion existence of Americans. The essays not only give basic historical data on the work, but also often refer to related or affiliated works and usually touch upon the cultural context of its creation and popular usage in the United States. All of the essays are presented in a lively, offbeat, and, it is hoped, entertaining manner.

The essays are divided into nine functional sections: Dancing Songs; Marching Songs; Rural and Western Songs; Songs That Excite or Amuse (Lively, Uplifting, Dramatic); Songs That Soothe or Bring Tears (Graceful, Sentimental, Romantic); Children's Songs; Circus Songs; Drinking Songs; and College Songs. For the sake of simplicity, all works described have been loosely labeled "songs," though many of them are excerpts from longer works or even longer works in their entirety that are treated in popular culture in an informal manner. Among the nonsongs are: "An American in Paris," Beethoven's Fifth Symphony, 1812 Overture, *From the New World* Symphony, "Night on Bald Mountain," Rachmaninov's Piano Concerto No. 2, *Romeo and Juliet* by Tchaikovsky, and *Peter and the Wolf.* It is granted that the works represented here are an odd and heterogeneous mixture. But so is the United States and its culture. The key to all the works is that they are all regarded individually as small pieces of the American cultural puzzle and collectively as a large segment of the music of the country. To exclude some of the works covered because technically they do not qualify as a song or excerpt would do a disservice to the music of America. Similarly, to corrupt the title to literally reflect its content would be silly.

Since it would be impossible to write in any detail about the many songs or other musical works that noticeably have affected American popular culture and put it all in one manageable volume, five other volumes cover other aspects of the topic. *The Popular Song Reader* covers popular songs of the twentieth century, emphasizing older songs; *The Christmas Carol Reader* covers songs of that holiday period; *The National and Religious Song Reader* covers American and foreign national, patriotic, and religious songs; the anticipated *The Classic Rock and Roll Reader* will cover rock music of the 1950s, 1960s, and 1970s; and a planned volume, *The Big Band Reader,* will cover the swing era and the big bands, and to some extent, jazz. Both of these two future volumes will give more attention to the massive contributions of African-American musicians than has been done in other volumes.

The songs and other pieces of music that do not easily fall in the above five volumes, or fit better in the vague and broad category of Americana, are found in the present volume. Read, be informed, hum or tap your toes, and most of all, enjoy your musical voyage through American history.

SONGS OF CERTAIN STYLES
AND MOODS

After the Ball

If you see the claim "the world's greatest song writer," you would expect to see it attached to a certain name, for example, Irving Berlin, George Gershwin, Stephen Foster, Franz Schubert, or Paul McCartney, all of whom had outstanding achievements in at least one area of songwriting. But when you discover that a copyright record for a musician named Charles K. Harris included the description "the world's greatest song writer," the reaction has to be something like "Who is this overconfident person?"

Although Harris (1865-1930) was definitely not a failure at songwriting, he certainly had little if any justification for his claim. Born in Poughkeepsie, New York, Harris was a music publisher, president of the prestigious ASCAP (The American Society of Composers, Authors, and Publishers), and a popular composer of consequence. His most noted accomplishment was the creation of the ballad "After the Ball." Reportedly created for a minstrel show, the piece became world famous after it appeared in the 1892 musical *A Trip to Chinatown*. A fine, graceful waltz, "After the Ball" sold several million copies of sheet music, a feat not accomplished by any previous song.

There is no doubt that Harris's well-crafted "After the Ball" was a tremendous hit in the "gay nineties," perhaps aided by the innuendos about what may have occurred after the exciting and glamorous ball was through. On the other hand, "After the Ball" is seldom heard a century later, although it was inserted in the 1990s revival of

Show Boat, and no other song by Harris is even remotely well known today. Among his other compositions were: "Always in the Way," "Break the News to Mother," "Hello, Central, Give Me Heaven," "I've a Longing in My Heart for You, Louise," "'Mid the Green Fields of Virginia," "There'll Come a Time," and "Would You Care?" In Harris's case, there has come a time when few care or know about him and his single sensational song.

The Band Played On

When the first printing of a piece of music contains clear statements of authorship, that normally settles the matter. But such is not always true. The initial publication of "The Band Played On" in New York City in 1895 credited John F. Palmer, a New York actor, with the music and Charles B. Ward (1865-1917), an actor, composer, and publisher, with the lyrics.

Subsequently, however, there have been claims that Palmer wrote all of the lyrics and almost all of the melody, and, in contrast, Ward, who owned the company that published the song, was the composer of the melody. These differences may have arisen out of a personal feud between the apparent collaborators. While the feud played on, though, the song became one of America's more beloved pieces.

The Casey who waltzed "with the strawberry blonde" apparently had won the heart of his dancing partner. The other famous character in American culture with just the name Casey, on the other hand, managed only to strike out. But possibly the dancing Casey did not fare so well either. As one parody version, which starts with the vulgar lines, "Casey was hit with a bucket of s—," tells us, "He was so loaded he nearly exploded, while everyone watched with alarm." Following up on the parody lyrics, perhaps Casey got so drunk that after the band finally ended its gig, the blonde became angry, left with somebody else, and married the other guy.

After that romantic disappointment–as our highly speculative scenario wanders even further–Casey decided to join the U.S. Armed Forces and reportedly was part of another band, Theodore Roosevelt's Rough Riders, as they charged up San Juan Hill in 1898. If this was so, he had the opportunity to hear the playing of "(There'll Be) a Hot Time in the Old Town Tonight" during the spirited military charge.

That 1896 composition by lyricist Joseph Hayden and composer Theodore A. Metz (1848-1936), written for the theatrical production

Me and Bessie, was also a piece for dancing. But the wild and belligerent sounds of "Hot Time," in contrast to the smooth and graceful strains of "The Band Played On," would have been closer to the mood of poor rejected Casey whether he was a Rough Rider or just had a rough time after the big dance.

Blue Danube

The name Strauss seems to be almost synonymous with the art of music. There were a batch of talented nineteenth and twentieth century composers with that last name or a close variant. First came Johann Strauss the elder, then his three sons Johann the younger, Josef, and Edward. In varying degrees, they were all skilled creators of Viennese-style music. Next came Richard Strauss, who was not related to the others, but who was a famous German composer of operas and other classical works. Finally, there was Oscar Straus (one "s"), a Viennese musician whose works were in the same grand tradition as the four Strausses previously mentioned.

The most famous Strauss, of course, was Johann the younger (1825-1899), the waltz king. The most famous of his waltzes was "Blue Danube." Published in 1867 under the title, "On der Schönen, blauen Donau," this gorgeous slow waltz, which describes the legendary river flowing past Vienna, the capital of polished and graceful music, is the epitome of its three-quarter time genre. Without doubt, it is the most renowned waltz ever written.

American use of "Blue Danube" over the past century or so has been practically endless. One of its most striking adaptations was for an animated cartoon showing a group of swans deliberately and elegantly making their way along the Danube to the succulent rhythms of Strauss's masterpiece.

In spite of his undisputed coronation as the king of waltz makers, not everyone has looked upon Strauss as a great composer. Some persons with a distinct streak of snobbery have regarded Strauss as being affiliated with a "less than serious" art form. Yet the celebrated composer Johannes Brahms, one of the "three B's" (Bach, Beethoven, and Brahms) of "serious" German music, is reported to have lamented that "Blue Danube" was "unfortunately not by Brahms."

"Can Can" by Offenbach

Artistic descriptions of Hell usually have not depicted the under-world as a fun place. For example, Peter Ilich Tchaikovsky's musical picture of Hell in his 1877 symphonic fantasy "Francesca da Rimini" expresses dreariness and tragedy along with dark, stormy winds. Therefore, those of us who have been told to go to Hades have wisely ignored the command.

One blatant exception to the typical portrayal of the devil's domain is Jacques Offenbach's "Can Can," or galop, from his 1858 operetta *Orphée aux Enfers* (*Orpheus in the Underworld*). Bold, vivacious, vigorous, and just plain wild, the "Can Can" dance openly and unabashedly suggests that Hell can be a lively and pleasurable spot. Of course, the scene is obviously intended to be satirical, especially when you note that the piece immediately preceding it was a highly contrasting gentle, peaceful minuet.

The "Can Can" is probably the best-known piece by Offenbach (1819-1880), the highly successful Parisian theatrical composer who has left us with many good melodies, including the dynamic one used for "The Marines' Hymn." The incredibly bouncy and deliciously wicked rhythms of "Can Can" have been borrowed for a wide variety of purposes, all nonserious. The French composer Camille Saint-Saëns, in a clear tongue-in-cheek mood, slowed "Can Can" down so that tortoises could dance to it in his 1886 amusement, "Carnival of Animals." The celebrated creator of Broadway musicals, Cole Porter, borrowed the title for his 1953 show, *Can-Can* (which had a rambunctious title number in the true spirit of Offenbach's classic). Also, comedy scenes in movies and television have been funnier by the background presence of the "Can Can," dancing cartoon pigs have strutted to its compelling tempo, and it has become the stereotype music for "naughty" stage dancing by an ensemble of attractive young women. Because of its style and usage, it probably will never be performed during a religious service. But then, "A Mighty Fortress Is Our God" and "Rock of Ages" are probably not standards in bars and nightclubs either.

Dance of the Hours

One of the most popular pieces of serious music at pops concerts in the United States is the lively and melodic "Dance of the Hours." It is also a favorite in American popular culture, appearing in animated cartoons, including the masterful 1940 Walt Disney full-length film, *Fantasia* (where hippopotamuses danced to its strains), nonanimated movies, television advertisements, radio programs, and theatrical productions. Its slower opening section was even borrowed for a 1963 novelty song, "Hello Muddah, Hello Fadduh," by Allen Sherman and Lou Busch. Among the more informal or unplanned occasions on which this author has heard the music are athletic events, group dancing, and a simulated sword fight by young men.

This widespread appeal of "Dance of the Hours" is quite understandable. It is an active and amiable concoction of motion and mirth, with a decided degree of playful punch. By far the most famous creation of Italian composer Amilcare Ponchielli (1834-1886), "Dance" is a ballet sequence from the 1876 opera *La Gioconda*. The title of the production literally means "joyful girl," and the work has nothing to do with Leonardo da Vinci's famous painting, Mona Lisa, which is sometimes referred to as La Gioconda. Da Vinci's great masterwork is a portrait of a female with a puzzling little smile, perhaps, if you believe the theory of one researcher, a reflection of the artist's sense of humor. According to the theory, the Mona Lisa is actually a modified mirror image of the artist himself.

Ponchielli must have had a good sense of humor, for no career grouch could have conceived a joyful and vivacious minimasterwork like "Dance of the Hours."

Dance of the Sugar Plum Fairy

The term sugar plum, used to describe sweet sugary goodies on special occasions such as Christmas, was commonly used in the nineteenth century, but less so today. In the world-famous and influential 1822 poem "A Visit from St. Nicholas" or "'Twas the Night Before Christmas," Clement Moore included the line, "While visions of sugar plums danced in their heads."

Seventy years after Moore penned that familiar line, Russian composer Peter Ilich Tchaikovsky (1840-1893) included the "Dance of the Sugar Plum Fairy" in his extremely popular 1892 ballet, *The Nutcracker*. Using a delicate instrument, the celesta, to evoke the delicate dance movements of the sugar plum fairy, that number is perhaps the best-known part of *The Nutcracker*. "Sugar Plum" is a favorite piece for skaters, matching the graceful and subtle maneuvers of a solo female on ice.

With its annually repeated story about how the Christmas gift of a nutcracker by a mysterious uncle leads to an exciting and magical dream adventure for young Clara, *The Nutcracker* is primarily performed during the December holidays (in America and elsewhere). Yet with a number of other memorable sections in addition to "Dance of the Sugar Plum Fairy," for example, the also popular "Waltz of the Flowers," *The Nutcracker* is really a production for all seasons. Indeed, the "Waltz of the Flowers" has been a staple in American animated cartoons and various other types of entertainment all year around.

The Hokey Pokey

One might think that a well-known and highly successful American song appearing after World War II would have brought fame and fortune to its author. Yet the reputed creators of the dance piece "The Hokey Pokey," with its commands to put in and put out various parts of the human body, are very obscure and did not become very wealthy because of their novelty composition. Roland Lawrence (Larry) LaPrise (1913?-1996), in his later years a postal worker, and two musician associates, Charles P. Macak and Tafft Baker, reportedly wrote the song around 1948 and recorded it in 1949. In 1953, they sold the rights to bandleader Ray Anthony who turned "Hokey" into a 1950s dance rage and a minor national institution enduring into the 1990s.

However, there are some persons who claim that the story of Laprise's composition of the song is pure "Hokey Pokey," or trickery. These doubters, American World War II veterans, say the piece was very popular in England around 1943. But no matter what the ultimate truth may be, Laprise copyrighted the song in the United States in 1950 and Anthony made it very famous. In reality, Laprise and Anthony, not some nebulous unknown earlier person, were the true "fathers" of this modern cultural phenomenon.

Another American dance craze song of the 1950s was "The Bunny Hop," which was written in 1951 by Ray Anthony and Leonard Auletti and recorded by Anthony that year. This author participated in the mass fun of the "Hop" only once, in 1957, while attending the University of Connecticut. The occasion was a warm spring evening when roughly 5,000 students did "The Bunny Hop" in a very long wiggly line throughout part of the campus. Even *The New York Times* printed a story about the incident. Less than a decade later, if many students gathered on a campus other than for a sporting event or graduation it would normally mean a protest and perhaps a riot. In time, both the large-scale campus protests and the performance of "The Bunny Hop" would become less frequent.

With his co-composition of "The Bunny Hop" and his smash recordings of that song and "The Hokey Pokey," Anthony kept the 1950s both pokey and hopping. He also helped liven up the 1970s. At the end of the hilarious 1974 Western film *Blazing Saddles*, Mel Brooks satirized "Hokey" in the song "The French Mistake." For a number which has the dancer remain in place while moving, "hokey" does seem to cover a lot of territory.

Hootchy Kootchy Dance

As has been reported on occasion, U.S. Congressmen have been known to pay too much close attention to suggestive oriental hootchy kootchy dancing and the young women who perform the dance. Strangely, it may have been a Congressman who actually wrote the famous "Hootchy Kootchy Dance," which most of us have heard, but few of us can identify.

Sol Bloom (1870-1949), who was a representative from the state of New York from 1923 to 1949, claims to have written the little pseudo-oriental melody in 1893. Bloom was the press agent for the Chicago World's Exposition. When some music was needed for a "Little Egypt" show on the midway, Bloom, who also worked in the music publishing business, created an impromptu little dance.

Whenever you have seen a belly dancer in a night club, in a carnival, on a theater stage, or in a movie or television production, the accompanying music may very well have been the "Hootchy Kootchy." In a completely different context, college bands throughout the United States adopted the first bar of "Hootchy Kootchy" as their favorite repertory piece starting in the early 1980s, and sometimes performed the five notes over and over and over again. (The notes were actually the opening of a rock arrangement of the composition.)

You may also be familiar with the well-known parody lyrics, "Oh they don't wear pants in the southern part of France, But they do wear grass to cover up their a——." Despite the vulgarism, this is, as parodies go, a pretty good one. And the dance, as impromptu pieces go, is also quite good.

Invitation to the Dance

Carl Maria von Weber (1786-1826), a German classical composer, conductor, and pianist, is far from a household name in the United States. Although the names of Bach, Mozart, Beethoven, Chopin, Wagner, Tchaikovsky, and others are known well beyond the concert halls of America, the name Weber is not. He wrote several outstanding compositions, including the operas *Der Freischütz* (*The Marksman with Magic Bullets*) (1821) and *Oberon* (1826), yet his accomplishments are recognized primarily by individuals associated with serious music.

However, one of his pieces, "Invitation to the Dance," an 1819 piano work, has been appreciated by a famous person in American popular culture and has become a semi-hidden classic of the big band era. Originally, the composition (in German, "Aufforderung zum Tanz") was a delightful waltz preceded and followed by slow tempo sections. In 1935, musician Fanny Baldridge and lyricists Joseph Bonine and Gregory Stone reworked the brilliant waltz section into "Let's Dance," which was to become the theme of the great bandleader Benny Goodman. With the sweet sounds of "Invitation to the Dance" emanating from the sweet tones of Goodman's clarinet, the swing era of the 1920s, 1930s, and 1940s, which emphasized dancing, had one more good reason to dance. Weber thus not only created *The Marksman with Magic Bullets*, but significantly propelled the career of the musician with magic clarinet valves.

The Merry Widow Waltz

When Americans think about waltzes from Vienna, the usual association is with the famous Strauss family of musicians, most notably Johann Strauss Jr., the creator of "Blue Danube," "Tales from the Vienna Woods," and a number of other fine, graceful, and expansive compositions in three-quarter time. Yet the Strausses are far from the total picture of delicate dance music from the capital of Austria. Obscure composers such as Otto Nicolai (1810-1849) and Richard Heuberger (1850-1914), and better-known composers such as Oscar Straus (1870-1954) and Franz Lehár (1870-1948), contributed substantially to the music from Vienna.

Nicolai's 1849 opera *Die lustigen Weiber von Windsor* (*The Merry Wives of Windsor*), Heuberger's 1898 opera *Der Opernball* (*The Opera Ball*), Straus' operettas *Ein Walzertraum* (*A Waltz Dream*) (1907) and *Der tapfere Soldat* (*The Chocolate Soldier*) (1908), and several operettas by Lehár all have enhanced the musical form mastered by the Strausses. The best-known non-Strauss waltz is almost certainly "The Merry Widow" by Lehár. From his 1905 operetta *Die lustige Witwe* (*The Merry Widow*), this familiar piece has been used in films and other productions, and has appeared in many songbooks as an "old favorite." Schools, clubs, and other groups have collectively lofted its lilting, lyrical lines, often with words other than those in the original.

The fortunes of "The Merry Widow" in the United States have declined in recent decades like so much other fine older music, but the song does live on. Indeed, the name "The Merry Widow" appears to be known even to many who cannot hum, identify, or appreciate Lehár's beautiful masterwork.

Missouri Waltz

During his tenure as president (1945-1953), Harry Truman, like so many public figures, was the subject of contemporary humor. Two especially memorable standing television gags about the man from Missouri included one that shows the White House in the background and an unseen pianist not-so-competently playing the strains of the "Missouri Waltz," and one in which Truman shouts to an unseen pianist, his daughter Margaret, to "stop playing that infernal song!" (or something like that). Since the fine composition reminiscent of the best of Vienna was the unofficial theme of Truman's administration, the jokes were appropriate to the situation (as were jokes about heat and kitchens because of Truman's famous statement, "If you can't stand the heat, stay out of the kitchen!").

The "Missouri Waltz" was created when Truman (1884-1972) was just a young man. In 1914 Frederic Knight Logan (1871-1928) wrote the piece as a piano instrumental, quite possibly borrowing from an anonymous black composer. The lyrics were created in 1916 by James Royce (1881-1946) using the pseudonym James Royce Shannon. (The name John Valentine Eppel pops up in some versions of the history of the song as the "discoverer" of the melody.) Although the dignified "Missouri Waltz" may seem a bit lofty for earthy "give-'em-hell Harry," the independent man from Independence, Missouri was definitely a class act worthy of such a piece.

Two other songs with both state names and dance form names in their titles are well known throughout the United States. "Tennessee Waltz," a strongly enduring 1948 blend of country western and three-quarter time modes was written by Redd Stewart and Pee Wee King (1914-). "Pennsylvania Polka," a lively, very danceable favorite written in 1942 by Lester Lee and Zeke Manners, is one of the very best American polkas. It has often been used as a theme for various state-related activities, including as a "fight song" for the

Pittsburgh Steelers professional football team. However, in spite of "Tennessee's" and "Pennsylvania's" good artistry and public acceptance, "Missouri" is the king of state dance songs because it is closely associated with a president and is also an official state song. "Tennessee" is a state song, but has not yet been linked to a presidency, and "Pennsylvania," as loveable as it is, has so far failed at both tests.

"Pizzicati" from *Sylvia*

Pizzicato is a musical term to describe the plucking of certain stringed instruments, such as the violin, viola, and cello, instead of the normal bowing these instruments receive. One of the most famous usages of the pizzicato technique in classical music is in the third act of the 1876 ballet, *Sylvia*. That delicate yet lively section of the ballet has been widely used in American everyday culture. Television advertisements, comedy routines, and animated cartoons have often included the distinctive melodies from *Sylvia*. Probably the situation that best matches the style of the music is the stalking of a mouse by a cat in animated films.

Music from the same act of *Sylvia* was borrowed for the theme of the mid-1980s American television program, *Knight Rider*. Pops concerts also include other excellent excerpts from *Sylvia*, especially its powerful and emphatic opening march, as well as other music by the composer of *Sylvia*, French master Léo Delibes (1836-1891). Other famous works by the primarily theatrical composer were *Coppélia* (1870), one of the all-time elite ballets, and *Lakmé* (1883), an enduring but not great opera. Though definitely not in the first rank of serious composers today, Delibes was one of the musical stars of Paris in the second half of the nineteenth century.

Delibes's music and life clearly indicate a fine sense of humor. (During a Paris production of an operetta by his friend Jacques Offenbach, in which a coin is tossed on the stage as part of the plot, Delibes threw in a confusing second coin from the wings at the same time.) One wonders, however, whether he would be particularly amused by being best known in America from scenes of cartoon cats chasing cartoon mice.

Sabre Dance

Throughout history, warriors and civilians have performed various types of sword dances. Whether in an advanced civilization or a less-developed culture, swords either brandished in the air or placed on the ground have been part of ceremonial or recreational dancing, mostly by men. Sword dances are typically used to demonstrate the power of the individual or group, or to celebrate some occasion. By no means are such dances always associated with war, but frequently some past victory provides at least some background for the event.

At one end of the sword dance spectrum are the playful sword-on-the-ground dances performed by Celtic peoples accompanied by the playing of bagpipes. At the other end are vigorous, almost savage sword-handling dances like the "Sabre Dance." With one of the most pulsating and dynamic rhythms of any musical work, a kind of driving and relentless linear attack, "Sabre Dance" instantly grabs your attention. It is a piece that cannot easily be ignored while being played loudly, which is the usual manner, and is one of the easier pieces of music to remember or recognize. It is a truly distinctive composition that has appeared in American television programs and advertisements, movies, and live performing arts. At times it is used satirically, to accompany frantic comedic scenes.

The creator of "Sabre Dance" was the noted Soviet composer Aram Khachaturian (1903-1978), who was of Armenian descent. "Sabre Dance" was the centerpiece of his excellent 1942 ballet *Gayne* or *Gayane,* which was his most famous work. (Another fairly well-known composition by Khachaturian is his "Galop" from the 1944 symphonic suite *Masquerade.*) One of the English titles for *Gayne* is *Happiness,* which is the typical response of many persons hearing its famous dance. Of course, if the sabre wielder is coming after you, the typical response would be terror!

Simple Gifts

The Shakers were a religious group who began as part of a Quaker revival in England in 1747, and then spread to the United States under the name Shaking Quakers. Under the leadership of Ann Lee, the Shakers founded a colony in New York State in 1776, and in time, other colonies were founded throughout the country as far west as Indiana. By the end of the nineteenth century, the movement declined, in large part due to their policy of celibacy, which necessitated recruitment of all new members from the general population. Among the artistic accomplishments of this group that separated itself from the outside world were fine handicrafts and furniture, and at least one very good song.

Shaker worship included marching, singing, and dancing. (The sexes were strictly segregated.) A collection of Shaker hymns was published in 1940 by Edward D. Andrews under the title *The Gift To Be Simple*. From this collection, noted American classical composer Aaron Copland (1900-1990) borrowed a dance melody that he aptly described as "calm and flowing" and inserted it toward the end of his excellent 1944 ballet *Appalachian Spring*. The use of the tune, called "Simple Gifts" or "The Gift To Be Simple" in the ballet and a subsequent orchestral suite, made the song fairly well known to non-Shakers. Other uses include a 1963 adaptation by Sydney Carter, "Lord of the Dance," and a 1977 adaptation, "Turning (Shaker Hymn)," for the Broadway musical *The Act,* created by composer John Kander and lyricist W. Fred Ebb and sung by Liza Minnelli.

"Simple Gifts" was possibly influenced by the anonymous seventeenth-century German hymn tune "Lasst Uns Erfreuen," and very possibly created in the middle of the nineteenth century (1848) by Joseph Brackett (1797-1882) at a Shaker community in Alfred, Maine. It has found its way, always in a modest manner, into late twentieth-century American popular culture. Its appearances in everyday life include a 1990s series of television advertisements for a make of automobile. This usage is quite ironic, for the original Shakers probably would not have approved of the worldly influences of either television or cars.

Slaughter on Tenth Avenue

The title of this brilliant dance number, "Slaughter on Tenth Avenue," coupled with a description of the piece, may be enough to keep some people from listening to it. An extended jazz composition, accompanying an intense plot in which a couple dances in apache style (that is, a violent dance for two derived from Parisian hoodlums and other rough types) and with a homicide as the end result, "Slaughter" is a fascinating combination of the good and bad in society.

The good is the excellent choreography plus the exceptional score by composer Richard Rodgers (1902-1979). "Slaughter" was the best as well as the most striking number in the 1936 musical *On Your Toes* (note the suggestion of dancing in the title). That production was one of the better shows of the 27 created by Rodgers and his lyricist collaborator Lorenz Hart (1895-1943) between 1920 and 1942. Their best musical was perhaps *Babes in Arms* (1937), which not only had another reference to human anatomy in the title but also included the enduring well-known songs "My Funny Valentine," "The Lady Is a Tramp," "I Wish I Were in Love Again," "Where or When?," and "Johnny One Note." Another of their productions, *Pal Joey* (1940), is, however, better known in spite of a lesser score that included the classic "Bewitched, Bothered, and Bewildered."

For those who only associate the terms *slaughter* and *apache* with Western movies, "Slaughter on Tenth Avenue" is a piece well worth seeing (live or on video) or listening to. For artistic content and impact, it approaches the outstanding extended dance scene in Rodgers and Hammerstein's musical *Oklahoma!* (1943), the jazzy choreographic opening of Leonard Bernstein's musical *West Side Story* (1957), and the fantastic choreographic ending of the 1951 film, *An American in Paris*.

Sleeping Beauty Waltz

Peter Ilich Tchaikovsky (1840-1893), one of the greatest Russian composers, was three for three when it came to creating ballets. In 1877, he composed *Swan Lake*, the supreme classic of ballet. In 1890, he produced *Sleeping Beauty*, another classic that closely approached the excellence of *Swan Lake*. Two years later, *The Nutcracker* appeared, which in time was to become the perennial favorite of the Christmas season in the United States and elsewhere.

The *Sleeping Beauty* concept, however, has not fared especially well other than in the ballet. The original story of the young princess who went into an extended slumber after being pricked by the spindle of a spinning wheel is very familiar, but is not one of the "supertales" of Western culture. The 1959 movie *Sleeping Beauty* certainly was not among the best animated cartoon features from Walt Disney Studios. Although a technically competent film, its most artistic component was the use of various sections of Tchaikovsky's ballet score. The key piece in the movie was "Once Upon a Dream," a conversion of the lilting, gorgeous "Sleeping Beauty Waltz" into a love ballad by the addition of new lyrics by Sammy Fain (1902-1979) and Jack Lawrence (1912-).

Tchaikovsky had three choreographic home runs in three times at bat, with a smaller stick, a conductor's baton, being extensively used over the next century. "Sleeping Beauty" only scored once: in the 1890 ballet. On the other two artistic occasions, it was stranded somewhere around second base.

Tales from the Vienna Woods

"Whither the zither?" is not a question to be asked in association with the great waltz, "Tales from the Vienna Woods." One of the most beautiful and suitable arrangements of the song employs the zither as a solo instrument to convey the soft, reserved tones of the beginning and the ending. As a contrast to the sophistication of the full Viennese orchestra, the simple plucked-string instrument, which is of Central European folk origin, seems to be completely at home in a composition about the rural environs of Vienna.

The original instrument for this waltz, however, was not the zither. In 1868, Johann Strauss Jr. (1825-1899) published "Geschichten aus dem Wienerwald" for the piano. A year later, the orchestral score was published and "Vienna Woods" was on its way to becoming one of world's best-known waltzes. Together with "Blue Danube" (1867), "Emperor Waltz" (1888), "An Artist's Life" (1867), "Wine, Women, and Song" (1869), "The Voices of Spring" (1883), "Roses from the South" (1878), and other glittering compositions, "Vienna Woods" has made Strauss a symbol of the finer things in life.

Although there are no tales specifically connected with "Tales from the Vienna Woods," its lilting strains have been used to accompany a wide variety of imaginary and media adventures. In the United States and elsewhere, dancing animals, romantic couples, carefree peasants, graceful athletes, goofy comedians, and cartoon rabbits have all been known to cavort through the forested countryside or other locales courtesy of the genius of Johann Strauss. The appearance of the musical rabbit, Bugs Bunny, was courtesy of the Warner Brothers, perhaps geniuses in another art form, filmmaking.

The Voices of Spring

High society and low society tend not to associate frequently. If the two socioeconomic strata are as diametrically divergent as the Three Stooges and the well-to-do party attendees in one of the Stooges' old films, then disaster may strike as it did in those movies.

With a society matron bellowing "The Voices of Spring" to a not completely enthusiastic audience in one of the scenes, and Moe, Larry, and Curly making a shambles of the place in typical fashion, Johann Strauss Jr.'s famous waltz certainly did not convey the impression of beauty and grace. But at the same time, the use of the intricate song as a tool for comedy in the middle of the twentieth century was a sign that "The Voices of Spring" had attained a degree of stature in Western culture.

Strauss (1825-1899) published the waltz in 1883, accompanied by lyrics by Richard Genée (1823-1895). Its original German title was "Frühlingsstimmen," which literally means "spring voices." Apparently, Genée felt that the rapid and accelerating rhythms of "Voices" imitated the rapid and vigorous growth of new life in the spring. If he had chosen another season for the title, he may have been referred to the then young Viennese doctor Sigmund Freud for observation. Only a madman or a rebel would have matched the hot doldrums of summer, the reflective peacefulness of autumn, or the blustery discomfort of winter with the lively and upbeat mood of "The Voices of Spring."

Waves of the Danube

Al Jolson, the legendary American entertainer, was involved with the performance or composition of a large number of popular songs. Among the well-known pieces to which Jolson (1886-1950) directly contributed were "Avalon" (1920), "California Here I Come" (1924), "Me and My Shadow" (1927), and "Anniversary Song," also called "Anniversary Waltz" (1946).

"Anniversary Song" was not an entirely new creation. The lyrics were by Jolson and perhaps his associate Saul Chaplin, but the music was adapted, apparently by Chaplin, from a classical piece. The original work, an 1880 waltz without lyrics, was entitled "Valurile Dunări," Romanian for "Waves of the Danube." Its composer was Ion Ivanovici (1845-1902), a significant Romanian musician.

Most waltzing tributes to the magnificence of the Danube River have come from the city of Vienna, hundreds of miles away near the other end of the waterway. It's a good thing that Ivanovici was not so awed by Vienna that he was unable to compose his Vienna-style smooth imitation of waves. Otherwise, sentimental couples would never have been able to enjoy the memories of "Oh, how we danced, On the night we were wed."

MARCHING SONGS

Funeral March of a Marionette

Most persons would prefer not to be associated with the devil. But the celebrated French composer Charles Gounod (1818-1893), though personally not particularly diabolical, has had two of his three most famous works in one way or another connected with things dark.

His most important creation, the 1859 grand opera *Faust*, directly deals with the story of the man who sold his immortal soul to the devil. Another of his leading compositions, "Funeral March of a Marionette" (originally "Marche funèbre d'une marionnette"), seems to be completely innocent of Lucifer's influences, but does have an indirect tie with darker matters. The 1872 piece, at first a piano solo, was adopted by and made more famous by the two television mystery series produced by Alfred Hitchcock. From 1955 to 1962 and from 1963 to 1965, millions of viewers heard "Marionette" introduce Hitchcock and his devilish tales of murder, mayhem, and the macabre.

Fortunately for Gounod's reputation, the third of his famous trio is totally unaffiliated with the master of the underworld. In fact, it is in purpose and in style quite heavenly. The same year that witnessed the premier of *Faust* with its devil theme also saw the publication of Gounod's "Ave Maria," a beautiful religious composition created by the superimposition of one of his melodies on top of one of Johann Sebastian Bach's.

In the Hall of the Mountain King

Some persons have said that the music of Edvard Grieg (1843-1907), the most renowned Norwegian composer, reflects the icy cold winters of Norway. That is, it is reserved and far from fiery. To an extent, such criticisms are valid, for Grieg is known best for gentle, soft, and melancholy music. One exception to this is "In the Hall of the Mountain King," an oddly active, heavy-footed, rather grotesque march that is part of Grieg's *Peer Gynt* Suite No. 1 (1876). (*Peer Gynt* Suite No. 2, which is less famous, was also written in the same year.) "Mountain King" is heard from time to time in American popular culture in situations befitting its delightfully bizarre and brilliantly ponderous rhythms which have a resemblance to a marching, then running, grizzly bear. Animated cartoons with or without bears are just one example. One late twentieth-century cartoon show that used "Mountain King" as a theme was *Garfield and Friends,* featuring a cat that caused more trouble than any one bear. Speaking of trouble, a 1957 television musical based on the old story, *The Pied Piper of Hamelin,* incorporated "Mountain King" and other *Peer Gynt* music in the production. With its immense rat problem, Hamelin could have used Garfield and his feline friends.

Grieg's *Peer Gynt* is based on the play of the same name by the great Norwegian writer Henrik Ibsen. Another well-known piece from *Peer Gynt* Suite No. 1 is "Morning," a tender and lyrical tribute to the first part of the day. More typical of Grieg's style, "Morning" is a stereotype for musical depiction of the sun rising and birds singing. It often appears in American television programs and advertisements, movies, animated cartoons, and other forms of entertainment and communication.

But Grieg doesn't have a total monopoly on classical music used in the simulation of mornings in popular culture. On occasion, the "Morning" passage from Gioacchino Rossini's masterful opera

William Tell, which depicts sunrise over the Swiss Alps in contrast to Grieg's description of morning arriving in Norway, can be heard in American everyday life. Rossini (1792-1868) wrote *William Tell* (or *Guillaume Tell*) in 1829.

Although flamboyant Rossini and reserved Grieg do not have a lot in common, the two masterworks mentioned above do. In addition to the morning passages included in both, each is about a national hero, the imaginary Gynt and the legendary Tell, and each has a dramatic ending, the mountain king sequence in one and the ride of the Lone Ranger in the other.

I've Been Working on the Railroad

Four for the price of one–that's what you get with "I've Been Working on the Railroad." First you get a brawny, masculine song with sweep. Then, starting with "Dinah won't you blow," come a few lines in bouncy minstrel style. Following that is a little march-like melody beginning with "Someone's in the kitchen with Dinah." Another melodic episode about strumming on a banjo ends this musical mishmash.

"I've Been Working" is a delightful piece of nonsense, but it reminds us of the old joke about a camel being a horse assembled by a committee. You can never know for sure, but "I've Been Working" sounds like a deliberate attempt to assemble a medley of short individual pieces, or even a collective college prank. (The lyrics for the section about Dinah in the kitchen may have come from an earlier London lyric, "Someone's in the house with Dinah.") Since its first known printing, under the title "Levee Song," occurred in an 1894 collection of Princeton University songs, either the medley or prank theory (or both) may be valid. The original title, and parts of its style, suggest origins in a minstrel show. It could easily be speculated, furthermore, that the composition (or pasting together) of "I've Been Working" may have taken place a decade or more before 1894, for college songs tend to loosely hang around for some years prior to actual publication.

In 1903, the scene shifted from New Jersey all the way down to Texas. A student minstrel show held at the University of Texas in Austin performed "The Eyes of Texas," using the melody of "I've Been Working." The new lyrics, based on a speech by the university president, were by John Lang Sinclair (1880-1947). The new piece officially became a part of the university in 1918 when it was printed in a University of Texas song book.

With this mixed background, you could call "I've Been Working" a railroad song, a folk song, a college song, or a minstrel ditty. But no matter how you may try to describe it, there is no doubt that it is a first-rate fun song.

Love for Three Oranges March

The Federal Bureau of Investigation, the highly respected and very competent national law enforcement agency, has at least two quite bizarre facets to its history. The first one involves J. Edgar Hoover, the tough longtime director of the FBI who more than anyone else made the agency what it is today. Hoover, it appears, was a cross-dresser and may have had a sexual preference for men.

Just as strange was the piece of music that served as the theme for the radio program *This Is Your F.B.I.*, which began in 1945. The program was sanctioned by the strongly anti-Communist FBI, and used material from actual FBI cases. Yet in spite of the clear political leanings of the agency and the poor relations between the United States and the Soviet Union during the run of the program, the theme was derived from the music of a prominent Soviet composer.

That composer was Sergei Prokofiev (1891-1953), perhaps the most celebrated of all Russian musicians during the Soviet regime. Prokofiev cannot be described as a true Soviet artist, for he was absent from Russia between 1918 and 1933 and was often in trouble with the Soviet authorities after 1933.

It was during his flight from his homeland, in 1921, that his notable opera *Liubov k trem apelsinam* (*Love for Three Oranges*) was produced. The brilliant and famous march from the orchestral suite of this satirical work was to become the basis for the theme of *This Is Your F.B.I.* a generation later. The use of the music for a program extolling the FBI is not the only odd facet of this story. The plot of the opera came from Italy, the language of the production was in French, and the place of its premiere was Chicago, Illinois. One famous person who witnessed the Chicago production was long-time Chicagoan and author Ben Hecht, who described the work as "fantastic lollipops."

March of the Toys

Three famous persons from three countries are involved in the history of the beloved composition, "March of the Toys." Most directly connected is composer Victor Herbert (1859-1924). Born in Ireland, Herbert emigrated to the United States in the late nineteenth century and soon became one of the top composers in his adopted nation. With outstanding operettas such as *Naughty Marietta* (1910) and *Babes in Toyland* (1903), Herbert was the most dominant theatrical composer of the first decade of the twentieth century. *Babes in Toyland*, his most celebrated production, included the miniclassics "Toyland," a Christmas favorite, and "March of the Toys," a brisk piece in pseudo-military style that is brilliantly understated to match the situation of little toy figures coming to the rescue.

The two other well-known persons associated with "March of the Toys" were also brilliant in their area of American culture, but could hardly be described as understated. Stan Laurel, born in England, and Oliver Hardy, an American, were without a doubt the most successful film comedy team prior to World War II. The buffoonery of Laurel and Hardy is still very much appreciated today, and perhaps was at its peak in the 1934 movie *Babes in Toyland* (also known as *March of the Wooden Soldiers*), based on Herbert's show. Bumbling and fumbling Laurel and Hardy got into a variety of messes in the film, while the marching toys, propelled by Herbert's timeless composition, were the heroes.

Another lesser-known march by toys was "Parade of the Wooden Soldiers." Leon Jessel (1871-1942), a German composer, wrote the piece in 1911 as an instrumental, and it later became part of the 1922 Broadway musical, *Chauve souris*. American Ballard MacDonald (1882-1935) wrote the lyrics used in the production. MacDonald also collaborated with lyricist Bud DeSylva and composer George Gershwin on the classic song "Somebody Loves Me" (1924). Thus the great creator of the 1920s and 1930s musicals, Gershwin, is in this strange roundabout way connected with Herbert, the great creator of musicals of the generation before.

Maryland! My Maryland

The American Civil War, 1861-1865, was not only a bloody conflict but also a complex one. Although slavery was the most fundamental cause, states' rights, economics, and other factors were involved. In addition, it was not always easy to determine who was on the Confederate side and who was on the Union side. Some persons from the North sympathized with the South, and some persons from the South sympathized with the North. Families often had split loyalties. Particularly confusing was the status of border states such as Kentucky and Maryland, which were not clearly on one side or the other.

Maryland, despite being adjacent to the federal capital and not being a true Southern state, had many Confederate sympathizers. One of these was James Ryder Randall (1839-1908). Distressed with the developments around the beginning of the war in 1861, Randall penned some fervent lyrics that were decidedly pro-South. Later his "Maryland! My Maryland" was set to the famous melody earlier used for the anonymous sixteenth- or seventeenth-century German Christmas carol "O Tannebaum" ("O Christmas Tree"), and the combination became the official state song. Another official state song using this exceptional melody is "The Song of Iowa," created by Samuel Hawkins Marshall in 1897.

Because of its rousing melody, "Maryland! My Maryland" is still a proud and attractive song. Yet the lyrics seem quite out of place in our current American society.

Old Time Religion

Most songs in Western culture probably can only be placed in one or two reasonable or logical categories. Lunatics or overly imaginative writers, on the other hand, can take a comparatively simple composition and give it multiple musical classifications or historical/cultural roles.

Take, for example, "Old Time Religion," also known as "Give Me That Old Time Religion." Like many anonymous black spirituals, it was published around the end of the Civil War–in this case, 1865. This splendid work of folk genius goes far beyond the status of a slave spiritual. It was also a key hymn for the mainly Protestant white settlers in the West after the war, as various films and television programs have portrayed over the years. The song was also very popular in the East, Midwest, and South during the second half of the nineteenth century, and throughout the whole country for at least the first half of the twentieth century. Although created and widely sung by blacks, it was also strongly embraced by whites. Far more than just a hymn, it is a real cultural icon that has helped make the expression "old time religion" a permanent part of U.S. civilization. For example, in the 1960 film version of Jerome Lawrence and Robert E. Lee's drama *Inherit the Wind,* "Old Time Religion" was the background music in the opening scene.

Going beyond the status of a spiritual/hymn/icon, it is also a very good and very energetic march for many occasions. Like another anonymous nineteenth-century hymn, "Shall We Gather at the River?" (a slower, less artistic, and less enduring icon from white America) its survival is due less to its theology than its moving march rhythms and its noteworthy contributions to the historical rhythms of America.

On the Mall

In the last decades of the twentieth century, "hanging out" at the mall has been a favorite activity for Americans of all ages. From 1924 to well over a half century later, listening to the gusty march "On the Mall" was a favorite activity for some Americans. The rousing composition, with its very distinctive chorus in which the audience is invited to sing "la la la la, la la la la, la la la la la!" as loudly as they wish, has filled the atmosphere at many outdoor band concerts.

The creator of this unique 1924 march, which still livens up performances of local bands, was Edwin Franko Goldman (1878-1956). A native of Louisville, Kentucky, Goldman was born into a musical family, his uncles being noted conductors. Following the paths of his uncles, and no doubt inspired by the world-famous band of John Philip Sousa that was around its peak at the time, Goldman organized his own band in 1911. In 1918, he began outdoor concerts on the green at Columbia University in New York City. The repertoire of the Goldman Band included over 100 marches written by Goldman.

In a definite act of poetic justice, about ten years or so after Goldman's best-known work first appeared, the Goldman Band began to perform in New York City's Central Park. When their concerts were presented on the mall in the Park, there can be little doubt that "On the Mall" was frequently on the schedule.

Toreador Song

The story of *Carmen*, arguably the world's most famous opera, is not a pleasant one. A poor working girl, a cigar factory, hate, jealousy, tragic love, a bullfight, and the murder of the heroine are not the ingredients of an idyllic plot.

The music of *Carmen*, on the other hand, is sparkling, lush, colorful, and brilliant. Composed by French master Georges Bizet (1838-1875), whose own life was not a lot longer than that of the young woman he immortalized, the 1875 production boasts one of the finest opera scores ever conceived. Although Bizet did not write a lot of music because of his short life span, he also created some other creditable operas including *The Pearl Fishers* (1863) and an excellent pair of orchestral suites based on incidental music for the 1872 play *L'Arlésienne.*

Of all his creations, Bizet has received the most attention for his bullfight scene composition, "Toreador Song." Like so much of *Carmen*, "Toreador" is very melodic, rousing, and succulent. An exceptional portrayal of the drama of bulls versus bullfighters, "Toreador" is one of our most familiar marches. It is such a stereotype that bullfight music and "Toreador" are almost synonymous. It has also, incidentally, been used as a boxing song, "Stand Up and Fight" in Oscar Hammerstein's 1943 musical, *Carmen Jones,* which was based on Bizet's opera. And of course, various parodies have also appeared in the bull ring. The most notorious is surely the apparently American barroom phenomenon, "Toreador, Don't spit on the floor, Spit in the cuspidor, That's what it's for." When you sing it in the shower tonight, don't forget to give two beats to the four line-ending "-or" words.

"Triumphal March" from *Aida*

The "Triumphal March" from the great 1871 opera *Aida* has been described by some music lovers as an old warhorse. Because of its brilliant, dynamic, and uplifting qualities, it has been immensely popular and accordingly has been performed an enormous number of times. On top of being played in the opera, it is a favorite concert piece and has been substantially adapted for hymns and other purposes such as movie themes and television advertisements. Therefore, according to some, it has become as tired and overused as a worn-out nag that has been through too many battles. But other music lovers, including this author, feel that the march is still vital and invigorating and ready to challenge the conductor's baton many more times.

If one is inclined to use terminology such as "old warhorse" to describe the "Triumphal March," the phrase "old war elephant" might be a better choice. At its premiere in Cairo, the opera with the Egyptian theme featured elephants in the production. (You don't just "insert" elephants in any production. Their massive presence overwhelms everything else on the scene, including loudly played grand marches of triumph.)

Aida and a number of other famous operas were created by the extraordinary genius of Giuseppe Verdi (1813-1901), the foremost Italian operatic composer. Verdi was in talent a very uncommon man, writing highly successful operas as late in life as age 80. In contrast, Verdi was by background completely common, coming from a family of modest means and having a name which, if translated into English, is as plain and ordinary as can be. What is more everyday and proletarian than Joe Green?

When the Saints Go Marching In

Somewhere along the line, someone got the idea that when Christian saints go to get their reward in Heaven, their entrance through the pearly gates will be accompanied by march music. It's not an absurd idea at all. Certainly a march seems more appropriate to the occasion than dance music, a love ballad, or an operatic aria. It would be fascinating to know if such a processional will occur, but unfortunately, many of us will never have the chance to be firsthand witnesses.

The person or persons who transferred this concept into music via the famous song "When the Saints Go Marching In" is unknown. The dominant theory is that by about 1900, black bands in New Orleans had established "Saints" in their repertory of funeral songs. On the way to the cemetery, when the loss of a loved one was being grieved, the beat was slow. On the return, when the loved one's entrance into Heaven was being celebrated, the rhythm was much faster. If this anecdote about New Orleans is valid, the song is almost surely of New Orleans black origins, and probably from the second half of the nineteenth century.

But there are also other opinions. The earliest known print version, with the title "When the Saints Are Marching In," was published in 1896. James M. Black of Williamsport, Pennsylvania, was credited with the music and Katharine E. Purvis was credited with the lyrics. Whether Black and Purvis discovered the New Orleans song, or whether New Orleans musicians obtained a copy of Black and Purvis' creation seems to be unprovable. The chronological closeness, though, is most interesting, as are the similarities between "Saints" and an 1893 hymn by Black, "When the Roll is Called Up Yonder."

It wasn't until Louis Armstrong recorded "Saints" in 1930 that the song became widely popular. (This delayed mainstream popularity and the initial recordings being made by a New Orleans-born black artist tends to support African-American New Orleans origins for the song.) After Satchmo lovingly applied his pleasant gravel voice and his hot trumpet to the jazz classic, "Saints" became a leading standard on the American pop music scene. Perhaps some day Armstrong and the song's creator will get together to collaborate on a final rendering of "Saints" when they go marching in.

The Yellow Rose of Texas

Nothing is known about "J.K." except that he or she wrote the lyrics and music for the lively old favorite "The Yellow Rose of Texas." An obvious inference might be that J.K. was born in or had lived in the Lone Star state, but such a presumption really cannot be safely made.

It is known that J.K.'s ballad was written for minstrel show use and was published in New York City in 1858. "Yellow Rose" was very popular in the minstrel circuit and with both the North and the South during the Civil War. Various parodies also popped up, and in addition the tune was lassoed and tied to "The Song of the Texas Rangers." About a century after its birth, "Yellow Rose" proved that it was no short-lived, fragile flower by once again scoring high with the public. A 1955 version recorded by Mitch Miller and his chorus resulted in a million rings of the cash register.

There is one minor peculiarity about "Yellow Rose," though. Musically, it could be described as a love march. Romance and marching are a rare blend in musical compositions, and perhaps this novelty was one key to "Yellow Rose"'s wide public acceptance. Such a combination, however, is far from unique to the 1853 song. For example, 20 years earlier, in 1838, a similar love march, "She Wore a Yellow Ribbon," was anonymously created. (This song was the featured music in the 1949 John Wayne movie of the same title.) It is quite possible that this first "Yellow R" was the artistic parent of the second and better known "Yellow R." Even when both were repopularized in the mid-twentieth century, "Yellow Ribbon" preceded "Yellow Rose."

RURAL AND WESTERN SONGS

The Arkansas Traveler

In the 1990s, Bill Clinton might have been described as "The Arkansas Traveler" who journeyed to the White House and many other places in the world in his role as president of the United States. But before then, "The Arkansas Traveler" (also spelled "Traveller") was a charming and lively folk piece highly popular in rural America.

The song is based on the legend of a country fiddler who over and over again repeated the same notes on his violin. The Arkansas Traveler, it is told, came upon this strange phenomenon during his various wanderings. The musical composition emanating from this curious tale was almost surely written in the first half of the nineteenth century, and was published in 1851.

Probably written in or around Arkansas, "Traveler" is anonymous, although such obscure composers as Joseph Tosso have been mentioned as possible authors. The piece, undoubtedly the most famous composition with "Arkansas" in the title, became an official state song of Arkansas in 1987.

Another charming and lively piece strongly connected with rural fiddling is the square dance "Red Wing" (1907) by lyricist Thurland Chattaway and composer Kerry Mills. One more rural-style song connected with motion and the color red is Red Foley's reflective 1950 hymn, "Just a Closer Walk with Thee." With the mention of these two songs, we seem to have traveled far from Arkansas.

The Big Rock Candy Mountain

Utopias come in as many varieties as there are persons to dream about them. For the hobo, vagabond, or traveling bum in the United States, "The Big Rock Candy Mountain" is an especially inviting utopia. Filled with hobo references such as "jungle fires" (the hobo jungle at night) and "down the track came a hobo hiking," (meaning, of course, the railroad track that hobos for many years have used as their avenue for free transportation anywhere), "Big Rock" tells of "a land that's far away beside the crystal fountain."

The creator of this well-known ballad was most likely Harry Kirby McClintock (1882-1957), who probably wrote the piece early in his life, around the beginning of the twentieth century. From this song, and another attributed to McClintock, the comedic "Hallelujah, I'm a Bum" (1928), which was based on the traditional hymn, "Revive Us Again," it is obvious that he had considerable experience riding the rails with other homeless wanderers. "Mac" McClintock's hobo handle, "Haywire Mac," also suggests this. (Incidentally, another song with the title "Hallelujah, I'm a Bum" was written by Richard Rodgers and Lorenz Hart in 1932, and an Al Jolson movie also used the title.)

A still-popular country favorite, "Big Rock," was revived with much success in 1949. If McClintock had collected the proper royalties from his "Big Rock" song, he would never have had to use the lines from his "I'm a Bum" song, which ask the listener to "give me a handout, to revive me again."

Buffalo Gals

Shakespeare's wise question, "What's in a name?," has special applicability to the old song, "Buffalo Gals." Originally entitled "Lubly Fan," it has also been known as "Louisiana Gals," "Pittsburgh Gals" and similar variations, and was many years after its creation adapted into the pop hit, "Dance with a Dolly."

This lively composition with a hot beat was written by Cool White in 1844. White and his Serenaders turned the song into one of the most popular pre-Civil War minstrel show numbers. It was so familiar as a part of American culture that it was mentioned in Mark Twain's famous 1876 novel, *Tom Sawyer.*

About a century after Cool White introduced his song into the world of the minstrel show, "Dance with a Dolly (with a Hole in Her Stockin')" swung into the 1940s world of popular music. With new lyrics written and old music adapted by Terry Shand, Jimmy Eaton, and Mickey Leader in 1940, and energized by a lively 1943 recording by the Mills Brothers, "Dolly" was at home in her era as were the "Buffalo Gals" in theirs.

In fact, if the tune were to be reinstated during the rock era, it probably would again feel completely comfortable. Such a transition would be quite easy because the "Buffalo Gals" melody is sort of a precursor or ancestor of the rock music style. But the rock lyrics, unfortunately, would almost surely be much more sexually explicit than their nineteenth-century predecessor. Could you imagine a contemporary rock song subtly asking Buffalo Gals to "come out tonight and dance by the light of the moon?"

Clementine

Probably the most famous fictional heroine of the Old West is Clementine, the daughter of "a miner, forty-niner." Her tragic tale is one of the most popular Western ballads of all time.

Probably the most famous real lawman in the West was Wyatt Earp. Many legends have accumulated around Earp and his associates, including the notorious Doc Holliday. Earp has been the main or a secondary character in a number of movies and television programs, and a successful television series featured him as the hero.

The best movie about Earp as well as one of the best Westerns to ever come out of Hollywood brought these two famous figures of the West together. In the 1946 film *My Darling Clementine*, the distinguished actor Henry Fonda played the role of Earp, who was smitten with the lovely Clementine, played by Cathy Downs. That production was such a classic that a screening of it was the focus of one of the episodes of another classic, the TV comedy series *M*A*S*H*.

In spite of all the attention that has been paid to Clementine, she remains a shadowy figure. The song does not reveal a lot about Clementine the imaginary person, and history has not really been able to clarify the details of the song's creation. The lyrics and music were first published together, under the title "Oh My Darling Clementine," in 1884. The authorship credit was given to Percy Montrose. A slightly different version appeared the following year under the title "Clementine," with authorship credited to a Barker Bradford. In addition, the lyrics alone had been published in 1863, with H. S. Thompson indicated as the creator. To even further confuse the issue, "Clementine"'s melody is quite similar to two other American melodies printed in the 1860s. Clementine may be perpetually darling, but she and her origins, like so much else in the folk domain, may also be perpetually mysterious. As Tom Lehrer, who created a spoof of "Clementine" has commented, the only thing wrong with folk music is that it was written by folk.

Git Along Little Dogies

When you're tired and bored, and away from the usual sources of amusement, just about anything can entertain you. So for a cowboy on a trail drive, pushing thousands of reluctant cattle to Abilene or some other cowtown, a ditty like "Git Along Little Dogies" can sound pretty good. It is far from a great song, but it apparently had a special appeal to the typical lonely cowhand. Part of this appeal was the plaintive quality of the lyrics. When the cowboy sang about the "dogie," the poor, unloved, undernourished, motherless calf, he was to some degree touching upon his own fate.

What makes the song so personal and poignant is its probable legitimate origins in a trail drive, possibly in the 1880s, in Texas. It was not, like many cowboy ballads, a slick composition originating in a big eastern city. Highlighted by its unique line "Whoopee ti yi yo," it is a natural, realistic, spontaneous, exuberant folk piece with an underlying layer of sadness. All these qualities have made it a definite classic of Western America.

Its status as a cowboy standard has been reinforced by a comic book-level joke that has been around for at least two generations. There are a number of variations, but one form is: "In what way are a cowboy and a radio advertisement selling dachshunds the same?" The answer: They both say "Git a long little dogie."

Home on the Range

"Home on the Range" is the official state song of Kansas. It has been called "the cowboy's national anthem." It surely is the best-known Western song in the United States. It also is, incidentally, one of this author's least favorite compositions.

"Home on the Range" is so familiar that it has become a stereotype. The lines "Where the buffalo roam," "Where the deer and the antelope play," "Where seldom is heard a discouraging word," as well as the title phrase, have been considerably parodied and are deeply ingrained in American popular culture. Even the most fair-minded observer cannot describe it as an especially good song, but it would be folly to deny its long-standing popularity.

The original home for "Home on the Range" was the wide-open range. The lyrics, probably by pioneer physician Brewster M. Higley (1823-1911) were published in the *Smith County Pioneer* (Kansas) in 1873 under the title "Oh, Give Me a Home Where the Buffalo Roam." (Printings with the titles "Western Home" and "Colorado Home" were also issued.) The music was first published (along with the lyrics) in 1904, with yet another geographical relocation to "Arizona Home." The melody is now usually ascribed to Daniel E. Kelley (1843-1905), a musician and entertainer, but at the time of the song's first publication, was credited to William H. Goodwin.

For years, the controversy surrounding various authorship claims, including lawsuits, was as hot as a kitchen range just before Sunday dinner. Although the skies may not be cloudy all day where the deer and the antelope play, the legal and historical issues relating to "Home on the Range" have definitely been overcast and stormy.

Jesse James

In the aftermath of the American Civil War and the social upheavals it caused, many men, already accustomed to fighting with guns, became outlaws in the West. Among these were Missouri-born Jesse James and his older brother Frank, who had ridden with Quantrill's Raiders, a vicious gang siding with the Confederates.

Daring and bold, Jesse and his own gang held up trains and banks in the late 1860s, the 1870s, and the early 1880s. Jesse became a folk hero to many everyday Americans not possessing the wealth of the railroads and banks. Jesse, in hiding and using the last name Howard, was assassinated in April 1882 by Robert Ford, a member of Jesse's band. Partly because of Jesse's murder by one of his own, Jesse James became one of the icons of popular culture in the United States. One of the ingredients contributing to the ongoing hero worship was the ballad, "Jesse James." Sometimes attributed to a Billy Gashade, the song appeared in Springfield, Missouri soon after Jesse's death. Along with all the Jesse James stories, movies, and myths (such as the recently debunked one that Jesse was not killed in 1882 and had lived for many years after), the ballad helped assemble what may be the biggest body of lore from the old West.

Reportedly, Bob Ford's sister, upset with the unflattering lines about her brother, assaulted an old blind woman who was singing the sad tale on a Missouri street. A somewhat similar confrontation, probably with no basis in fact, occurred in the 1948 film, *I Shot Jesse James*. Bob Ford, played by John Ireland, warily stopped in a saloon in a small western town. A wandering balladeer offered, for a little monetary consideration, to sing the most popular song at that time. Wishing for some diversion from his troubles, Ford agreed to the request. The balladeer proceeded to sing "Jesse James," including the memorable lines, "But the dirty little coward that shot Mr. Howard, has laid Jesse James in his grave." When Ford, who was totally unknown to the men in the saloon, reacted painfully to the song, the singer asked what the problem was. Ford replied tersely, "I'm Bob Ford." The onlookers expected Ford to shoot the unlucky troubadour, but instead, he asked for more of the song, which had now become a difficult task for the singer. Ford then paid the man, and departed quietly.

Jim Crack Corn

Gettysburg is a place of great historic importance. Near that southern Pennsylvania city in July 1863, the most crucial battle of the American Civil War bloodily altered the conflict in favor of the Union cause. In November of the same year, President Lincoln went to Gettysburg to dedicate a memorial cemetery. The short speech he delivered on that occasion became one of the world's most famous orations.

It is said that while at Gettysburg, Lincoln requested the playing of "Jim Crack Corn" or "The Blue Tail Fly." A favorite of minstrel shows and folk singers as well as our sixteenth president, "Jim Crack Corn," sometimes known as "Jimmy Crack Corn," was published in Baltimore in 1846.

Authorship of this lively classic with a distinctly rural flavor is uncertain. There is some belief that it was composed by Daniel Decatur Emmett (1815-1904) of Ohio. If this is so, the anecdote about Gettysburg, Lincoln, and "Jim Crack Corn" has an ironic sidelight: Emmett is best known as the composer of another and more famous minstrel piece, "Dixie," the musical symbol of the South during the Civil War. (Some sources suggest, however, that Emmett may have borrowed the song from an anonymous black musician. If this debt is valid, there is another irony involved, the composition of a confederate song by a black.)

Mississippi Mud

One of the more interesting songs about a region of the United States, "Mississippi Mud" appears to refer to the southern half of the Mississippi River Valley, which, of course, includes the state with the long name as well as the long river. Its bouncy, folk-like melody and its spontaneous lyrics, with the opening line "When the sun goes down, the tide goes out," makes it seem to be a nineteenth-century concoction from somewhere on the banks of the river.

Yet it is definitely a twentieth-century phenomenon, published in nonrural New York City in 1927, the same year that the most famous song about the Mississippi "Ol' Man River," first appeared in the great musical, *Show Boat*. While the poignant "Ol' Man River" was written by two very famous artists, composer Jerome Kern and lyricist Oscar Hammerstein II, the frivolous "Mississippi Mud" was created by Harry Barris (1905-1962), a popular composer of modest achievement. (He also wrote the 1931 hit "Wrap Your Troubles in Dreams [and Dream Your Troubles Away]" with Ted Koehler and Billy Moll.)

Yet his 1927 ditty, though not especially well-crafted, does catch the feel of life for everyday people in the rural Mississippi Valley. Its memorable signature sentence, "It's a treat to beat your feet on the Mississippi Mud," describes the composition perfectly. The song is a treat, it makes you want to beat your feet, and it helps to carry you off to the more peaceful and unsophisticated environs of America's greatest river. In other words, it in some ways transports us back to the fuzzy pleasantries of the era of Tom Sawyer and Huckleberry Finn.

Oh, Susanna

There is a lot of nonsense connected with "Oh, Susanna." The lyrics are, of course, a batch of delightful nonsense connected to a sprightly, toe-tapping tune. When we sing the concoction, we tend to forget about the silliness of the lyrics because we are too busy trying to keep up with rapidly rambling rhythm.

A certain degree of goofiness was also exhibited by Stephen Foster (1826-1864) after he wrote his first famous song and probably the best known of all his works. Because he was afraid that this type of unsophisticated black dialect composition would damage his artistic reputation (up to then he had little), he initially didn't want his name associated with the piece.

The biggest batch of silliness related to "Oh, Susanna," however, took place in the western part of the United States. Soon after the song's 1847 premiere as planned entertainment in a Pittsburgh ice cream parlor and its 1848 New York City publication and minstrel performance, gold was discovered at Sutter's Mill in California. Tens of thousands of lemming-like prospectors flocked to California in the big Gold Rush of 1849. On the way, the favorite song of the forty-niners was "Oh, Susanna," sung both in the original version and in various parodies. Although few struck it rich in the new land, they did at least have some fun on the trip there. Other early travelers to the West also took a special liking to this smash hit of 1848. It can be truly said that during the middle of the nineteenth century, the imaginary Susanna was the prospector's and pioneer's most pleasurable traveling companion.

The Red River Valley

The story of the excellent Western folk ballad "The Red River Valley" contains a lesson in geography. Nemaha and Harlan, both cities in western Iowa, are indicated on the earliest manuscript of the lyrics, along with references to the years 1879 and 1885. The initial printing of lyrics and melody together (1896) gives another title, "In the Bright Mohawk Valley," along with credits to a James J. Kerrigan. Thus, Iowa in the Midwest is mentioned in the first version, and New York State in the East is referred to in the second.

But since the oldest known title is "The Red River Valley" and the Red River Valley is located in Texas, Oklahoma, Arkansas, and Louisiana, the southern states must be the real locale for the song, right? This guess, as well as the references to Iowa and New York, gives a completely false trail in the hunt for geographical truth. The apparent inspiration for the composition is either Manitoba, Canada, or the U.S. region just south of it. There is a Red River, also called "Red River of the North," which flows from the Dakotas and Minnesota into Lake Winnipeg.

Therefore, "The Red River Valley" is quite possibly of Canadian origin. It may have been sung during an 1869 rebellion in the Northwest Territories of Canada. Yet American folk origins are also just as possible because of the Iowa manuscript, the first printing of lyrics with music in New York City, the fact that the Red River is partially in the United States, and the stylistic similarities with other songs of the American West. In function, it is a classic standard of the Old West, and thereby essentially American. Even if it is in reality Canadian, it still could be categorized as a "Western," since Manitoba is a prairie province in the western portion of the vast domain of Canada.

The Streets of Laredo

The city of Laredo, Texas was founded in 1755 and the ballad that helped make the community famous had its origins only a few decades later, around the 1790s. However, the first manifestations of this well-known composition about a cowboy dying on the streets of Laredo had nothing to do with Texas or cowboys. The tortuous path of "The Streets of Laredo" started with an Irish street song called "The Unfortunate Rake," and then went to England where "The Trooper Cut Down in His Prime" related the sad tale of a dying young British soldier. Other versions evolved, including the American black jazz piece "St. James Infirmary" and "Laredo," which was written anonymously around 1860. Lumberjacks and sailors have also appeared in other variants, all of which have a mournful flavor.

A classic of the Old West, "Laredo" is still sung well over a century later, spawning a successful 1993 Western novel, *The Streets of Laredo,* by Larry McMurtry. In 1949, it also spawned a notable Western film "The Streets of Laredo," starring two famous actors, William Holden and William Bendix. If you remember both of these men, you will have no trouble figuring out who the good guy was.

Turkey in the Straw

In the late twentieth century, "turkey" is a slang expression to describe a person with little appeal. In the first half of the nineteenth century, "zip coon" was used as a derisive term to describe pretentious, fashionably dressed, black "Broadway swells."

The classic of square dance pieces, "Turkey in the Straw," was originally called, curiously, "Zip Coon." Introduced by New York City minstrel Bob Farrell in 1834 and subsequently a feature of George Washington Dixon's minstrel productions, "Zip Coon" was claimed by both Farrell and Dixon. There is a good chance that one of the two created this strange phenomenon, but debt to an Irish folk tune has also been mentioned.

"Zip Coon"'s nonsense lyrics, which included lines like "Possum up a gum tree, Coony on a stump," were fortunately forgotten in time. In 1861, the Thanksgiving bird came onto the scene. A new song entitled "Turkey in de Straw," with lyrics and melody unrelated to "Zip Coon," was published in that year. At the end of the printing of "Turkey" was attached the wordless melody of "Zip Coon." The old melody and the new "Turkey" title became thus linked together in the minds of the American public and the two did a permanent "do-si-do" into U.S. music history, accompanied by a similar anonymous square dance favorite of the same period, "Skip to My Loo" (around 1844). The two songs make an ideal duo, for the meaningless word "loo," apparently used simply to rhyme with "shoo," is a perfect companion to the delightful meaninglessness of the lyrics of "Turkey in the Straw."

SONGS THAT EXCITE OR AMUSE

An American in Paris

It is not very common for two different artistic forms with identical titles and a basically different content to both be extraordinarily good. But in the case involving Gene Kelly, the very talented dancer who also was a good actor and singer, it happened twice. In 1952, he starred in the outstanding movie *Singin' in the Rain* and danced to and sang its outstanding title song in an unforgettable extended scene. The song, however, was first performed in another film musical, *Hollywood Revue of 1929*. The only connections between the 1952 movie and the 1929 song by lyricist Arthur Freed and composer Nacio Herb Brown, however, were the one scene and the shared titles. Though both the film and musical number were first-rate, they were just joined together to attract audiences.

The other incident relating to Kelly occurred one year earlier, in 1951. The film *An American in Paris* also featured a musical composition with the same title. As in the case of *Singin' in the Rain,* the song was not essential to the plot, yet was the best part of the film. In an eerie coincidence, "An American in Paris" was written one year before "Singin' in the Rain," paralleling the one year difference between the films that showcased them.

"An American in Paris" was, of course, the 1928 masterpiece of that name by the great George Gershwin (1898-1937). "American" combined classical and jazz styles, with the opening section presenting touches of Paris, including car horns and a little French march very noticeable because of its bold and aggressive tempo. The polished 1928 inspiration was almost as fine as (some say better than) Gershwin's more spontaneous early masterwork, "Rhapsody in Blue" (1924). In an also unforgettable multiscene ballet sequence at the end of the movie, Kelly and Leslie Caron danced all over Paris to the mostly lively rhythms of "American," ending with a full reconciliation of the two young lovers. There was no rain in that sequence, just brilliant dancing, choreography, and music.

The Anvil Chorus

The concept of a chorus of anvils pounding on metal in rhythm is a clever one. If you have ever seen a first-rate blacksmith skillfully and methodically work on a red-hot horseshoe or ornamental piece of ironwork, you may have sensed a certain monotonic musical beat accompanying the task.

This is what Italian composer Giuseppe Verdi (1813-1901), with his definite penchant for genius, apparently recognized when he wrote "The Anvil Chorus" for his 1853 opera *Il Trovatore* (*The Troubadour*). Although medieval troubadours and their modern counterparts have generally performed on simple everyday instruments such as mandolins or guitars, the "instrument" that made Verdi's opera so famous was the "musical" anvil. Verdi, of course, was a world-famous composer who created masterful operas such as *Rigoletto* (1851), *La Traviata* (*The Woman Gone Astray*) (1853), *La Forza del Destino* (*The Force of Destiny*) (1862), and *Aida* (1871), as well as *Il Trovatore*.

"The Anvil Chorus" has found its way into American culture in various ways. Its distinctive tones have been heard in television advertisements, animated cartoons, and recordings by a famous big band. The Glenn Miller Orchestra, whose short but meteoric existence under Miller from 1939 to 1944 (succeeded by continuing versions after Miller's death in late 1944) put them at the top of the bands of the swing era, recorded "The Anvil Chorus" with their usual skill, zest, and sense of humor. Verdi's brilliant music, as adapted with equal brilliance by the Miller Orchestra, was one of the ensemble's favorite numbers.

Beethoven's Fifth Symphony

Probably the most famous four notes in the world, the distinctive opening of Beethoven's Fifth Symphony (1808) is hummed or whistled by persons who may have no idea of its source. The four notes, three short and one long, are a firm part of the everyday culture of the world including that of the United States. They even found their way into Walter Murphy's 1976 rock tribute, "A Fifth of Beethoven," 20 years after another homage composition in rock style, Chuck Berry's 1956 "Roll Over Beethoven." Other works by Beethoven (1770-1827), arguably the greatest composer ever, have penetrated the easily accessed domain of American popular culture. These include his piano works and his magnificent Ninth Symphony (1824), with its rousing choral, "Hymn to Joy."

But his Fifth Symphony, with its dramatic four-note signature, is perhaps his best effort. Extremely well-crafted and original throughout, it is as impeccable and fulfilling as any major work ever written. His Ninth Symphony has finer moments, perhaps, but nothing else has the consistent and persistent mastery of the Fifth.

There have been various interpretations of the symphony and its "dee dee dee *dah*" beginning, including the presence of fate and a struggle with destiny. One very fascinating ramification of the renowned opening is its usage as a form of defiance against the Nazis in World War II. In Morse code, invented after Beethoven's death, three dots and one dash signify the letter "V." With a code rhythm similar to Beethoven's four notes, "V," as made famous by Winston Churchill's memorable finger-positioning, was the symbol for victory over the Nazis. Beethoven's theme thus became closely allied with the Allied war effort.

"V" also means "five" in Roman numerals, another connection with the "Fifth." In case you haven't noticed, we have touched upon the numbers one through five–one dash, World War II, three dots, four notes, and symphony number five.

Camptown Races

The Camptown Racetrack was a strange place. First, the track was "five miles long," while the typical track today is closer to one mile. Second, they either scheduled a ridiculous amount of contests or else the horses were unbelievably slow, for as the song says, the animals were "Gwine to run all night, Gwine to run all day." (Sounds like the last glue pot you bet on, right?)

Stephen Foster's nonsense lyrics are much of the charm of this bouncy and enduring bit of Americana. Written in 1850 and introduced by the Christy Minstrels, "De Camptown Races" was a big hit with minstrel troupes throughout the country. Soon after, a well-known nautical folk song, "Sacramento," with the first lines "A bully ship and a bully crew, Doodah, Doodah," used "Camptown's" melody and obviously also was influenced by Foster's lyrics. Another probable nautical derivative was the anonymous "A Capital Ship" (around 1875), which apparently borrowed its refrain from "Camptown." And among the parodies that developed was a pro-Lincoln curiosity which appeared during the 1860 presidential campaign between Lincoln and Stephen A. Douglas. Part of those lyrics were "I'll bet my money on the Lincoln hoss, Who'll bet on Stephen A?"

Perhaps the best way to describe the song's current status would be to paraphrase Foster:

The Camptown Races still are fun,
Doodah, Doodah,
A favorite song of everyone
Oh, doodah, day.

Chopsticks

Chopsticks are wooden sticks the Chinese use as eating utensils. *Chopsticks* the musical curiosity is not as easily defined. Published in 1877 in both London and Glasgow, Scotland, as "The Celebrated Chop Waltz," this strange composition has mystified musicologists ever since. With preexistence implied by the title, and the 1877 edition stating arrangement by Arthur de Lulli, it would appear that the piece was older. Yet there is no evidence of earlier origins. Arthur de Lulli was actually the pseudonym of Euphremia Allen (1861-1949), the sister of Mozart Allen, who published "Chopsticks" in Glasgow. In 1877, Euphremia was a sixteen-year-old.

With the hyperbole of having "celebrated" in the title, and the odd instructions to hold both hands in a chopping motion, "Chopsticks" was most likely a prank by a typical and talented teenager. Euphremia was probably the tongue-in-cheek composer, but her private joke in time became a public phenomenon in the United States and elsewhere.

But the story doesn't end there. In the same year, 1877, another young lady, the daughter of the Russian master Alexander Borodin, also played or composed four bars of notes that her father used one year later as the basis for a composition. The daughter's little piece was similar to "Chopsticks." That alone would not have been particularly remarkable if it weren't for the name given to the "Chopsticks" sound-alike. Borodin called the Russian version "The Coteletten Polka." Côtelette is French, meaning "cutlet" or "chop." This has to be a bizarre coincidence, for it is extremely unlikely that a minor piece from Scotland would find its way to distant Russia, or vice versa, almost overnight. In any case, the highly repetitive "Chopsticks" has delighted American youngsters and sent some American parents away screaming for over 100 years.

Donna Diana Overture

One of the favorite old radio programs in the United States was the action series *The Challenge of the Yukon,* also known as *Sergeant Preston of the Yukon.* In the radio broadcasts (1947-1955) as well as a later television version (1955-1958), Preston, a Mountie, and his sled dog, King would traverse the frozen North and maintain law and order in the Canadian Wilderness. Among the elements that made both versions successful was the striking theme music, which conveyed the impression of boldness, freedom, airiness, and openness. In other words, it fit in very well with the atmosphere and geography of the program.

As is so often the case, the original composition had little in common with its later function. The brilliant, stimulating music used for the dramatic adventures of Sergeant Preston was written for a comedy set in a much warmer climate, namely Spain. It was part of the overture to *Donna Diana,* a comic opera by Emil Nikolaus von Rezniček (1860-1945), an Austrian composer and conductor. Produced in Prague, Czechoslovakia, early in Rezniček's career (1894), it brought him considerable success and fame. Subsequent works, however, did not approach the popularity of *Donna Diana.*

As a result, Rezniček is far from a household name throughout the world. If it weren't for the fortunate adaptation of his partly Viennese and partly Spanish overture as the introduction to the radio and television episodes of Preston and King, few Americans would ever have heard his sole significant creation.

1812 Overture

Under the autocratic regime of the Russian Czars, serious Russian composers were "encouraged" to use Russian national themes in their music. For example, the great master Peter Ilich Tchaikovsky (1840-1893) used the fine Russian national anthem, "God Save the Czar," in two of his better-known works. In his "Marche Slave" ("Slavic March") (1876), Tchaikovsky used the Russian national anthem plus bits from two Russian folk songs. This excellent march sometimes finds its way into American popular culture.

The second famous work incorporating "God Save the Czar" was *1812* Overture. Written in 1880 and first performed in 1882, *1812,* which relates the story of the Russian victory over invading Napoleon in 1812, borrows from both the Russian national anthem and the superlative French national anthem, "La Marseillaise." Although Tchaikovsky was a bit anachronistic in usage of the 1833 "God Save the Czar" in his musical reproduction of 1812 events ("La Marseillaise" was historically correct, being created in 1792), neither Tchaikovsky, the Czar, or the many music fans who love the powerful overture seem to care.

In fact, *1812,* perhaps the most popular of all of Tchaikovsky's works, is sort of a cult favorite among American outdoor concertgoers. It is also popular at indoor concerts, but the very loud ending with accompanying cannon booms is more conducive to open air environments than concert halls. A particular favorite at Fourth of July celebrations where fireworks are exhibited, the pyrotechnics are sometimes employed as a substitute for live cannons. Whether the emphases to the overture's ending are provided by cannons, fireworks, percussion instruments, or explosives (as in the finale of the 1980 film *Caddyshack),* such performances of the work are a deservingly emphatic tribute to the outstanding Russian musician.

Fingal's Cave Overture

The romantic and colorful land of Scotland has been represented in music many times. Usually the portrayal is in the form of ballads or bagpipe pieces. In the case of the brilliant German composer Felix Mendelssohn (1809-1847), the music inspired by the homeland of Robert Burns included a symphony and a first-rate overture. Obviously affected by an 1829 trip to Scotland, Mendelssohn wrote his Symphony No. 3 (1842), called the *Scotch* because of the Scottish melodies used and the Scottish scenes pictured.

Ten years before, in 1832, Mendelssohn produced an even more vivid memory of that northern British country. Named for a famous cave in the Hebrides Islands, *Fingal's Cave* or *The Hebrides* is an overture so well crafted that the first-time listener is often transfixed by its intricate yet powerful tones, which have the feel of circular or cyclical activity. One can almost literally hear and touch the forward and backward flow of the mighty ocean in its relentless physical interchange with the cave. This superlative image is the reason why *Fingal's Cave* is frequently used in various performing arts in the United States and elsewhere to add a sense of drama and power, particularly when relating to the forces of nature. It has sometimes been utilized to represent a storm, which it does well, but it really is symbolic of the march of time and tides. In other words, *Fingal's Cave* is an indirect tribute to both Mother Nature and Father Time.

The Flight of the Bumblebee

There is an old absurdity about the tuba player who tried to play "The Flight of the Bumblebee" in its normal tempo. Of course, such a task is impossible. Even with instruments designed to accommodate high-speed music, the performance of this extremely fast-paced, delicate, and intricate morsel requires a considerable amount of skill. "The Flight of the Bumblebee" is an exquisite artistic simulation of the hyperactive daily routine of this highly beneficial insect. Not many composers have had the capability to carry out such musical mimicry so realistically.

"Bumblebee's" creator was Nikolai Rimsky-Korsakov (1844-1908), the great Russian composer. Rimsky-Korsakov included his widely known piece in a 1900 opera, *The Tale of Tsar Saltan.* "Bumblebee" has since been utilized in a large variety of situations—animated cartoons, advertisements, comedy routines, radio and TV programs, and other occasions. One of its more famous adaptations was for the old radio show *The Green Hornet,* which ran from 1936 to 1952.

A television version was also produced in 1966-67, starring Van Williams as the Hornet and Bruce Lee as the faithful oriental associate, Kato. Later on, Lee became quasi-legendary for his starring roles in a series of martial arts films. With superhuman combat powers, Lee would eradicate an abundance of bad guys with stinging force reminiscent of his former affiliation with the hornet and bumblebee.

The Flying Dutchman

No, the Flying Dutchman is not about a man from Amsterdam in a plane or hot-air balloon. Instead, it is the sad tale of a phantom ship that is destined to sail the seas forever and ever, on occasion reappearing within view of living humans. The great German master Richard Wagner (1813-1883) transferred this dreary scenario into a fairly good opera, *Der fliegende Holländer* (*The Flying Dutchman*) (1843). Perhaps the best part of the opera is its overture, which starts with some tense and terse notes from horns to suggest the drama about to unfold. The horn notes are followed by an excellent simulation of a storm at sea, clearly depicting a sailing craft sharply moving from side to side, matching the surges of the angry ocean.

Wagner's storm sequence in *Dutchman* has often been used in acted or animated movie scenes where an old two- or three-masted ship is tossed around by inclement weather. Indeed, in America and throughout the world it is the stereotypical music for artistic occasions involving what I call the four S's: sea, ship, sails, storm, and at times, a fifth "S": sunk or stranded.

Two more "storm" sequences from serious music that pack a wallop in American popular culture appear in the opera *William Tell* (1829) by Italian master Gioacchino Rossini (1792-1868) and in the overture *Fingal's Cave* or *The Hebrides* (1832) by the German master, Felix Mendelssohn (1809-1847). Rossini musically follows a land storm from its beginning to its end; Mendelssohn is not literally trying to reproduce a storm, but with dramatically ebbing and flowing sensations, his creation succulently portrays the power of the ocean.

"Humoresque" by Dvořák

You may or may not know much about Antonin Dvořák (1841-1904), who is perhaps the greatest composer from Czechoslovakia. Dvořák (pronounced like "Dvorjak") is well known internationally for his Symphony No. 5, *From the New World* (1893), which brilliantly reproduces his impressions of America; his *Slavonic Dances*; and the little piano piece, "Humoresque."

Actually, "Humoresque" was number seven of a group of *Humoresken* published in 1894, and proved to be a very lucky seven for the enduring reputation of Dvořák. Although many of his other works are much more significant, his lively "Humoresque," conceived while visiting the United States, is quite possibly recognized by more persons than any of his other compositions. A favorite recreation for five or ten fingers at the piano, it is also played orchestrally.

A great many of us have heard "Humoresque," even if we didn't know the name. In the United States, it has been adapted for many purposes, including dancing, television, and the movies. In case you haven't been able to identify the melody yet, the following identification should probably rectify that. (At times like this, it would be handy to be able to hum on paper.) "Humoresque" is the tune used for (brace yourself) the undistinguished nonclassic "One-sy, two-sy, I love you-sy, three-sy, four-sy, I adore-sy."

"Hungarian Rhapsody" by Liszt

As a performer, Milton Berle was unique. He was perhaps the
most significant personality in the early days of television. After a
notable period on radio, the buffoonery of "Uncle Miltie" brought
hysterics to American audiences in the 1940s and 1950s. (In later
years, Berle also proved to be a capable movie and TV actor.)

Berle's TV shows appeared under various names. The first, called
The Milton Berle Show, ran from 1948 to 1953. Following that came
The Buick-Berle Show (1953-1955), another *Milton Berle Show*
(1955-1956), *The Kraft Music Hall* (1958-1959), and yet another
The Milton Berle Show (1966-1967). By far the most popular of
these programs was the original one, also called *The Texaco Star
Theater.*

The introductory music on that show was "Hungarian Rhapsody
No. 2" (1851) by Franz Liszt. While millions were awaiting the
arrival of their favorite comedian, a group of men in gas station
attendant uniforms extolled the virtues of the sponsor's gasoline to
the tune of the "Rhapsody." (Uncle Miltie himself didn't need to get
gassed up. He was always ready to induce a laugh at the drop of a
stolen joke.)

Liszt (1811-1886), a Hungarian-born composer and pianist, was
one of the outstanding and most influential musical figures of the
nineteenth century. A full liszt of his accomplishments is quite
impressive: great virtuosity at the keyboard, a number of fine compositions, and various technical innovations. Among his works is
the 1854 symphonic poem "Les Préludes," which was used on
another media classic of the same period. "Les Préludes" was the
"bridge" music between scenes of *The Lone Ranger* radio series.
So, more or less, Liszt simultaneously kept both the Ranger riding
and introduced the outlandish Berle-esque routines of Uncle Miltie.

Hunt Theme

Humans have hunted for food since they first existed. Hunting for sport began much later, and has received its share of criticism, especially in more recent centuries. Among the least defensible forms of hunting is the horses and hounds custom practiced by landed gentry in Europe and elsewhere. This particular activity is troublesome in part because a pack of dogs track down a solitary fox or similar animal, and then a brave member of the hunt party shoots the cornered and fatigued creature. Another difficulty is that the aristocrats who participate in this "sport" sometimes have denied the right of hunting for food to the poorer and less powerful inhabitants of the area.

Despite the problems associated with this type of hunting, it has been much glamorized over the years in literature, theater, film, and so on. Part of the glamorization of the custom is a short piece of music known as the "Hunt Theme." With its rousing call to the hunt, sometimes accompanied by the words "Tantivy! Tantivy! Tantivy! A-hunting we will go!," it has become a most familiar symbol of the hounds chasing the fox and of red-coated horsemen shouting "Tally-ho!" In the United States, it has been used for animated cartoons, various films, the live theater, and many other venues.

The tune appears to be a folk composition of eighteenth-century England. Around 1782-1792, a "Hunt Theme" composition very similar to the present form was published with the title "Tantivy, My Boys, Tantivy" and the notation "A favorite hunting song." About a century later, in 1884, the familiar arrangement of the music accompanied by the "A-hunting we will go" lyrics was printed as part of a larger work. The composer of the work was the minor English musician Procida Bucalossi (1833?-1918), whose only claim to fame is the few bars of the "Hunt Theme." Since Bucalossi most likely only adapted the earlier folk melody, and may have also taken the brief lyric from the folk domain, his contribution to posterity is as dubious as the hunting custom it glorifies.

Light Cavalry Overture

The cavalry is light, the music is light, the mood is light. Therefore, the *Light Cavalry* Overture can be confidently described as a light composition. Written by Viennese composer Franz von Suppé (1820-1895) for the 1866 horse opera *Leichte Cavalrie* ("Light Cavalry"), the piece has been a favorite of concert audiences for generations. Its energetic simulation of men on horseback and its freewheeling atmosphere have made it a perennial of the light classical repertory. Suppé's 1854 *Poet and Peasant* Overture, likewise a vigorous composition, is a concert standard too.

Light Cavalry has been used frequently in movies and other situations when serious or comedic musical renditions of horsemanship are required. If the Light Brigade that made the suicidal charge in the Crimean War of 1853-1856 had had *Light Cavalry* available to it, it may well have used it as its comedic relief battle song. (It is possible that this historical incident was the inspiration of the later opera.)

Poet and Peasant and *Light Cavalry* may also have influenced two subsequent light compositions. In the introductory section of *Poet and Peasant*, there is a passage that is reminiscent of the opening line of the American classic "I've Been Working on the Railroad," which was published in 1894. The opening lines of *Light Cavalry*'s main theme, furthermore, are similar to the 1871 melody attached to "Jack and Jill went up the hill to fetch a pail of water." The young couple's bucket of H_2O is the first nonlight thing connected with this whole session of horsing around.

Listen to the Mocking Bird

It has been said that society's direct or indirect resistance is the reason there have not been more outstanding female composers. There is at least some truth to such an assessment, yet, like most explanations for human behavior, the statement is far from universally valid. An interesting example of this is the case of the American composition, "Listen to the Mocking Bird." When the song was published in 1855, the name attached to the song was Alice Hawthorne. The presence of a female name did not prevent the composition from becoming one of the most popular pieces of its era. Although the publisher may have known that Alice Hawthorne was actually the pseudonym of a man, Septimus Winner, the general public was not aware of this. Furthermore, when Winner wrote the tender hymn "Whispering Hope" in 1868, he again used the Hawthorne pen name with considerable success. It might even be postulated that for these two particular songs–a ballad about a songbird and a delicate anthem–using a woman's name may have been to Winner's advantage because of the lyrical and soft natures of the pieces.

In contrast, when Winner (1827-1902) concocted his two well-known novelty or comedy songs, "Oh Where, Oh Where Has My Little Dog Gone," and "Ten Little Indians," he used his real male name. "Oh Where," also known as "Der Deutcher's Dog," was published in 1864. Winner wrote the lyrics and probably adapted the music from the third movement of Ludwig van Beethoven's Symphony No. 6 (1808), also known as the *Pastorale.*

The music for "Ten Little Indians" (1868) was perhaps based on an old chantey, "The Drunken Sailor" or "What Shall We Do with a Drunken Sailor?," which was first published in 1891. Television fans may remember the scene from the 1965-1970 series *The Wild, Wild West,* in which the demented villain Dr. Loveless and one of his lovely female cronies sang "The Drunken Sailor" during one of his many escapades foiled by the hero James West. Both "The Drunken Sailor" and Winner's "Ten Little Indians" have silly or even nonsense lyrics, which is a large part of the reason they were quite popular in the late nineteenth and early twentieth centuries.

With the music for "Oh Where" and "Ten Little Indians" suspected to be borrowed from other sources, there is good reason to believe the reports that the music for "Mockingbird" was plagiarized by Winner from an African-American barber, Richard Milburn. Accordingly, one wonders if there is a whisper of a hope that his fine 1868 hymn was entirely original.

New World Symphony

Usually, a major work of music by a foreign composer that makes some kind of impact on American everyday life is known primarily in one or more excerpts. However, in the case of the *New World* Symphony, the most celebrated composition of Czech master Antonin Dvořák (1841-1904), the whole work is in a way totally American. Also known as Symphony No. 5 or *From the New World,* it was created in the New World, premiered in the New World, was strongly influenced by the New World, and is very popular in the New World. Dvořák came to the United States in 1892 after receiving an invitation to become director of the National Conservatory of Music in New York City. Greatly impressed by America, Dvořák put his greatest creativity into the new symphony, which premiered in New York City in December 1893. It was such a triumph that only two weeks after its introduction by the New York Philharmonic, the Boston Symphony Orchestra also performed it.

There has been some debate over whether *New World* was an American work written by a foreigner, or a foreign work influenced by American music. Although the latter seems to be more the case, either scenario would make the masterpiece just as good. American music and music in American style pop up throughout the symphony. In the first movement, there is a theme resembling that of "Swing Low, Sweet Chariot." In the second movement, a theme strongly reminiscent of a black spiritual is heard, and from that passage, the notable song "Goin' Home" was derived, with 1922 lyrics by one of Dvořák's pupils, William Arms Fisher (1861-1948). The third movement contains a fast section that reminds one of a ritual dance of a Native American people. The last movement has a powerful and jubilant theme that could easily be interpreted as a tribute to the power and success of the United States. As noted at the beginning of this essay, the symphony is more or less pure Americana.

Dvořák's stay in the United States certainly was a positive experience for him. He wrote other American-related pieces because of his 1892 to 1895 sojourn across the Atlantic, and created his famous whimsical piano piece, "Humoresque" (1894), while in America.

A Night on Bald Mountain

If there was a perfect musical piece that depicts the evil spirits that roam the earth on Halloween, it might well be "A Night on Bald Mountain." Composed by Russian Modest Mussorgsky (1839-1881), "Bald Mountain" retells the legend of Bald Mountain near Kiev in Ukraine where all sorts of eerie phenomena gather to celebrate the Witches' Sabbath. The composition, written between 1860 and 1866 and first performed in 1886, is a memorable impact piece with considerable drama and vivid sensations of the supernatural. It is frequently used in the United States whenever a mood of excitement and uneasiness is intended. One of its most famous uses was in the 1940 Walt Disney animated masterpiece, *Fantasia.*

To Americans, the name "Modest" for an unorthodox, and in his last days, probably insane musician seems a bit laughable. The humor increases when Mussorgsky's two other best-known works are mentioned. His 1874 piano suite, *Pictures at an Exhibition,* now usually performed as a fully orchestrated composition, is both brilliant and awkward, with flashes of genius and definite touches of the grotesque. Parts of the unusual suite are occasionally found in television advertisements and other everyday situations. Mussorgsky's third famous work is the outstanding opera *Boris Godunov* (1874). The music of this production is more or less unknown outside of opera houses, but its name is indirectly familiar to the many Americans who are fans of the long-running Canadian animated cartoon show *Rocky and Bullwinkle.* The perpetual villain on the television series was named Boris Badinov (or however it is actually spelled), an obvious variation of Boris Godunov. That show, incidentally, has a striking theme perhaps assembled from the music of two classical masters, Franz Von Suppé and Richard Wagner. The rapid-fire, sort of jolting opening of the theme resembles several passages from Suppé's operas, and the dramatic second part is similar to the first notes of the prelude to the third act of Wagner's opera, *Lohengrin* (1850).

Another famous classical composition associated with Halloween is "Danse Macabre" ("Macabre Dance"), an 1875 symphonic poem by French musician Camille Saint-Saëns (1835-1921). With a decidedly wicked tone, especially during the violin solo (a chilling musical picture of Death dancing), it is a fitting vehicle for the spooky end-of-October holiday.

Reuben and Rachel

If you had to guess the original nationality of the musical curiosity "Reuben and Rachel," the United States would probably not be the initial speculation. With European-sounding names like Reuben and Rachel, references to the "northern sea," and a distinct folk music style, the best stab at locating the song might be in northern Europe, perhaps in Scandinavia.

Yet, as unlikely as it may seem, the strange conversation between "Reuben and Rachel" is completely American. William Gooch, the musician, and Harry Birch, the lyricist, published their comic duett (actual spelling) in Boston in 1871. By no means is it a superior composition, but the quaint, rivalry-of-the-sexes dialogue has had a certain degree of popularity.

The woman starts out saying, "Reuben, I have long been thinking" (or "Reuben, Reuben, I've been thinking"), "What a good world this might be, If the men were all transported, Far beyond the northern sea," and the man replies in kind. Part of its attractiveness, therefore, is that it dares to play around with a never to be resolved and always interesting issue. But the most significant feature of the duel, as once pointed out by a male music teacher, is that the man, Reuben, actually has the final word.

The Ride of the Valkyries

When the average American thinks about the music of the great German composer Richard Wagner (1813-1883), which is probably not very often, the recollections are most likely those of the "Wedding March" ("Here Comes the Bride") from his 1850 opera *Lohengrin* and "The Ride of the Valkyries" from his 1870 opera *Die Walküre* (*The Valkyries*). *Die Walküre,* which was completed in 1856, is part of Wagner's famous *Der Ring des Nibelungen* (*The Nibelung Ring* or *The Ring Cycle*). An extended, some say overblown, four-part operatic work, *The Ring Cycle* has been described by one critic as being either one of the greatest or one of the worst serious music efforts of all time.

Although *The Ring Cycle* does have sleep-inducing sections more than occasionally, it also has some very lively passages. One of these is the above-mentioned "Ride of the Valkyries," which is a classic from the classics to many everyday working persons in the United States. With its attention-getting opening, air of excitement, and stimulating simulation of rapid motion, it is so well known that many who are not fans of serious music actually know the title. Among other uses, it has been heard in a Bugs Bunny cartoon and the 1979 film, *Apocalypse Now.*

In addition, its thrilling portrayal of the mythical Values (warrior maidens in Teutonic lore) frantically riding their steeds through the air fits in well with the music intended for Halloween. For that reason, it has sometimes become associated with that holiday's celebration, both in the classical music community and among mass audiences. Just about everybody, it seems, likes a good ghost story and good spooky music.

Row, Row, Row Your Boat

The history of "Row, Row, Row Your Boat" has similarities to its musical style. "Row Your Boat" is a round or canon which is sung in phases. One voice or group starts out with the initial line, and then another voice or group picks up the same line, and so forth.

When "Row Your Boat," an American ditty of possible minstrel origins, first got into print in 1852, its lyrics were almost the same as those we now know, but its melody was different. Another printing two years later kept the same lyrics, but offered yet another tune. A printing in 1881 finally got around to putting the present form of the lyrics and the present melody together. So, like the round in performance, there was a conflicting series of individual actions before all was settled in the end.

The first two versions did not at all identify the author of the nearly finalized lyrics. The "authoritative" 1881 printing mentioned someone named E. O. Lyte, but there was no indication whether Lyte was the creator or adapter. So, if you really want to know who wrote the nautical noodle "Row, Row, Row Your Boat," you're up the river without an oar.

Incidentally, "Row, row, row your boat, Gently down the stream" is not to be confused with the 1912 ballad with the opening lines "Row, row, row, Row up the river." (The 1912 "row" piece was by composer James V. Monaco and lyricist William Jerome.) The writer of the earlier song was either smarter or lazier, because he chose to navigate his little vessel with the current instead of fighting upstream like a neurotic salmon.

Sailor's Hornpipe

The term "stereotype" is often associated with things boring. But there is nothing dull about the spritely jig "Sailor's Hornpipe," which has to be the stereotypical song about nautical life. Often when a play, movie, or television program dealing with the sea is presented, the bristling chords of "Sailor's Hornpipe" bounce into the production. For example, it was a staple in the long-running *Popeye the Sailor Man* cartoons. (Another famous nautical song heard in cartoons is the anonymous English or American ditty "Pirate Song" or "Fifteen Men on a Dead Man's Chest–Yo! Ho! Ho! and a Bottle of Rum." Although rum has been popular for centuries, this piece about rum is most likely from the nineteenth century.)

Their closest rival for captain of the musical ship is the 1880 composition "Sailing, Sailing, Over the Bounding Main" by the English musician James Frederick Swift (1847-1931), who was also known as Godfrey Marks. But the quaint "Hornpipe" is probably the best internationally known of the three, even if the majority of those familiar with it do not know its actual title.

Ironically, however, this most nautical of songs may not have been created with the ocean in mind. It is anonymous and probably from eighteenth-century England or Ireland. When first published in the United States in 1796, it had the title "College Hornpipe," and this same title was used in its first English printing two years later. This type of devil-may-care dance seems a bit incongruous with the collegiate atmosphere, although students have been known to do just about anything for recreation.

The song not being at all associated with college life today is an indicator that its career on campus was not long-lived. At some unknown point in time, it became exclusively connected with sailors. Quite possibly it was always a sea song, with the first printings only a temporary diversion from its true purpose.

The Sidewalks of New York

The thousands of miles of sidewalks in New York City are very familiar to this writer. Born near the city and having spent a quarter century in its vicinity, the concrete pathways of the metropolis are by no means strangers. In the early 1960s, this author even traversed the entire island of Manhattan on foot, south to north, on one fine summer day.

Among the millions of other feet which have trod on New York City's pavements were those of vaudevillian Charles B. Lawlor (1852-1925) and hat salesman and lyricist James W. Blake (1862-1935). Lawlor, a Dubliner who emigrated to New York City, and Blake, a native New Yorker, collaborated on the 1894 composition that is the Big Apple's most famous musical tribute.

"The Sidewalks of New York," also known as "East Side, West Side" (from the opening of the chorus), has been frequently used in connection with America's largest community. Musicals, movies, and TV shows often include it. Notable among these are the 1927 stage production, *The Sidewalks of New York*, and the 1957 film biography of former Mayor James J. Walker, *Beau James*, in which Jimmy Durante and Bob Hope merrily sang and tap danced. It also was used as the official campaign song for the 1928 presidential campaign of New Yorker Al Smith. Smith lost the election to Herbert Hoover, who eventually was also a loser by being blamed, incorrectly, for the Great Depression of the 1930s.

The Sorcerer's Apprentice

One of Mickey Mouse's most renowned media appearances was in the 1940 Disney cartoon, *Fantasia*. There was nothing "Mickey Mouse" about that film, however, for *Fantasia* was so good that it could just as well be dubbed "Fantastica." A revolutionary blend of fine animation with some of the world's best serious music, *Fantasia* was a cinematic masterpiece.

Integrated into the film were Bach's Toccata and Fugue in D Minor, Beethoven's *Pastorale,* Mussorgsky's "Night on Bald Mountain," Ponchielli's "Dance of the Hours," Schubert's "Ave Maria," Stravinsky's "The Rite of Spring," Tchaikovsky's *Nutcracker Suite,* and most delightfully of all, Paul Dukas's "The Sorcerer's Apprentice." Originally composed in 1897 under the title "L'apprenti sorcier," the orchestral work was the most famous piece by the French composer. Born in 1865, Dukas died in 1935, just a few years before his animated composition was to become internationally beloved by association with the animated rodent.

While the senior sorcerer was away, junior magician Mickey Mouse managed to misuse the powers he had learned, create a flood of water, cause considerable chaos, and temporarily anger his mentor, all charmingly accompanied by Dukas's music. Mickey's mess, though, was a drop in the bucket compared to the catastrophe that may have occurred if Donald Duck had usurped Mickey's apprenticeship. And somehow the skillful notes of "The Sorcerer's Apprentice" would not at all fit with the mass confusion that would have been produced by the erratic fowl. Take the weirdest screech of dissonance, play it backwards and off tempo, and perhaps then the "music" would be compatible with the exasperating actions of Disney's dizzy duck.

Take Me Out to the Ball Game

There has been some argument as to whether or not baseball is America's national pastime. Football and basketball have each been seriously proposed as the leading sport in the United States, and various comedians have also offered other activities as the nation's number-one recreation.

No doubt exists, however, that "Take Me Out to the Ball Game" is the dominant song associated with baseball. Bellowed at ball games, played or sung in baseball motion pictures including the 1949 film *Take Me Out to the Ball Game,* and utilized in comedy routines and a broad assortment of other activities, it is such an established fixture that any suggestion to take it out of the baseball lineup might result in a fastball to the suggester's head. Its significance to the game is clearly confirmed by the presence of the original poem in the Baseball Hall of Fame in Cooperstown, New York.

As strange as a knuckleball, though, the authors of the summertime classic were apparently not even slight baseball fans. Reportedly, the lyricist Jack Norworth had not seen a major league game prior to the song's 1908 publication in New York City, and composer Albert von Tilzer did not see his first game until about 20 years after.

Philadelphia-born Norworth (1879-1959) was also known as the lyricist and co-composer (with Nora Bayes) for the 1908 romantic standard, "Shine On, Harvest Moon." Indianapolis-born Von Tilzer (1878-1956) was also known as the composer of the 1910 ballad "Put Your Arms Around Me, Honey" (lyricist, Junie McCree). These last two songs deal with what some of the previously mentioned comedians have characterized as our favorite national recreation.

Thus Spake Zarathusra

Any connection between the ancient prophet Zoroaster or Zarathusra, the founder of the pre-Christian religion Zoroastrianism, and space travel as depicted in the 1968 movie *2001* seems to be far-fetched. Yet as weird as this combination may appear to be, it actually happened. The instrument for bringing the two dissimilar elements together was composed by the celebrated German composer Richard Strauss (1864-1949).

In 1895, Strauss wrote "Also sprach Zarathusra" ("Thus Spake Zarathusra"), a symphonic poem. "Zarathusra" was used in the score of *2001*, along with other classical pieces including "The Blue Danube" by Johann Strauss (not a relative). The magnificent dramatic tones of "Zarathusra" caused much enthusiasm for Strauss's music among persons previously unacquainted with his works.

Unfortunately, most if not all of these new enthusiasts were probably disappointed when they delved further into Strauss. Their zeal surely waned greatly when they discovered that only the opening of "Zarathusra" is really exceptional. The rest of the composition is rather commonplace. Furthermore, the remainder of Strauss's music, though containing a number of fine sections here and there, is not consistently excellent. Strauss can go from exciting to boring in a relatively small number of bars.

But everything about Strauss is a bit weird. In appearance, he resembled a mousy businessman, but his music tended to be bizarre, sensuous, and provocative. His work was highly praised and just as strongly damned. He was linked with the Nazis because of a brief musical association with them, but was exonerated after World War II. Because of this Nazi connection and the general chaos in Germany during the last days of the Third Reich, the elderly Strauss feared for his life during that period in 1945. When encountered by American GIs, Strauss managed to communicate that he was the composer of *Der Rosenkavalier* ("The Rose Cavalier") his most famous opera, and thereby survived. Strauss was wise in choosing that work, for if he had mumbled something like "Thus Spake Zarathusra," the confused soldiers may have shot him.

"Troika" from *Lieutenant Kije*

The famous Soviet composer, Sergei Prokofiev (1891-1953), left Russia in 1918, soon after Czar Nicholas II had been deposed and the Russian Civil War had begun. He stayed away until 1933, returning after becoming more sympathetic to Soviet ideology. One of his first activities upon his return was to create a score for the 1933 film *Lieutenant Kije*. The music became a symphonic suite for orchestra in 1934.

The story of the satirical film was about a fictional officer accidentally created when Czar Paul I, a notoriously insane ruler during the late eighteenth century, accidentally reads a name on a military report as "Lieutenant Kije." (Kije is a nonsense word in Russian.) The Czar's courtiers, not wishing to embarrass the ruler, invent a life and eventual heroic death for Kije. Probably the finest section of the well-known work is "Troika," or three-horse sleigh, played to represent Kije's leaving on his honeymoon.

Lively and fast-paced, "Troika" is an exhilarating instrumental composition that is even better than Leroy Anderson's outstanding 1948 instrumental piece, "Sleigh Ride." Anderson's composition is a familiar component of American holiday culture, a perennial every December. Prokofiev's minimasterpiece understandably does not have the same high status in the United States as does Anderson's, but it can be heard in television advertisements, films, and other situations depicting winter excitement or a brisk sleigh ride. Although possibly becoming an increasingly significant element in American culture as time goes by, "Troika" may never become a big favorite in the United States until it acquires some good lyrics. "Sleigh Ride's" popularity increased after Mitchell Parish supplied effective lyrics for it in 1950. The same may be true for "Troika," although lyrics for this very spritely gem may actually ruin it.

William Tell Overture

What do Switzerland in the thirteenth century, Germany, France, and Italy in the early nineteenth century, the American West in the late nineteenth century, and Detroit, Michigan in the twentieth century have in common? The answer to this multiplace, multicentury riddle is the *William Tell* Overture.

William Tell was a legendary and possibly real figure of thirteenth-century Switzerland whose adventures were similar to those of the English legend, Robin Hood. In 1829, the famous Italian composer Gioacchino Rossini (1792-1868), who also gave us the 1816 opera *The Barber of Seville* and its famous character Figaro, produced an enduring opera, *Guillaume Tell* (*William Tell*), in Paris. The opera was based on an 1804 drama by the great German writer Friedrich von Schiller.

In 1933, radio station WXYZ in Detroit started to broadcast a Western adventure series, *The Lone Ranger.* The theme music for that long-running (1933-1954) and immensely popular program, and the similarly successful television series (1949-1957), was taken from the overture of *William Tell.* Because of the very familiar deeds of the Lone Ranger and his faithful Indian companion Tonto, the lively rhythms of the *William Tell* Overture, which resemble rapid horseback riding, are likewise very familiar to generations of Americans. Spike Jones and his City Slickers, for example, utilized the horse motif in their hilarious 1948 parody about a horse race won by "Beetlebomb." The excellence of the radio/TV dramas and the excellence of the theme helped to keep both at the forefront of American popular culture for a number of years. Even after the TV series starring Clayton Moore and Jay Silverheels ended, another Lone Ranger TV series in cartoon form ran from 1966 to 1969, and as a by-product of his role as the Ranger, Moore made many public appearances to fans of all ages.

The Lone Ranger and Tonto (which incidentally means "fool" in Spanish) were the inspiration for two subsequent series from the same radio station, *The Green Hornet* and *Sergeant Preston of the Yukon*. These two programs also used famous classical music, "The Flight of the Bumblebee" and *Donna Diana*, and had television sequels. So therefore, *The Lone Ranger* was the beginning of a favorable and successful cultural trend. In contrast, Rossini's *William Tell*, composed in the middle of his life, was the voluntary termination of his career as a composer of operas and just about anything else of importance.

Both Rossini and the Ranger had midlife career changes. Rossini switched to doing comparatively nothing and riding on his laurels. The Ranger switched to becoming the scourge of outlaws in the West and riding on his great horse, Silver.

The Worms Crawl In

Few songs are less elevating and uplifting than the morbid strains of the American parody, "The worms crawl in, The worms crawl out, They turn your guts into sauerkraut." A gentle classic, it isn't, but a perennial piece of musical humor, it is.

Also known as "The Hearse Song," "Rogues' March," "The Bums' March," "The Elephant Walk," and others, "The Worms Crawl In" is a song of uncertain origins. The first known publication of any of the variants, under the title "Army Duff" (which means "pudding") was in London in 1921. But it apparently was popular a few years earlier in World War I when, using "The Worms" title, it was a seriocomical description of one's fate if killed in battle and buried in the ground. It may even go back as far as the Crimean War of 1853-1856, when British soldiers supposedly were acquainted with it.

The various clues about its background indicate probable nineteenth-century English origins and affiliation with the military. It is quite understandable why this odd composition has never been claimed by anyone. Would you like to be famous just for this sluggish, uninspiring tune most commonly associated with body worms?

SONGS THAT SOOTHE
OR BRING TEARS

"Barcarolle" by Offenbach

For those who do not commute daily through the canals of Venice, a barcarolle is a boating song originated by Venetian gondoliers. Typically, it is slow and romantic. The most famous example of a barcarolle, undoubtedly, is the piece of that name derived from the 1881 opera *Les Contes d'Hoffmann* (*The Tales of Hoffmann*) by the illustrious French composer, Jacques Offenbach (1819-1880).

Actually, Offenbach had previously used the tune in an obscure 1864 opera, but fortunately, he resurrected it as the centerpiece of his most famous work. With its deliberately paced, sentimental, and dreamy style, it is an ideal vehicle for a love song. Its *Hoffmann* lyrics, telling of "the beautiful night, the night of romance" was definitely designed for lovers. So are the lyrics of the American ballad "Adrift on a Star," which say that "Here we are, Adrift on a star," accompanied by Offenbach's "Barcarolle." Edgar Yipsel Harburg (1898-1981) wrote those lines for the short-running 1961 musical, *Happiest Girl in the World*. (Less sweet and gentle is the parody "Here we are, all drunk in a bar.") Harburg's verses and any other lyrics yet tried, however, have been unable to match the subtle delicacy of Offenbach's melody.

To demonstrate the range of Offenbach's talents, which unfortunately are not highly regarded by some "serious" musicians, contrast the tender "Barcarolle" with the full-blooded and pulsating

93

melody used for "The Marines' Hymn" and with the raucous and rambunctious "Can Can." Three different styles producing three different little masterpieces—that certainly is a sign of something exceptional.

Beautiful Dreamer

Stephen Foster (1826-1864) was America's first musical genius. He was mostly self-taught, yet he managed to compose a large number of popular songs, several of which remain big favorites in the United States and elsewhere.

In some ways, he was similar to the pop genius of twentieth-century America, Irving Berlin. They both had little musical training, both were the dominant popular composers of their centuries, and both showed touches of classical music despite their limited backgrounds. In one major way, though, Foster and Berlin were entirely different. Berlin surpassed 101 years on earth, while Foster died at age 37. Foster had a chronic drinking problem, and succumbed to an accident while he was drunk.

Sometime during his last weeks, Foster wrote his last great song, and probably his best. In March 1864, about two months after he died, "Beautiful Dreamer" was published in New York City. The lovely sentiments of this smooth, placid ballad were a most appropriate final curtain call for this exceptional artist. Most of Foster's other famous songs had been created in the 1840s and 1850s. Possibly sensing his upcoming demise, Foster drew deep into the well of his talent not long before he, in a sense, became a permanent beautiful dreamer.

Beautiful Ohio

Wordsmith Ballard MacDonald (1882-1935) could hardly be called geographically confined. Around World War I, he wrote successful sentimental lyrics about three different states: Virginia, Indiana, and Ohio. In 1913, he collaborated with composer Harry Carroll on "The Trail of the Lonesome Pine," which referred to "the Blue Ridge Mountains of Virginia." In 1917, he and composer James F. Hanley cowrote "Indiana," also known as "Back Home Again in Indiana" and "My Indiana Home."

Then in 1918, MacDonald wrote the lyrics for "Beautiful Ohio" to go with a melody by Mary Earl (pseudonym of Robert A. King [1862-1932]). A fine waltz, "Ohio" refers to the river forming the long southern border of the midwestern state, not the entire state. However, the state liked the composition so much that "Ohio" was adopted as its official song.

In light of MacDonald's co-authorship of three notable songs about states, two of which, "Indiana" and "Beautiful Ohio," are very good, he could be dubbed the king of American state songs. Possibly that is why Robert King chose a pseudonym when he worked with MacDonald on "Ohio," the last of the three songs, recognizing that there should only be one "king."

Carry Me Back to Old Virginny

An old anecdote tells of a man who is listening to a not very talented woman sing the old favorite "Carry Me Back to Old Virginny." Part way through the performance, the man began to cry, and the more the woman sang, the more the man cried. After she was finished, the woman, noting the man's behavior, asked him, "Excuse me, sir, are you a Virginian?" The man responded with a deep sigh and the statement, "No . . . I'm a music lover!"

This tale not only reflects the longtime admiration for this song by the American public, but also hints at its very sentimental nature. The state song of Virginia for years, "Old Virginny" was created in 1878 by black American composer James A. Bland (1854-1911). For much of his life, Bland worked in the United States Patent Office, but also managed to keep the Copyright Office busy with his approximately 700 songs. His best-known song, other than "Old Virginny," is the enduring dance number, "Oh, Them Golden Slippers" (1879), which was a vaudeville favorite and which could be found occasionally on television in its earlier decades.

Ironically, the most famous song by this significant early black composer has lyrics that are considered by some as offensive to blacks. Notwithstanding, it is one of the better and more influential songs associated with any of the 50 American states.

Daisy Bell

Around 1815, the first primitive bicycle was invented in Germany. By 1892, the technology of the bicycle had progressed enough to allow women to easily operate the vehicle, and for a couple to ride together on a bicycle built for two. In that year, the popular English songwriter Harry Dacre, who was on a visit to the United States, published the famous ballad "Daisy Bell," also known as "A Bicycle Built for Two."

Dacre (probably the pseudonym of Frank Dean) brought a bicycle with him to the United States. When he had to pay custom duty on the bike, a friend quipped something about Dacre being lucky he didn't have "a bicycle built for two" because then he would be stuck with paying a double duty. Fascinated by the phrase, Dacre soon converted the inspiration from the customs incident into his enduring American popular song.

Speaking of bicycles and 1892, that was the year that two brothers named Wright opened their bicycle shop in Dayton, Ohio. Soon their interests turned to loftier aspirations and in 1903, their new project called the airplane got off the ground. After that, romantic songs like "Daisy Bell" changed to the new-fangled transportation, and ballads such as the 1910 "Come, Josephine, in My Flying Machine," by lyricist Alfred Bryan and composer Fred Fisher, flew into the hearts of the American public.

The Entertainer

Ragtime is an early form of jazz that features constant syncopation. Since ragtime varies considerably from the mainstreams of both popular and classical music, anyone called the "king of ragtime" is expected to be at least a little unconventional. However, Scott Joplin (1868-1917), the famous black American composer and pianist, was doubly different. Not only did he create a number of good serious jazz pieces at a time when such activity was quite unusual, he also gave many of his works the most imaginative and uncommon titles.

For instance, there were the piano rags: "Maple Leaf Rag" (1899), his first really successful work; "Elite Syncopations" (1902); "Palm Leaf Rag" (1903); "Gladiolus Rag" (1907); "Searchlight Rag" (1907); "Rose Leaf Rag" (1907); "Fig Leaf Rag" (1908); "Euphonic Sounds" (1909); "Stoptime Rag" (1910); "Magnetic Rag" (1914); and others of similar semantic style. There was also the march "Great Crush Collision" (1896), the waltz "Harmony Club Waltz" (1896), and the opera *Treemonisha* (1911). Joplin not only delights us with his music, but he also tickles our fancy with the creative naming of his works.

The most famous of Joplin's compositions is "The Entertainer" (1902). Accompanied by "Pine Apple Rag" (1908), "Easy Winners" (1901), and other Joplin pieces, "The Entertainer" was the featured music of the outstanding 1973 action and comedy movie, *The Sting*. The erratic and colorful rhythms of "The Entertainer" provided a most effective backdrop for the unpredictable story line of the Depression-era film, and in return, the production provided Joplin with a tremendous boost in popularity. After Paul Newman and Robert Redford masterfully executed "The Sting" before millions of moviegoers, "The Entertainer" and to a lesser extent, other creations by Joplin, became standard entertainers on the pop and semiclassical scenes.

Grand Canyon Suite

A familiar long-running radio and television advertisement of some years ago featured a cherubic short man dressed in a bellboy's outfit and calling for his sponsor's product. In the background ran an attractive bouncy melody that enhanced the presentation of the message. Today that type of scene is strictly passé, since cigarettes are no longer allowed to be advertised in those media. But the musical component of those ads has not had the same fate. Instead, Ferde Grofé's *Grand Canyon* Suite (1931) has developed into a standard light classical favorite. (Grofé also orchestrated another classical standard, George Gershwin's *Rhapsody in Blue*, for its 1924 premiere with the Paul Whiteman Orchestra in New York City.)

By far the most famous work of Chicago-born Grofé (1892-1972), *Grand Canyon* Suite and particularly the "On the Trail" section that was integrated into the ads goes appreciably beyond the world of classical music. It can also be found in everyday American popular culture whenever straightforward or satirical representation of the Grand Canyon or that section of the United States is needed. Such usage indicates that *Grand Canyon* has found a substantial niche in the collective imagination of the American public, and a more appropriate one than the above-mentioned advertising campaign. Even with the broadest and most tolerant of outlooks, the characteristics of tobacco products on one side and the strength, sweeping view, and open-air qualities of the Grand Canyon and its excellent orchestral soulmate on the other make for an almost perfect clash.

Green Grow the Lilacs

Have you ever seen lilacs with green flowers? While lilacs usually blossom only in white and bluish purple, the implication of the title "Green Grow the Lilacs" could be that the flowers are green. If the supposed meaning of "Green Grow the Lilacs" is that just the leaves are green, not the flowers, then the title, though poetic, is sort of meaningless due to redundancy.

The confusion and nonsense of the above paragraph is reflected in the history of this enduring song. The known path of the piece stretches from eighteenth-century Scotland to twentieth-century Oklahoma. In the eighteenth-century struggles over who should be king of England, the supporters of Scottish pretender Charles Stuart, better known as Bonnie Prince Charlie, sang an anonymous ballad with the line "We'll change the green laurel to the bonnet so blue." Irish-American soldiers in the Mexican War of 1846-1848 sang a version containing their homeland colors at the time, "orange and blue." (The song was published in the United States in 1846, while the war was still going on.) In time, the colors changed to the American national colors "red, white, and blue" and the plant changed from a laurel to lilacs, with the ending line becoming "And change the green lilacs to the Red, White, and Blue."

The person who changed the laurel to lilacs could have been Oklahoma author Lynn Riggs (1899-1954), who wrote a 1931 play called *Green Grow the Lilacs*. In 1943, the play was the basis for the plot of the great musical *Oklahoma* by Richard Rodgers and Oscar Hammerstein II. But considering the relatively late date of Riggs' play, there is reason to suspect that the change to "lilacs" took place well before 1931, and that Riggs borrowed her title intact from the song.

On top of the confusion of nationalities (Scottish, Irish, American, and Mexican) and colors (green, orange, blue, red, and white), there is an entirely spurious tale associated with "Green Grow the

Lilacs." Supposedly, Mexican troops, hearing "Green Grow" repeatedly began to call the Americans "gringos." This uncomplimentary expression signifying persons from the United States, it is told, became part of the Mexican vocabulary and has endured to this day. However, the true origins of the "gringo" term are in the Spanish word "griego" meaning "Greek," which in time came also to mean "foreigner." Now we have added two more nationalities to this musical melting pot.

Home, Sweet Home

"There's no place like home" is a very familiar sentence in many different countries, expressing a very widely held sentiment. After her fantastic adventures in Oz were over, Dorothy (Judy Garland) said it. Although few of us have had experiences to match Dorothy's, many of us have said it upon returning home. In 1823, John Howard Payne put it on paper accompanied by music.

Although the saying may have existed before 1823, Payne was the person who made it internationally famous. Payne (1791-1852) was a transplanted American who acted in, wrote, and produced several plays after moving to London in 1820. One of his dramatic efforts was the 1823 opera *Clari, or The Maid of Milan*. His collaborator on the libretto was the noted English composer and conductor, Henry Rowley Bishop (1786-1855).

"Home, Sweet Home" was the musical highlight of *Clari* and brought home very sweet recognition to both men. Although for a while the tune was thought to be a Sicilian folk air, Bishop was knighted by Queen Victoria in large part because of his extremely popular melody. He was the very first musician to receive such an honor. Payne, who didn't see a lot of "home, sweet home" during his lifetime, nor a lot of money for his world-famous lyrics, was the recipient of similar respect. In 1850, he was a special guest at the White House, where in the presence of President Millard Fillmore and other dignitaries, the renowned vocalist Jenny Lind sang "Home, Sweet Home" directly to Payne. Most appropriate of all, in 1873, a memorial statue of Payne was erected in New York City, his birthplace and the spot that he could call home.

I'll Take You Home Again, Kathleen

Rio Grande, a 1950 Western starring John Wayne and Maureen O'Hara, was one of the better movies Wayne appeared in, and one of the more sentimental. What makes this particular movie stand out from many others was the emphasis on the relationship between the cavalry commander, Wayne, and his estranged wife, played by O'Hara. There is an especially tender scene, in a period when the couple are beginning to come back together, where the gentle ballad "I'll Take You Home Again, Kathleen" is sung in the background.

Presuming that the movie is supposed to take place around the 1880s, the choice of "Kathleen" as the love song was quite appropriate. While historical films often include music written later than the period portrayed in the production, "Kathleen" was probably not an anachronism in *Rio Grande*. It was written in 1876, apparently in the west, by little-known American Thomas P. Westendorf. It was intended to cheer up his wife Jennie, who was homesick for the more familiar and more hospitable eastern part of the United States. Although Westendorf is known for nothing else, he produced one of the finer songs of the second half of the nineteenth century and a piece that is a significant part of a legendary Hollywood film.

I'm Always Chasing Rainbows

The music of Frédéric Chopin (1810-1849) covered the entire gamut of moods and emotions. At one end of the spectrum is his famous but morbid funeral march. At the other end are such compositions as the tune for "I'm Always Chasing Rainbows"–light, pretty, bubbly, and carefree with a touch of melancholy. The first category represents the end of life. The second suggests the full pursuit and enjoyment of our time in the cosmos.

The melody for "Rainbows" was derived from Chopin's 1834 piano work, "Fantaisie Impromptu." Composer Harry Carroll (1892-1962) adapted the French genius's sensitive music, Joseph McCarthy (1885-1943) added some lyrics, and a new song was created for use in the 1918 musical, *Oh Look!* (No, the lyricist McCarthy was neither the famous baseball manager nor the infamous communist-hunting senator from Wisconsin.)

"Rainbows" was the star of the otherwise forgettable production, and has remained a colorful and ethereal part of our culture ever since, inspiring Dorothy Parker's poetic pun, "I'm always chasing Rimbauds" (referring to the nineteenth-century French poet Arthur Rimbaud). It is one of two famous American songs about the romantic and elusive meteorological phenomenon. The other, of course, is the 1939 classic "Over the Rainbow" from the movie, *The Wizard of Oz.*

But compositions about rainbows did not end with "Over the Rainbow." For example, one of the most charming scenes from *The Muppet Movie* (1979) involved Kermit the Frog crooning a ballad about rainbows. We never seem to get tired of chasing our particular personal rainbows. Let's hope that we never do.

Indiana

The most famous sporting event in the state of Indiana, and also the most prestigious event of its kind, is the Indianapolis 500 automobile race held annually on Memorial Day weekend. Part of the elaborate ceremonies accompanying this test of endurance for car and driver is the performance of the beloved song, "Indiana." As a reflection of the regard in which this piece is held in the Hoosier state, the song is also known under two variant titles: "Back Home Again in Indiana" and "My Indiana Home." Created in 1917 by lyricist Ballard MacDonald (1882-1935) and composer James F. Hanley (1892-1942), "Indiana" is so well known that it has been thought to be the state's official song.

That distinction, however, goes to yet another outstanding Indiana ballad, "On the Banks of the Wabash." Honoring the river for which Hoosiers have a great affection, the nostalgic and sentimental "Wabash" was created in 1897 by Indiana-born Paul Dresser (1858-1906), the brother of the famous novelist Theodore Drieser.

The lyricist for "Indiana," MacDonald, also had a connection with a very well-known artist. In 1924 he wrote the popular classic "Somebody Loves Me" with co-lyricist Bud DeSylva and celebrated composer George Gershwin. He also wrote the lyrics for a nonclassic "The Trail of the Lonesome Pine" (1913), to go with a tune by Harry Carroll. The "old redhead," Arthur Godfrey, made this ballad about "the Blue Ridge Mountains of Virginia" familiar to the American public.

The composer for "Indiana," Hanley, wrote two other songs of consequence, "Second-Hand Rose" (1921) with lyricist Grant Clarke, and "Zing! Went the Strings of My Heart" (1935). Note that all songs mentioned in this essay deal with matters of the heart, both romantic and geographic.

Jeannie with the Light Brown Hair

The object of Stephen Foster's famous love ballad was actually Jane, not Jeannie. While temporarily separated from his wife Jane in 1854, Foster (1826-1864) composed this song apparently in hopes of a reconciliation. They did get together again, possibly because of Foster's beautiful portrayal of the woman of his affections.

So why didn't Foster openly insert the name "Jane" instead of "Jeannie?" Perhaps Foster wanted to be more subtle and discreet than that, or perhaps Foster simply recognized that "Jeannie" fit the rhythm of the melody much better than did "Jane." (Try singing "Jane" as two syllables in the line "I dream of Jane with the light brown hair.") He could, of course, have used "Janie," a two-syllable name relating to his wife, but for unknown reasons, he did not.

As a result of Foster's artistry, "Jeannie" has become a perpetual standard of American popular music and the sentence "I dream of Jeannie with the light brown hair" a permanent part of U.S. popular culture. Its influence as a piece of music is shown by its extensive usage on radio during 1941 when a disagreement between the song writers and the radio networks caused temporary removal of contemporary songs from the airwaves. The influence of the lyrics on American culture is shown by their utilization in commercials and in various jokes, and by a long-running television comedy program *I Dream of Jeannie* (1965-1970).

Meet Me in St. Louis, Louis

The story of this charming waltz-tempo ballad begins, in reality, in 1803. In that year, the United States, under President Thomas Jefferson, purchased a vast parcel of land from France. Stretching from the much-coveted port of New Orleans, which was the main purpose of the sale, north to Minnesota and Montana and west to the Rocky Mountains, the Louisiana Purchase included the Mississippi and Missouri River Valleys.

To celebrate the centennial of this major event in American history, a spectacular exposition was held in the city where the Mississippi and Missouri converge. The St. Louis Fair of 1904, officially the Louisiana Purchase Exposition, was the rage of the time. It directly caused the composition of a smash hit, "Meet Me in St. Louis, Louis" (1904), and a fine film, *Meet Me in St. Louis*, in 1944. The song's creators were lyricist Andrew B. Sterling (1874-?) and musician Kerry Mills (1869-1948). Sterling also wrote the lyrics for two other notable songs, "Wait Till the Sun Shines, Nellie" (1905) and "Under the Anheuser Bush" (1903), both with musician Harry Von Tilzer. Note that Sterling's 1903 song also has a St. Louis association, referring to a famous brewery in that city. Although he was not a great songwriter, Sterling's silver-toned lyrics had a golden touch during a short period of the very early twentieth century.

The movie based on the St. Louis Fair and the endearing song that honored it also produced several other good songs. The musical starred the great Judy Garland who very capably sang "Meet Me in St. Louis, Louis," "Skip to My Loo" (Anonymous, around 1844), and three other songs written for the film: "The Trolley Song," "The Boy Next Door," and "Have Yourself a Merry Little Christmas." The creators of these three pieces were wordsmith Ralph Blane and composer Hugh Martin.

The musical connections do not necessarily end with the 1944 film. In 1956, Richard Berry wrote a mambo, "Louie, Louie," which became a hit in 1963 when recorded by the Kingsmen. Since the last two words in the title of "Meet Me in St. Louis, Louis" are pronounced exactly the same as the title of "Louie, Louie," it is conceivable that there was some kind of subliminal or indirect connection with the title of the earlier song. Whether or not this last piece has the slightest association with the 1904 song or the 1944 movie, the Louisiana Purchase not only helped spawn the influential jazz of New Orleans, but also some enduring ballads touching upon another city further up the mighty Mississippi.

My Old Kentucky Home

Stephen Foster was not born in Kentucky (his birthplace was near Pittsburgh) nor did he ever live there (he worked and died in New York City). There is an unverified legend that in 1852, he briefly visited his cousin in Bardstown, Kentucky, and was so struck by its sights and sounds that in a very short time, he created the hymn-like classic, "My Old Kentucky Home." More likely, he was inspired by Harriet Beecher Stowe's 1851 novel, *Uncle Tom's Cabin*. In any case, the song was published in New York City in 1853 and introduced by the famous Christy Minstrels in the same year.

Foster (1826-1864) was entirely a Northerner, despite the mentions or suggestions of the South in many of his compositions. Furthermore, the black dialect commonly utilized in Foster's works was apparently developed only to meet the needs of white minstrel companies. In light of this, Foster's successful descriptions of Southern life and culture seem all the more remarkable.

Although he had no proven contact with the state of Kentucky, outsider Foster wrote the song that became the state's official anthem and also the theme for Kentucky's most renowned event, the annual running of the Kentucky Derby at Churchill Downs. On top of this, the "old Kentucky home" at Bardstown that allegedly inspired Foster became a historic shrine honoring both the state and the talented Yankee who helped make the southern locale more famous.

My Wild Irish Rose

"My Wild Irish Rose," introduced in the 1899 New York City musical *A Romance of Athlone*, is a famous Irish ballad. So are "Mother Machree" (1910) and "When Irish Eyes Are Smiling" (1912). Many persons, surely, would guess that these sentimental tributes to the Emerald Isle were either written in Ireland or by a person who was privileged to be from the land of blarney, four-leaf clovers, and leprechauns.

But, begorra, as so often is the case, what seems obvious or natural or probable is not. The composer of "My Wild Irish Rose" and a collaborator on the other two songs was born in Buffalo, New York (that doesn't sound Irish), and was named Olcott (that doesn't sound Irish either). Chauncey Olcott (1858-1932), a singer as well as a composer, apparently no more needed to be Irish to produce fine Irish-style compositions than Northerners Stephen Foster and Daniel Emmett (the presumed composer of "Dixie") needed to be from the South to create their Southern masterpieces. All it takes is some sense for the place, a fair amount of talent, and a popular artistic medium to propagate the creation.

For Foster and Emmett, the medium was the minstrel show, and for Olcott, it was the Irish tenor and an apparently hearty public appetite for things Irish. Another medium that helped make Olcott famous was the motion picture. In 1947, the film *My Wild Irish Rose* romantically portrayed the life of the popular non-Irish composer of Irish melodies.

Nobody Knows the Trouble I've Seen

"Nobody Knows the Trouble I've Seen" (also known as "Nobody Knows the Trouble I've Had") is supposed to be a very sad and depressing song, yet this author has witnessed laughter on several occasions when it was performed. The reason for this seemingly inappropriate behavior is that the mournful melody and plaintive lyrics are so blatantly on the downside that a reaction of laughter almost seems natural.

A black spiritual probably first published in the 1867 collection, *Slave Songs of the United States*, "Nobody Knows" is very possibly from the Charleston, South Carolina area. Another song which appeared in that collection was "Michael, Row the Boat Ashore," a much livelier piece suspected to be from the Port Royal Islands of South Carolina. Among the famous performers who have performed "Michael" are the Smothers Brothers, Tom and Dick, who playfully rendered this enduring black spiritual on their 1967-1969 television show, *Smothers Brothers Comedy Hour*. Because of the controversial social protest content of the program, the network finally cancelled the show. Yet Tom and Dick did not revert to singing "Nobody Knows the Trouble I've Seen" because in the long run, the causes they supported more or less gained the support of the American public. In other words, the Smothers did not have to, in the words of another black spiritual, "Look Down, Look Down that Lonesome Road." (The origins of sad and beautiful "Lonesome Road" are not known, though the song is probably from the first half of the nineteenth century.)

Yet another notable black spiritual, of uncertain origins, is "Let My People Go!" Although the song literally refers to the ancient Egyptian enslavement of the Israelites, the meaning could certainly also pertain to the situation of the slaves in the United States. It took a bloody Civil War to gain legal freedom for the slaves, and another century of lonesome roads to start to approach true and complete freedom and justice. It wasn't until well after World War II that the black people of the United States were really let go, so that Michael and all others of his race could finally row the boat ashore and begin to reduce the trouble they had seen.

Old Folks at Home

The very talented Stephen Foster (1826-1864) had an uncanny ability to write songs that would be eventually adopted as official or have a major cultural impact. Although he only made a short visit to Kentucky (if he visited the state at all), his "My Old Kentucky Home" became the official state song of Kentucky and the musical symbol of the Kentucky Derby. He never traveled in the west, yet his "Oh, Susanna" was widely heard in wagon trains and other caravans heading to California, Oregon, and similar western destinations. And he never visited Florida, but still his "Old Folks at Home" became the Florida official song.

"Old Folks," also known as "Swanee River," was published in 1851. It was entirely accidental that the Suwanee River in Florida became the focus of the song, for Foster's brother, while scanning an atlas, randomly suggested the Suwanee as a possible candidate for a song about a river. When Ed Christy of the Christy Minstrels asked Foster for an original song to be introduced by the Minstrels, Foster sent him "Old Folks." Because Christy requested that he be credited with the song in the initial printings, and since Foster was reluctant to be connected with what he described as an "Ethiopian Song," Foster sold the rights to Christy. The song was a tremendous success, but Foster did not profit greatly from it.

With the variant, "Swanee River" becoming the most commonly used title, the song, like the river, flowed on into history. "Swanee River" was a constant favorite with soft shoe and tap dancers. Irving Berlin inserted the words "Swanee river" in his 1911 ragtime masterpiece (and first big hit), "Alexander's Ragtime Band." And George Gershwin's first hit song was "Swanee" (1919), which obviously was influenced by Foster. So, when a movie was made about Foster's life in 1939, there was no surprise that the title "Swanee River" was chosen. Appropriately, one of the stars of the movie was Al Jolson, whose main theme during his career was "Swanee."

Jolson did not play the lead role of Foster, but instead was cast as a key secondary figure in the story, minstrel Christy. Don Ameche, who also portrayed another nineteenth-century legend in a film, Alexander Graham Bell, starred as Foster.

Polovtsian Dances

When most persons hear the lilting and exotic strains of the American popular song, "Stranger in Paradise," they probably can identify the piece. It was a very big hit in the 1950s and has remained a solid standard since then. A respectable number of individuals, in addition, probably know that "Stranger" was a number in the 1953 musical, *Kismet.* Not many, however, know the names of the two men George "Chet" Forrest (1915-) and Robert Wright (1914-), who wrote the lyrics for the musical and adapted the music used in it.

Some music lovers may know that the melody for "Stranger" was borrowed from the "Polovtsian Dances" or "Polovetsian Dances" by noted Russian composer Alexander Borodin (1833-1887), who, thanks to Forrest and Wright, received a very posthumous Tony Award in 1954 for best composer of a Broadway musical. This is because "Polovtsian" is a very popular piece, both in the classical music community and outside of it, as well as being Borodin's most famous work. (Incidentally, Borodin had a doctorate in chemistry and practiced this profession while composing as an avocation.) A few aficionados even know that "Polovtsian" is a part of Borodin's 1890 opera, *Prince Igor.*

However, it is doubtful that many Americans know what "Polovtsian" means or who Prince Igor was. "Polovtsi" is a Russian term to identity a nomadic East Turkish people, the Kuman or Cuman, who conquered southern Russia in the eleventh century. In 1185, a Russian army under the leadership of Prince Igor Sviatoslavich (1151-1202) was overwhelmed by the invaders. In the Borodin opera, the captured Prince and his troops were not killed by the victorious Polovtsi, but instead were entertained by a sumptuous banquet at which the Eastern style "Polovtsian Dances" were performed. The story of Prince Igor was told in the first notable literary work in Russian, *Slovo o polku Igoreve* (*The Song of Igor's Campaign* or *The Lay of the Host of Igor*), an epic written around 1187. Borodin used this work in creating his opera.

Rachmaninov's Piano Concerto No. 2

Sergei Rachmaninov (1873-1943) was one of the greatest Russian composers and one of the finest artists of his era. His lyrical, melodic, often melancholic, and very well-crafted music stands tall among his contemporaries, just as his six-foot-six-inch frame made him stand tall. Rachmaninov's music is especially popular in the United States, the nation to which he moved in 1935 after leaving Russia when the Soviet regime took over in 1917, and living in Switzerland for some years. (He became a U.S. citizen not long before his death.)

Probably the most beloved work by Rachmaninov, in the United States and elsewhere, is his Piano Concerto No. 2 (1901). A very fine romantic concerto, one of the best of its genre, it is appealing from the beginning to the end. However, one passage, from the third (and last) movement, is particularly notable. A soft, slow, and thoughtful section with a gentle yet consuming sweep, the theme is very familiar. In 1946, Buddy Kaye and Ted Mossman adapted the music and added some fairly good lyrics to create a hit of its time, "Full Moon and Empty Arms."

The Kaye-Mossman song is seldom performed today, but the brilliant theme they used can be found throughout Rachmaninov's adopted country. Its tender sounds can be heard in films, radio, television, and various other places where romance and/or quiet reflection is the mood of the moment. This author has more than once witnessed a scene where a somewhat knowledgeable but not sophisticated person has exclaimed something like "That-a-boy, Rocky" during the lovely strains of the famous concerto. The reference, of course, was not to Rocky Balboa, the boxer portrayed in film by Sylvester Stallone, or to Rocky the cartoon squirrel of the *Rocky and Bullwinkle* television show, both of whom have their own well-known themes. The Rocky being honored in this instance was the sensitive artistic genius Sergei Rachmaninov.

Rhapsody in Blue

From Brooklyn to a Manhattan alley to uptown—that was the lifelong New York City journey of the outstanding composer George Gershwin (1898-1937). From a lower-class family, Gershwin had barely reached manhood when he was making excursions into Tin Pan Alley, the popular music district of New York City. He became firmly entrenched in the figurative Alley after he produced his first hit song with lyricist Irving Caesar, "Swanee," in 1919.

After several very successful years as a popular musician, he raised his aspirations considerably and began to dabble in more serious music. In 1924, one of his great masterpieces, "Rhapsody in Blue," was performed at a jazz concert in Manhattan, with Gershwin himself at the piano. The next year, his "Concerto in F" for piano appeared, and a third masterpiece, "An American in Paris," premiered in 1928. His quartet of fine classical compositions was culminated in 1935 with his famous folk opera, *Porgy and Bess.* In all of these works, Gershwin combined traditional classical forms with jazz and folk elements.

After "Rhapsody in Blue," Gershwin's artistic reputation moved uptown, although he continued to visit his old Alley neighborhood. Even with his status as a serious composer reasonably well established, he still wrote popular songs and musicals, including the Pulitzer Prize-winning show, *Of Thee I Sing* (1931). But "Rhapsody" was the landmark event in Gershwin's life. On top of being his ultimate composition, one widely used in American everyday culture, including a long-running series of television advertisements for a major airline, it also in some ways reflected the tragic short existence of this genius. His artistic output was the beautiful rhapsody. His illness and early death was the blue note.

Romeo and Juliet by Tchaikovsky

The tragic tale of *Romeo and Juliet* by William Shakespeare is probably the world's most famous love story. It has inspired many derivative works, including at least ten operas and four ballets. The best known of the musical works based on Shakespeare's tragedy are probably the ballet *Romeo and Juliet* (1938) by the very prominent Soviet composer Sergei Prokofiev (1891-1953), and the fantasy overture *Romeo and Juliet* by the great Russian composer, Peter Ilich Tchaikovsky (1840-1893). Although Tchaikovsky wrote a large amount of music that could be applied to romantic situations, *Romeo and Juliet* is his most direct and glowing piece of love music.

Written in 1869 and first performed in Moscow in 1870, *Romeo and Juliet* was the first of a substantial batch of masterworks and/or popular compositions by Tchaikovsky. Many of his works and themes are familiar in American popular culture, including several mentioned elsewhere in this volume. Among the excerpts or adaptations from Tchaikovsky are John Denver's "Annie's Song" (1974), which was probably influenced by the second movement of Symphony No. 5 (1888), and a theme used to advertise convertible sofas in the 1950s, which was directly taken from "Serenade for Strings" (1882).

Romeo and Juliet is characterized as a "free overture," that is, not leading up to something else such as an opera or ballet. It also is very free with a range of sentiments from the most tragic to the most loving. The famous love theme, which appears toward the middle of the composition and is repeated later, is the piece of music you would most expect to find in movie, television, and stage love scenes in the United States and elsewhere. For example, in the mid-1990s, it was used in an American television ad that portrayed a pig who was enamored with a muddy four-wheel-drive vehicle. Its emotionally dripping passages are so well crafted yet so approachable that the love theme from *Romeo and Juliet,* ironically written by a man with a sexual preference for other men, has become a strong stereotype for heterosexual romance around the world.

Skaters' Waltz

It is winter and the ice on the local pond is frozen solid. Confident, accomplished athletes boldly glide across the open reaches of the cold surface, frequently diverting to figure eights, spins, and other manifestations of their highly developed skills. Interspersed with these ice eagles are various less proficient winter chickens, many of whom will never advance to a higher level of the snowbird kingdom.

Last of all are the love doves, who may have any level of skill, but whose main purpose for being on the ice is not the development of their physical conditioning but the development of their personal relationship. These are the persons for whom the "Skaters' Waltz" was especially composed. All who put on skates can enjoy the splendidly smooth rhythms of the glassy waltz, but the suggestions of romance in Émile Waldteufel's popular composition override the other facets of the skating scene.

Waldteufel (1837-1912), a French arranger and light composer, published "Les Patineurs" ("The Skaters") in 1882. ("Waldteufel," incidentally, means "forest devil" in German.) The anonymous, enticing lyrics, "Bright wintry day, Calls us away," which sometimes skate along with the tune, were created later, apparently in the United States. Of course if you are a super winter chicken like this author, the invitation of "chestnuts roasting on an open fire" is much more appealing than the thought of becoming "Frosty the Snowman" to the accompaniment of even the finest piece of music.

Tchaikovsky's Piano Concerto No. 1

Russian Peter Ilich Tchaikovsky (1840-1893) has a dual musical personality. He is one of the elite of the world's serious composers, yet so much of his music appeals to the everyday person who normally has little interest in what is commonly called "classical music." One example of this favorable interface between Tchaikovsky and the American public is the song "Tonight We Love." With lyrics written by Bobby Worth, and with music adapted by Ray Austin and bandleader Freddy Martin, the 1941 song was a hit and became a favorite piece of Martin's big band. The music borrowed from the splendid first movement of Tchaikovsky's Concerto No. 1 for piano and orchestra, or Piano Concerto No. 1, which premiered in Boston in 1875. (The work is perhaps the best and probably the most popular piano concerto in the world.) The romantic, very sentimental theme of the first movement was a perfect fit with the syrupy style of Martin's "sweet band."

No doubt buoyed by their success with borrowed music from the masters, Martin, Austin, and Worth tried again in 1942. The second time they used a theme from another piano work, Concerto in A Minor for Piano and Orchestra (1868) by the great Norwegian composer Edvard Grieg (1843-1907). Although Grieg's concerto is also one of the best of its kind, the resulting popular song, "I Look at Heaven," did not find as much public favor as "Tonight We Love." Two years later, however, Worth himself attempted yet another derivative of serious music. Writing new lyrics and adapting some music from the famous 1896 opera *La Bohéme* by Italian master Giacomo Puccini (1858-1924), Worth devised another song, "Don't You Know" (1954). Although Worth used the most popular piece from *La Bohéme* and one of the best-known operatic excerpts, "Don't You Know" was not a big hit.

But, for what it's worth, Bobby Worth along with Ray Austin and Freddy Martin did attempt to bridge the cultural gap between the masters and the masses. In the one case of "Tonight We Love," they succeeded well.

While Strolling Through the Park
One Day

In 1884, six years before the start of the "gay nineties," a song was published that fit in well with the carefree and nicely naughty spirit of the decade. The light and flirtatious "While Strolling Through the Park One Day," originally known as "The Fountain in the Park," livened up the 1880s, 1890s, and the whole twentieth century. While its lyrics are not heard very often at the end of the twentieth century, its pleasant slow waltz melody is still heard in a variety of places. Over the years, it has appeared in films, animated cartoons, theatrical productions, and television. (Another extremely popular slow waltz from the end of the nineteenth century, incidentally, was "The Bowery" (1892), with lyrics by Charles H. Hoyt and music adapted from the Neapolitan folk song, "La Spagnola" by Percy Saunt. The song, which lightly and satirically portrayed negative experiences in that section of New York City, had a negative influence on land values there.)

A sort of classic, "Strolling" was written by two nonexistent persons. That is, one of the names associated with the composition of "Strolling," Ed Haley, is probably fictitious, and the other name, Robert A. Keiser, is a pseudonym. Robert A. King (1862-1932) was the sole creator of the enduring ditty, as well as the co-author of another memorable song, "Beautiful Ohio" (1918). King wrote the music for the 1918 waltz, again using a pseudonym, "Mary Earl." Ballard MacDonald (1882-1935) wrote the "Ohio" lyrics. It is interesting to note that King created a placid song about a river when he was close to 60, and created a song about young love when he was barely in his twenties. Different interests come at different ages.

To demonstrate how much difference a century or so can make, the original lyrics of "Strolling" are given below, followed by an updated set of lyrics that reflect the realities of late twentieth-century America.

122

1884 lyrics :

> While strolling through the park one day
> In the very merry month of May
> I was taken by surprise
> By a pair of roguish eyes
> In the very merry month of May

1997 version

> While running through the park one night
> Far away from any city light
> I was taken by surprise
> By a pair of angry guys
> No more going through the park at night!

SONGS FOR SPECIAL PERSONS
AND OCCASIONS

CHILDREN'S SONGS

Brahms' "Lullaby"

To persons not very familiar with classical music, Brahms' "Lullaby" is the most famous composition of the renowned composer. To some persons quite familiar with classical music, much of Brahms' other music has the same sleep-producing effect as the "Lullaby."

To be fair, Johannes Brahms (1833-1897), one of the three prominent B's of German classical music along with Bach and Beethoven, did write some very invigorating and stimulating pieces, such as his "Hungarian Dances." But as a whole, Brahms is far from the most exciting musician in history. His "Lullaby," originally entitled "Wiegenlied," was first printed in 1868. The German lyrics, which date back to 1808, and the familiar English lyrics, "Lullaby, and good night," which may well be American, are both anonymous.

Countless children around the world have been pleasantly transported into a period of rest (for both parents and child) by the soothing strains of the world's most famous lullaby. Accordingly, Brahms, who never married, is owed a little debt by millions of couples who did tie the knot and have children. In spite of his not marrying, Brahms did demonstrate some understanding of the problems of child rearing, as well as a sense of humor, when he suggested to his publisher that "Lullaby" should be issued in a special minor-key (and less pleasant) version for children who had misbehaved.

Hansel and Gretel

The brothers Grimm, Jakob (1785-1863) and Wilhelm (1786-1859), were aptly named. The famous German tales that they collected and retold in their world-famous work, *Grimm's Fairy Tales* (1812-1815), often have a grim, dark, or sinister plot or aspect. The beloved children's tale *Hansel and Gretel,* with its portrayal of two lost siblings and their encounter with a wicked witch, is typical. Of course, without the elements of evil and trouble, the stories would be dull and the Grimms' book unread.

Engelbert Humperdinck sounds like a name from a Grimm brothers tale. Yet it was the real name of a late nineteenth-century/early twentieth-century German classical composer and the assumed name of a pop vocalist in the second half of the twentieth century who was born in Madras, India. While the singer, popular in the United States and elsewhere, is possibly best known for the adoption of a curious name, the German composer (1854-1921) is definitely best known for his 1893 fairy-opera, *Hänsel und Gretel* (*Hansel and Gretel*). The production was a very big success, largely because of its attractive melodies.

The best melody from the opera is a gentle, softly flowing piece that is often used as a lullaby to put children to sleep and sometimes as a Christmas song. Since the passage was written for a scene where Hansel and Gretel fall asleep safely protected by guardian angels, the lullaby's role is natural and obvious. Its usage as a Christmas favorite, however, seems less natural and obvious because there is no direct artistic connection with that holiday. Yet it can be found in some American Christmas anthologies partly because its pleasant and peaceful tones coincide with the more tender sentiments of the celebration, and partly because of tradition. The opera's premiere was on December 23, therefore its most famous song has been loosely associated with the holiday period.

But an evil old witch active at Christmastime? Even in our often weird late twentieth-century American culture, which includes the tale of the Grinch stealing Christmas, witches seem a bit out of place during the December holiday.

Happy Birthday to You

Probably the most frequently sung composition in the United States, and possibly in the world, is "Happy Birthday to You." Thousands and thousands of birthdays are celebrated each day, and most of the time the little four-line curiosity is sung to honor the birthday person. But as very public as this song has been over the years, it still is not in the public domain. Since "Happy Birthday" remains under copyright protection about a century after its conception, its title could easily be altered to "Happy Copyright to You."

"Happy Birthday," which is therefore in some ways on the top of the musical hill, was created in 1893 by two women named Hill. Mildred J. Hill (1859-1916), an organist, pianist, and composer from Louisville, wrote the music. Patty Smith Hill (1868-1946), a professor of education at Columbia University and also from Louisville, wrote the lyrics. Originally, the title was "Good Morning to All."

For about 40 years after publication, there was a common belief that "Happy Birthday" was in the public domain and therefore could be used freely. After a 1934 lawsuit involving the insertion of "Happy Birthday" in Irving Berlin's musical "As Thousands Cheer," the song was copyrighted again in 1935, this time with the title "Happy Birthday to You." With the copyright renewed in 1963, the unusual situation of seemingly unending copyright continues. Someday the legal protection of the ubiquitous little ditty will finally cease, but it is doubtful that partying groups will stop the beloved generations-old practice of off-key serenading on birthdays.

Mary Had a Little Lamb

Did Mary really have a woolly pet that followed her everywhere? Apparently, Sarah J. Hale's little lines about a little lass and a little lamb were actually based on a true personal incident. Hale (1788-1879), a New Hampshire-born author and editor, published her world-famous minipoem in 1830. Originally, there were several stanzas scratched out about the ever-loyal beastie, but only the first one is commonly printed. Few other authors have been remembered in history for something as meager as four small spurts of children's verse. When Thomas Edison also made history by producing the first sound recording around 1878, the words he uttered were Hale's enduring lines.

Only one year after its initial printing, "Mary Had a Little Lamb" had received enough attention to be set to music (but not the present melody). The marriage of the now very familiar melody and the lyrics took place in an 1868 collection of college songs. In that publication, Hobart College in Geneva, New York, was identified as the completed song's place of origin.

The tune had been taken from an 1867 printing of "Goodnight, Ladies." (This bouncy and energetic anonymous work is not to be confused with another smoother and slower "Goodnight, Ladies" by lyricist Harry H. Williams and composer Egbert Van Alstyne, published in 1911.) The first part of the earlier song appeared in 1847, and 20 years later, another version added a second part, "Merrily We Roll Along." The melody for the new second section was the one used for "Mary Had a Little Lamb." So the tail end of a tune was tied to a tale about the tail that tailed the mistress. It also may have been the inspiration for the first part of the uninhibited musical theme for Warner Brothers' "Looney Tunes and Merry Melodies." So the next time you see Bugs Bunny or Daffy Duck, give a little side thought to Mary's little lamb.

Mulberry Bush

When this author was a child, "Here we go 'round the mulberry bush" and the games that went along with it were considered to be dumb. A number of years later, this opinion has not been altered an iota. It cannot be denied, however, that "Mulberry Bush" has persevered as a continuously popular recreation of the younger set. Children's books, recordings, and musical toys frequently include the lyrics and/or music, and merry-go-rounds and ice cream trucks also sometimes dispense its notes.

The melody, which was originally issued with lyrics entitled "Nancy Dawson" after a well-known dancer of the period, was published in London in 1760. The "bush" lyrics were first printed in New York City in 1883, accompanied by the 1760 tune, although an earlier version without any "mulberry bushes" had appeared in Edinburgh, Scotland, in 1842. The music and all versions of the lyrics are anonymous.

A parody (probably American), "Here we go gathering nuts in May" has appeared from time to time, including in the mass entertainment media. Or is it a parody? For a parody to exist, there has to be some implication that the original is worth satirizing or imitating. Instead, "Nuts in May" should be regarded as simply another semi-meaningless lyric attached to an old mediocre melody.

Old MacDonald Had a Farm

How old do you think MacDonald's strange farm is? Well, believe it or not, it goes all the way back to 1706, almost 300 years ago. Originally, the farm had no name, but it did have the same eccentric characteristics as the present establishment. In a London comic opera, *Wonders in the Sun,* or *The Kingdom of the Birds,* an untitled country life song by Thomas D'Urfey (1653-1723) contained these memorable lines:

Here a Boo, there a Boo, everywhere a Boo
Here a Whoo, there a Whoo, everywhere a Whoo
Here a Bae, there a Bae, everywhere a Bae

Soon other barnyard sounds such as "Coo," "Gobble," "Cackle," "Quack," and "Grunt" also appeared in print. By 1862, the funny farm, still without the name MacDonald, had moved from England to the United States. Various versions were published during the 1860s and 1870s, including the titles "The Gobble Family" and "The Gibble Gobble Family." In 1917, the current lyrics and tune were printed together under the title "Ohio," with "Old *MacDougal*" owning the farm. (Now we know where the farm is actually located.) The tune may have come from an 1859 college song from Yale University. (Harvard graduates, please note!)

But how did the name of the farm change from one Scotsman to another? Nobody seems to know this answer for sure, but there is a fascinating possibility. The London publisher of the familiar 1917 version was none other than Erkine *MacDonald.* Performers or a subsequent printer may have gotten confused by the closeness of the publisher's and farmer's names or else a person with a playful sense of humor deliberately switched the two. (Watch out for this latter type.)

Incidentally, the farm flourished under the new management and there was so much productivity by the 1950s that some grandsons decided to go into the fast-food restaurant business.

Peter and the Wolf

One of the best and most endearing serious works specifically written for children is *Peter and the Wolf.* Originally *Petia i volk,* it was created in 1936 by the outstanding Soviet composer Sergei Prokofiev (1891-1953). Other noted works by Prokofiev include the 1921 opera *Love for Three Oranges* and the orchestral suite *Lieutenant Kije* (1934).

Also a favorite with adults, *Peter and the Wolf* is a delightful musical tale for children. With an original script written by Prokofiev himself, *Peter and the Wolf* consists of a narration with interludes of music. Each of the characters–Peter, his grandfather, the wolf, the duck, the cat, etc.–has its own musical theme, which is inserted into the scenario whenever that character appears.

Perhaps the finest English version of *Peter and the Wolf* is one narrated by the renowned actor Boris Karloff, who for good or bad, is most famous for his movie portrayal of Frankenstein's monster. The clear, resonant, and expressive voice of Karloff considerably enhances the creative score and the lovable story about the boy who captures a wolf and parades it off to a zoo. Again applying his narration skills, Karloff also inserted a large amount of class into another children's classic, the 1966 animated holiday cartoon *How the Grinch Stole Christmas*, based on the story by Dr. Seuss. Karloff's "Grinch" is more famous in the United States than is Karloff's *Peter and the Wolf* (or any other version). Partly this is because of the Grinch's association with Christmas and Dr. Seuss, two much-beloved aspects of American culture. Yet *Peter and the Wolf* is far from an obscurity to Americans, young and old, appearing in many young persons' and pops concerts year after year.

Pop Goes the Weasel

There are a number of strange songs and musical curiosities described in this book. They are so plentiful, in fact, that to be uncommon or abnormal is commonplace and normal. But even among this gathering of eccentrics and oddballs, "Pop Goes the Weasel" stands out above the rest.

You would expect a comic or nonsense song to have silly or gibberish lyrics. That is certainly true for "Weasel." What sets "Weasel" 's lyrics apart from similar concoctions is that first, the lyrics really are not very amusing, and second, various commentators have tried to justify the verbal garbage by explaining that a "weasel" was a metal tool used by hatmakers. Whether the weasel was a tool, a sneaky animal, or a sneaky undesirable human, the lyrics still do not make sense even in the context of humor. There is no particular significance to the familiar lines "All around the cobbler's bench, The monkey chased the weasel." Since that version is one of the more recent variations (published in 1914 in New York City), it may only have been a matter of timing that those are the lyrics now used. Other versions such as "All around the chicken coop, The possum chased the weasel" (New York City, 1901), "All around the chimney top, The monkey chased the weasel" (source unknown), or "All around the cobbler's house, The monkey chased the people" (Boston, 1858) are no better or worse.

The sprightly, animated nature of the tune is, of course, the only real reason the song is preserved. First published in 1853, it is a simple English dance quite possibly dating from the eighteenth century. The style suggests folk or rural origins. The bizarre thing about the tune is that it was apparently a hit among the upper classes of Victorian England and even appeared at the balls sponsored by the Queen. Somehow, the sophisticates and nobility of imperial Britain frolicking to the tune of this children's favorite seems a bit incongruous. Perhaps the stuffy and conservative veneer of the Victorian period was even thinner than we have previously believed.

Rock-a-Bye Baby

For over two centuries, Mother Goose rhymes have entertained young children and have assisted parents and baby-sitters in escorting the little dears to Slumberland. (The origins of the term "Mother Goose" have been under dispute, with French, American, and English sources all being mentioned as possibilities.) Around 1872, a 15-year-old sitter named Effie I. Crockett was having difficulty putting a baby to bed. With other techniques having failed, Crockett resorted to an age-old stratagem, music. She improvised a little tune accompanied by the old nursery rhyme "Hush-a-bye, baby, on the tree top." with the opening modified to "Rock-a-bye, baby."

The original "Hush-a-bye" lyrics, along with other familiar Mother Goose concoctions, had been published by John Newberry in London in 1765. The adapted "Rock-a-Bye" lyrics, along with the sweet lullaby that saved the night for the teenage sitter, were published in Boston about 1884 under the pseudonym Effie I. Canning. From this private, extemporaneous beginning, "Rock-a-Bye Baby" quietly has become a standard lullaby in America and elsewhere.

Maine-born Crockett (1857-1940), who later became an actress, was related to the famous Davy Crockett who died defending the Alamo in 1836. Davy, for his big chunk of heroism, is fondly appreciated by Texans and others who have struggled for their freedom. Effie, for her little piece of creativity, is fondly but anonymously appreciated by anyone who has struggled with the daily routine of bedtime.

Sing a Song of Sixpence

It is uncertain whether the rye in "Sing a song of sixpence, A pocket full of rye" refers to the grain or the beverage. No matter what the unknown author of this familiar children's poem may have consumed before penning those lines, a fairly imaginative little morsel of bird pastry was the result. It is entirely possible, incidentally, that the creator of "Sing a Song" also was responsible for "London Bridge," another good juvenile poem published in the very same 1744 London songbook.

The composer of the tune most commonly identified with "Sing a Song" was the English musician James William Elliott (1833-1915). In the 1871 London collection in which Elliott published the melody for "Sing a Song," there also appeared the usual settings for "Hey, Diddle Diddle," "Humpty Dumpty," "Jack and Jill," "Little Bo-Peep," "Little Jack Horner," "See-Saw, Margery Daw," and other nursery rhymes, all by Elliott. Therefore, Americans and many others in English-speaking countries have happily sung several of Elliott's tiny musical bits, whether they or others were the children. If there was a special prize for composition in the realm of children's songs, Elliott most certainly would have received an award.

Three Blind Mice

Throughout history and literature, groups of three have not always worked out well. In addition to the unlucky three on a match and the always awkward three's a crowd, there have been the famous triumvirate of ancient Rome who were supposed to rule the Empire together but instead fought with each other, the troublemaking three witches in Shakespeare's *Macbeth*, and the three musketeers who really didn't do anything exceptional until they became four. There also have been the three little pigs who were hounded by the wolf, the three members of the Axis who badly lost World War II, the three monkeys who spoke, heard, and saw no evil, the goofy three Marx brothers who were really five, and the hapless and hopeless Three Stooges: Moe, Larry, and Curly.

Let us not forget to mention the three blind mice who were chased by the farmer's wife and lost their tails as a result. The musical tale (tail) of the rodent trio is a very old one. Both the lyrics and melody were published in London in 1609 (during Shakespeare's lifetime). The song is anonymous and almost surely was not written by the incomparable bard from Stratford-upon-Avon. Not only has it survived almost four centuries, the quaint little piece has another distinction. Of nonreligious songs famous today, it was one of the earliest to be printed. So "Three Blind Mice" is a historical curiosity as well as a musical curiosity.

As we all know from the song, the three mice had as much luck as did the Three Stooges in their many comedy films. Perhaps that is why the ending theme for the Three Stooges' escapades was, quite appropriately, "Three Blind Mice."

Twinkle, Twinkle, Little Star

Mother, Mozart, a carpenter's bench, the alphabet, a sheep, and a star–such is the diverse cast of characters in the complex saga of one tune.

As in all births, the first contact was mother. In 1761, an attractive, wordless little melody was published in Paris. Four years later, the music and the lyrics "Ah! Vous dirai-je, maman" ("Oh! I will tell you, Mama") appeared on a manuscript. In 1778, Wolfgang Amadeus Mozart came upon the tune while visiting Paris, and created a dozen variations for piano.

About 1830, "Ist das nicht ein Schnitzelbank?" ("Is this not a carpenter's bench?") was printed in Germany, and in 1834 "The Schoolmaster," also known as "ABCDEFG," was published in Boston. Both of these children's diversions used the "maman" melody or a close variant. In 1879, "Baa, Baa, Black Sheep," originally an anonymous 1744 English lyric, was attached to our French mama in Philadelphia.

Finally, and perhaps most suitably, "Twinkle, Twinkle, Little Star" was printed with the well-traveled tune in an 1881 New York City collection. "Twinkle" had been written in 1806 by the English poet Jane Taylor (1783-1824).

Have you had enough lyrics for one essay? If not, here's something else to add to the confusion. Taylor's "Twinkle, Twinkle, Little Star" is not the only poem with that name. There are at least several other lesser stars that have twinkled from the pens of various imitators.

CIRCUS SONGS

Barnum and Bailey's Favorite

P. T. Barnum (1810-1891), the unabashed American showman, supposedly said, "There's one born every minute." He of course was referring to the suckers who were quite willing to part with their money to see the curiosities and gimmicks so imaginatively provided by slick P. T. Of his many popular attractions, the longest lasting and most famous was the internationally celebrated circus known for years as "Barnum and Bailey's." Founded in 1871 and still continuing today, "The Greatest Show on Earth" is one of Barnum's entertainments that usually gives the customer his/her money's worth.

"There's one born every minute" may have applied to the gullible rube with a pocketful of cash, but it certainly doesn't apply to good circus music. Since the circus band is a central part of the various big top acts, a ready supply of suitable music is a must. Barnum and Bailey's has used countless compositions in the past century or so, but the piece having a special meaning to that show is a lively 1913 march entitled "Barnum and Bailey's Favorite."

Karl L. King (1891-1971), an Ohio-born musician, wrote "Favorite" while he was a member of Barnum and Bailey's band. "Favorite" became the circus's favorite, at least in that period, and King went on to a successful career as a bandmaster (including a 1917-1918 stint as head of Barnum and Bailey's music) and a composer of marches (He was not to be known as the "March King," though, for that title was already taken by a fellow named Sousa.)

Curiously, King and Barnum and Bailey's had a strange chronological connection in addition to the musical composition that contributed to the fame of both. King was born in the year that Barnum died, and died on the one-hundredth anniversary of the founding of Barnum's circus. Perhaps somebody born in 1971 will carry on the circus creativity chain started by Barnum and continued by King.

Be a Clown

Circus clowns as we know them today have been a part of the modern circus almost as long as that form of entertainment has existed—that is, about two centuries. These public buffoons have one basic purpose—to make people laugh. Yet in spite of their very significant roles in circuses, most clowns are anonymous. So why would anyone want to be a clown?

For some persons, performing the lowbrow zany antics of the clown to please audiences is an irresistible urge with intrinsic rewards. That is more or less the message of the 1948 song "Be a Clown." Although clowns tend to be obscure figures in bizarre or gaudy costumes under the bright lights of the circus, the three persons most associated with "Be a Clown" were all celebrated artists who basked in the bright lights of fame. The composer of the song was the very accomplished creator of musicals, Cole Porter (1891-1964), and the stars of the film musical *The Pirate* in which the song premiered were the very talented singer and actress Judy Garland and the equally talented dancer, actor, and singer Gene Kelly. (A similar song, "Make 'Em Laugh," by lyricist Arthur Freed and composer Nacio Herb Brown, was a memorable number in the outstanding 1952 film, *Singin' in the Rain*, again starring Gene Kelly.) Incidentally, perhaps the best known of all American circus clowns was also named Kelly. Sad-faced Emmett Kelly (1898-1979) was an outstanding performer with Ringling Brothers in the middle years of the twentieth century.

Although less than two generations old, "Be a Clown" has become an almost stereotypical song to represent the circus. Another much earlier composition, roughly two centuries old, has similarly represented the atmosphere of circuses and carnivals. "The Carnival of Venice" ("Il Carnevale di Venizia"), originally a popular Venetian song, "O Mamma Mia," probably dates from around the eighteenth century. The noted Italian composer Nicoló

Paganini (1782-1840) helped make it famous throughout the world by creating some piano and violin variations of the simple yet quite appealing melody with its gently rolling rhythms. These were published after Paganini's death. Paganini's variations, created by 1829, caught on quickly, for the melody was published in the United States in the 1840s, and has become a favorite of cornet players. Among its manifestations in America have been the music of the hand-cranked hurdy-gurdies that used to be common on city streets and the bustling and cheerful carousels that used to be so very popular throughout the land.

Other classical composers besides Paganini with an interest in circus-affiliated music were notable, innovative composer Charles Ives (1874-1954) and the Russian master Igor Stravinsky (1882-1971). Ives created "The Circus Band" (around 1894), also known as "The Circus Band March," and Stravinsky wrote "Circus Polka" in 1942, three years after he moved to the United States. "Circus Polka" is also known as "Polka for Circus Elephants," evoking an image even a bit bizarre for the gloriously unreal world of the circus.

Comedians' Galop

Horses gallop and apparently comedians (or clowns) also do. The antics of some types of comedic entertainers sometimes require a very fast-paced physical routine in which running, jumping, tumbling, kicking, flipping, or similar energetic maneuvers are employed to evoke laughter from audiences. If music is involved in the routine, it could be in the form of a galop (one "1"). A galop is a double or more time dance that tends toward the wild and tends to catch the attention of listeners. One famous galop is the "Can Can" from the 1858 French operetta, *Orpheus in the Underworld* by Jacques Offenbach.

Another well-known one is the "Comedians' Galop" from a children's play, *The Comedians*, by Russian composer Dmitri Kabalevsky (1904-1987). Published in an orchestral suite in 1940, "Comedians' Galop" or just "The Comedians" is Kabalevsky's most famous work. It has appeared in the United States in various manifestations, including circus music, background music for television advertisements, and as the opening theme for a well-known game show, *To Tell the Truth,* in early television.

With its spirit of free abandon and the rapidly descending notes of its main theme, "Comedians" is an ideal vessel to introduce clowns, cute animal acts, or anything else active and amusing. The xylophone, an instrument used to produce light and lively tones, is prominently used in the composition, fully compatible with the piece's delightfully frivolous nature. Incidentally, another galop by a Soviet composer is the "Galop" from *Masquerade* (1944), a suite by Aram Khachaturian (1903-1978). One way the 1944 galop differs from the 1940 galop is that the main theme of the later piece starts with briskly ascending notes. The galop from *Masquerade* would be a fine circus piece if it hasn't already been used as such, for circus fans do not care whether the music goes up or down, as long as fun is involved.

The Flying Trapeze

It is easy to understand why the ladies were pleased by "the daring young man on the flying trapeze." He was young and by necessity, athletic, muscular, and slim. He was also unafraid to take risks, and artistically graceful. Furthermore, he was associated with a tantalizing make-believe world into which anybody could escape from the realities of the real world for a while.

Today, the exploits of the trapeze artist are as exciting and romantic as they were over 100 years ago when "The Flying Trapeze" or "The Man on the Flying Trapeze" first came upon the scene. The song was initially published in London in 1868, credited to George Leybourne, the pseudonym of the English comic singer Joe Saunders. (The flying trapeze had been introduced to London just shortly before.) There is good reason to believe that Leybourne was not the composer, but instead the music hall popularizer of an English folk piece, and so the song like the man swinging high above our head must remain an anonymous delight.

"The Flying Trapeze" not only performed amazing feats of popularity in nineteenth-century Britain and America, but also swayed audiences in the twentieth century. It appeared in the 1934 Academy Award-winning movie, *It Happened One Night*. In the same year Pulitzer Prize-winning author William Saroyan gave a collection of short stories the title *The Daring Young Man on the Flying Trapeze*. In 1939, a revival of the song actually made the radio hit parade. Another related hit, recorded in 1948, was a parody version produced by Spike Jones and his City Slickers on the flip side of the famous "Beetlebomb" rendition of Rossini's *William Tell*.

It's quite a versatile song. Not many songs can be inspirations to the circus, music halls, movies, fiction, the radio, and parody creators.

The Gladiators

There is a shameless old anecdote with several different versions. One variant concerns a brave young female gladiator in ancient Rome. This amazing Amazon had handily defeated every male opponent in the arena. Then she was challenged by a huge, hungry lion. After several uneventful minutes of lady/lion struggle, the cat managed to strike a massive paw across the back of the human's head and knock her unconscious. With an ear-shattering roar of triumph, the beast swallowed his opponent whole. An obvious expression of contentment was fixed on his face as he slowly returned to his lair. The Roman historian who later reported this incident wrote only the following: "Ferocious feline fells fierce female–Gladiator!"

An appropriate piece of music to accompany this ludicrous tale would be "The Gladiators," a very popular circus march often associated with the antics of clowns. Although not specifically written for big top shenanigans, "The Gladiators" has become the most famous of all circus songs. When energetically played on a steam calliope, it can make one's senses sizzle with delight.

At first, "The Gladiators" was an orchestral piece published in 1900 by Czech composer and bandmaster Julius Fučik (1872-1916). The original title "Einzug der Gladiatoren" ("Entry of the Gladiators"), which must have been satirical in light of the frivolous, mocking style of the music, fits in well with the various usages of the composition. On top of circuses, American professional wrestling and other comedy scripts have also adopted the tasty morsel of–to use an expression for the annual NCAA basketball tournament–march madness.

Over the Waves

If you have attended American circuses to any extent, you may have noticed that a certain smooth waltz is frequently played during high-wire and trapeze acts. That particular piece, however, is more than just a musical accompaniment. Its beauty and polish enhances the delicacy and intricacy of those daring esthetic performances under the big top. For a large number of seasons, the commonly used tune and countless circus troupes have worked together very satisfactorily. As a result, the combination has become sort of a show business cliché, but a very pleasant one.

The little waltz has proven to be a most versatile musical tool. As well as being a staple of circus bands, it has been used as a skating theme, as background for comedy sketches, as a school song, and for various other purposes. Because of its grace and sophistication, one might well believe that its origins are the banks of the Danube in Vienna or at least some kindred locale such as Paris. Yet its 1888 creation occurred far from those centers of art, both geographically and culturally.

From 1864 to 1867, the nation of Mexico had an Austrian emperor, Maximilian, imposed upon the land. One of the positive legacies of that short historical aberration was the introduction of the waltz as a musical form. About a generation later, a full-blooded Mexican Indian composer and violinist, Juventino Rosas (1868-1894), successfully responded to the partial transplantation of Vienna and published the melody as a piano piece in Mexico City.

The song's original title was "Sobre las olas," which literally means "Over the Waves." The composer's chosen title, then, is very compatible with the gentle, rolling, rhythmic pattern of the music. It is unlikely, however, that Rosas ever envisioned that his nautical composition would become closely associated with aerial performances in a land-based form of entertainment.

Auld Lang Syne

On the occasion when we usually sing "Auld Lang Syne," on New Year's Eve, many of us are fuzzy-headed because of the time of day or the amount of alcohol consumed. But why shouldn't we be fuzzy when "Auld Lang Syne" carries us off into the new year? Everything else about the song is fuzzy too. Even its performance for many years by Guy Lombardo and his Royal Canadians had a soft, sweet, fuzzy style.

Outside of Scottish origins, little is known about this perennial favorite. The tune is apparently from the folk domain, and could date as far back as the sixteenth century. The music was printed with lyrics in 1799, and by itself in a slightly different form in 1687, but almost surely is older than the late seventeenth century. The lyrics most likely come from the seventeenth century, but a somewhat earlier or later dating is also conceivable. (The earliest known form of the words found its way into print in 1711.) The first verse, the only one sung extensively, is of folk creation, and so are some of the other verses. In 1788, the celebrated Scottish poet Robert Burns (1759-1796) added two verses of his own making, and because of this the misconception that Burns wrote the whole poem has sprung up.

Added to this vague historical background is the total lack of information about when and why "Auld Lang Syne" became a New Year's Eve tradition. The song does not openly or blatantly belong to that particular holiday, although the nostalgia in the verses and even the literal translation of the title ("Old long since") does make it understandable why New Year's Eve became the ballad's perpetual resting place.

Fuzziness is also the feeling one gets when the piece is being sung. A slight amount of mental fuzziness is present because we really don't comprehend the lyrics very well. A large amount of psychological fuzziness, of the sweet and warm variety, also overcomes us because of our own personal sentimentality for the year that has just passed into "old long since."

Drink to Me Only with Thine Eyes

Anybody who has ever been in love knows very well the importance of eye contact and eye communication in affairs of the heart. When the famous English poet Ben Jonson (1572-1637) wrote the immortal lines "Drink to me only with thine eyes, and I will pledge with mine," he was surely reflecting his own romantic experiences. But he was also echoing the emotions of legions of lovers in the past, present, and future.

"Drink to Me Only with Thine Eyes" is perhaps the best-known and best-liked love poem in the English language. You would think that the verse masterpiece of 1616 would be a natural for conversion into song within a few years after its appearance, but the first known efforts to convert it into a romantic ballad were attempted around the year 1750. After several musical settings were attempted without any appreciable public approval, a slow, wafting, and sensitive melody published in multiple editions around 1785 proved to be an ideal mate for Jonson's lines.

The creator of the tender and beautiful melody is unknown, although British origins are almost certain. J. W. Callcott, an English composer born in 1766, has been mentioned as a likely candidate. The earliest printings of the music were almost exclusively in glee form (an unaccompanied part song). Callcott was writing glees for a club by 1784. (Now you understand the origins of the term "glee club.") A collection of musical pieces published around that time and which included the famous melody was claimed to be entirely composed by Callcott. So Callcott may be the person who in combination with Johnson has put so much glee into the voices and eyes of lovers and hopeful lovers in the United States and all other places where romance remains in vogue.

Drinking Song

In a real sense, any song performed in a drinking atmosphere is a drinking song. From very limited personal experience, this author has witnessed a wide variety of musical pieces sung in drinking spots. No piece, even an anthem such as "The Battle Hymn of the Republic," is necessarily exempt from tavern usage. Yet there have been a number of songs specifically written for the context of the group consumption of alcoholic beverages.

One of the very best of these is "Drinking Song" or "Drink, Drink, Drink," a lively and fun-filled number from the 1924 operetta *The Student Prince*. With a robust melody emulating Central European music styles and a clever and somewhat tongue-in-cheek set of lyrics including the famous lines "Here's a hope that those bright eyes will shine, longingly, lovingly, soon into mine," "Drinking Song" is the best number of a production that ranks at or near the top of American operettas. Composer Sigmund Romberg (1887-1951), who no doubt dipped into his Hungarian background for inspiration for the score, also wrote two other superior operettas, *The Desert Song* (1926) and *New Moon* (1928). Overall, he was among the very best theatrical composers in the United States in the first third of the twentieth century. Lyricist Dorothy Donnelly (1880-1928) is not associated with any other musical work of consequence, yet she provided splendid lyrics for *The Student Prince*, exhibiting a good understanding of its European setting.

Ironically, "Drinking Song" is too complex and challenging for most persons. Therefore, this playful piece with the most appropriate title is seldom performed in real-life drinking situations. However, the three-word line from the opening of the song, "Drink, Drink, Drink," all by itself, has been heard more than occasionally on television, on the stage, in the movies, and in taverns.

For He's a Jolly Good Fellow

"For it's a jolly good tune, dear, For it's a jolly good tune, dear, For it's a jolly good tune, dear, That's why it's often used!"

That just-written parody is a reasonable facsimile of the history of this very familiar song. First comes the original French version "Malbrouk s'en va t'en guerre" ("Malbrouk has gone to war"), whose folk lyrics and music date from the second half of the eighteenth century, and possibly somewhat earlier. Next comes the variant lyric "We Won't Go Home till Morning!," obviously a theme of partying night owls, which appeared in England in the 1840s. One Charles Blondel is apparently the author of these carousing lyrics attached to the rousing melody.

Following that was "For He's a Jolly Good Fellow," almost surely an English folk song, which was first printed in 1870 and is probably not too much older. In 1920, the scene switched to America where the tune was published with still another set of anonymous lyrics, "The Bear Went Over the Mountain."

The same vigorous melody was used to see Malbrouk off to war, to help a group stay up all night, to show appreciation for a beloved comrade, and to provide yet another nonsense song for the world. In this last particular bit of musical mischief, all the bear ever does is repeatedly traverse one mountain only to discover one more mountain and so on to infinity. Most other nonsense pieces such as "Ninety-Nine Bottles of Beer," which comes to a merciful end after reaching one bottle of beer, eventually have a conclusion. But the bear's ballad has no definite point of termination.

So the next time you encounter a bear in the woods or in your backyard, you should have gained some insight as to why he's so grouchy. If you had to do what he has been doing, you'd be tired and angry too! However, if the bear you come upon is a teddy bear having a picnic, as in John W. Bratton and James B. Kennedy's 1913 children's piece, "The Teddy Bears' Picnic," there would be no danger except possibly overeating.

How Dry I Am

"How Dry I Am" could be called a theme song of the Prohibition Era (1920-1933). Because the Eighteenth Amendment made the consumption of alcoholic beverages illegal, the complaint "Nobody knows how dry I am" was probably widespread. But either the complainer was trying to deceive others about his forced abstinence or else was naïve about the true availability of liquor at the time. Prohibition did little to stop the flow of booze; it just altered the distribution from the taverns and main street liquor stores to the speakeasies and back alley vendors. The excitement of skirting the law gave the Roaring Twenties some of its howl.

Soon after the start of Prohibition, the 1921 musical *Up in the Clouds* presented an early version of "How Dry," which was partially different from the present form. The music was by Tom A. Johnstone and the lyrics by Will B. Johnstone. (One source gives Phillip Dodridge as the lyricist and Edward F. Rimbault as the composer of the 1921 version. However, since Rimbault (1816-1876) died 45 years before the 1921 musical, his authorship is obviously impossible and Dodridge's authorship is therefore unlikely.) Around the end of Prohibition, the current anonymous version was published in New York City in 1933. Although they were working with lyrics that most likely preceded the "dry years" and with a melody that ironically dated back to an anonymous 1855 American hymn "O Happy Day," the composite composers of "How Dry" took the entire Prohibition period to perfect their musical gripe. Maybe they were having so many "happy days" because of intoxication that completion of a dry song seemed less relevant than finishing another bootleg beer.

It would be noted that after prohibition was over, new lyrics connected with the tune turned to even less lofty themes. The prime example of this tendency to sink distinctly lower is the folk non-classic "My dog has fleas, Oh scratch him please."

Another piece, incidentally, which combines nonloftiness and drinking, is an anonymous curiosity of uncertain origin and title. It starts out, "For it's beer, beer, beer, that makes me want to cheer." Progressively, the lyrics become more and more risqué, usually in proportion to the amount of alcohol consumed. A college student favorite in the Northeast in the 1950s, and possibly originating in World War II, it is uncertain whether it has ever appeared in print. If it hasn't been published, the reasons are obvious.

> For it's beer, beer, beer
> That makes me want to cheer
> In the corps, in the corps
> For it's beer, beer, beer
> That makes me want to cheer
> In the quartermaster corps
> Refrain:
> My eyes are dim
> I cannot see-e-e
> I have not brought my specs with me

Subsequent verses substitute another alcoholic beverage for beer, with the second line adjusted to rhyme. For example, one of the tamer verses starts out:

> For it's whisky, whisky, whisky
> That makes me feel so frisky

Another verse is slightly more explicit, with the opening:

> For it's vodka, vodka, vodka
> That makes me feel I gotta

Let's stop now, while we are not too far beyond the twilight zone of good taste.

Little Brown Jug

When the Universities of Minnesota and Michigan play football each autumn, the winner of the contest not only improves its Big 10 standing but also gets to take home for a year the traditional "little brown jug." (The jug is not filled with any spirited liquids, for athletes are required to stay dry during training.)

The football brown jug is therefore associated with a winner, and so is the musical brown jug. Joseph Eastburn Winner (1837-1918), a Philadelphia composer and publisher also known as R. A. Eastburn, wrote the bouncy little concoction "Little Brown Jug" in 1869. It is unknown whether Winner was relating to his own personal experience or was just letting his imagination run free, but in either case (pun intended) he created one of the most popular of American drinking songs. His "Ha, ha, ha, you and me, Little brown jug how I love thee" is a picturesque portrayal of a solitary drinker sitting on the back porch or under the big oak with a partially emptied jug as a companion.

It is such an invigorating shot of fun that even nondrinkers have been known to participate in its jolly spirits. In the 1940s, renowned bandleader Glen Miller distilled "Little Brown Jug" into one of the favorite dance pieces of the swing era. Miller recognized the famous jug for what it really is, a full container of musical delight for generations of Americans.

Ninety-Nine Bottles of Beer

If sung to its theoretical end, which may have been done on occasion, "Ninety-Nine Bottles of Beer" would take roughly 15 minutes. Each of the verses of this monotonous reverse counting song takes about ten seconds to sing, and only the very bored, the very determined, or the very drunk would ever try to choke out all 99 verses nonstop.

Yet the amount of known history connected with this ongoing curiosity of American popular culture is even briefer than the chant-like verses. The concoction is definitely American, and most likely predates World War II, but there is absolutely no indication of authorship. (If you had written this piece, would you claim it? To have collected all the royalties from its use would have been nice, but since most of the time it has been sung spontaneously by informal and unofficial groups or lone individuals, probably very little money would have been forthcoming anyway.)

Another anonymous American song with "beer" in the title is "In Heaven There Is No Beer," a polka-style song probably created after World War II. "No Beer" is a favorite in communities such as Milwaukee, which have large German or Polish populations. Its first known recording, an unabashed rendition by Frank Yankovic (who may well be the song's creator), was in 1965. Although the polka's lively melody is a big part of its continuance as a favorite in recreational situations, its main appeal is no doubt the wry pseudotheological excuse to consume more brew. The lines "In heaven there is no beer, That's why we drink it here" are a unique bit of popular culture.

There Is a Tavern in the Town

Whether it is a small dot on the map with one local pub and little else, or a huge metropolis with a seemingly endless array of watering holes, most communities in America can relate to the familiar song, "There Is a Tavern in the Town." With some exceptions, where there is a town there is also at least one place to buy a drink.

From the feel of the anonymous piece, with its echoes "in the town," "sits me down," and so on, the impression that "Tavern" may have been actually composed during a session at the bar is as strong as the voices that raise up in unison. This theory is reinforced by its being first published in a collection of student songs (Cambridge, Massachusetts, 1883) and by a subsequent first printing in Britain (1891) in a similar volume. It just sounds like something put together by college students directly on the premises.

Whether or not "Tavern" was actually authored by students, it has long been a favorite at American colleges. In the late 1920s, Yale man and perpetual college kid Rudy Vallée (1901-1986) revived the song via radio and records and made this possible Harvard composition very popular among the general populace. Another interesting sidelight is its usage as a whistled recognition code in the 1942 adventure movie *Pimpernel Smith*. Smith was a college professor who, with the help of his students, smuggled scientists out of Nazi Germany following the example of the fictional Scarlet Pimpernel of the French Revolution. In real life and in fantasy, "There Is a Tavern in the Town" and college students seem to be often involved with each other.

Vive la Compagnie

France is the reputed locale for an old anecdote. During a session of the French National Assembly, an orator made the proclamation "And there is a difference between men and women!" Spontaneously, the entire body stood up and shouted, "Vive la difference!" (Long live the difference!")

France has also been associated with the familiar song, "Vive la Compagnie." Yet while the anecdote about the difference may have actually occurred in France, the similar-sounding song title apparently has no connection with that country. The present version, with the opening lines "Let ev'ry old bachelor fill up his glass, Vive la compagnie," was published in Baltimore in 1844. But the music was first published in Germany in 1838, along with an earlier German form of the lyrics. The German title was "Ich nehm' mein Glaschen in die Hand" ("I take my glass in my hand"). The German lyrics go back at least as far as 1818, when a large portion of the lyric was published.

But as complicated as the story has been so far, it gets even murkier. A similar melody, called "Lincolnshire Poacher," which may date from the late eighteenth century, was printed in London in 1840, only two years after the German publication of the tune. Whether there is any connection between the two tunes is uncertain, and which nation was the actual source for the melody is also equally unsure.

The German/English melody with German lyrics converted into an American lyric has certainly not been a tremendous favorite in the United States, but has enjoyed a certain degree of popularity over the years. Part of the reason is the tune's lively rhythm, and part is the inclusion of the two French phrases "Vive la compagnie" ("Long live the company") and "Vive l'amour" ("Long live love"). Now we're back to the anecdote at the beginning.

COLLEGE SONGS

Down the Field

Yale University has been honored by well over a dozen songs. Perhaps the best of these is "Down the Field," a smooth and much-borrowed fight song that is among the elite of college songs. With a fine melody by Stanleigh P. Freedman and good lyrics by Caleb W. O'Connor, this 1911 classic marches its way into football games throughout the United States. Among other places, the tune is used at the University of Tennessee and the University of Oregon.

Another famous Yale fight song is "Yale Boola," written in 1901 by A. M. Hirsch. The lively echoes of "Boola, boola, boola, boola" that rock the stadium in New Haven also reverberate in other places; in Norman, Oklahoma, for instance, the tune is used for the University of Oklahoma's rousing fight song, "Boomer Sooner."

Even the great Broadway composer Cole Porter (1891-1964) contributed two songs while he was a student at Yale: the bouncy 1911 novelty, "The Bull Dog," and the popular "Bingo Eli Yale" (1910).

Yale's longtime rival Harvard University also has some good songs, most notably "Our Director March," using an excellent tune of that name written in 1926 by F. E. Bigelow. The same tune is also used for the alma mater of Rice University, "Rice's Honor."

After following this complicated trail of college songs throughout the United States, we come to the Ohio State University in Columbus. Though at Yale and other universities the football teams march down the field, at Ohio State the team marches "Across the Field." An active and smooth fight song of that name by W. A. Dougherty Jr. has pleased fans in Columbus since its composition in 1915.

Far Above Cayuga's Waters

In upstate New York, there are eleven "Finger Lakes" that are both historic and attractive. In 1872, 20 fingers (two writers) created the lyrics that have immortalized the longest and perhaps most important of the Finger Lakes, Cayuga. With sentimental attachment to the cliffs that overlook the lake at Ithaca, two Cornell University students, Archibald C. Weeks (1850-1927) and Wilmot M. Smith (1852-1906) penned the famous verses of Cornell's alma mater.

Weeks and Smith were not the only ones to recognize the merits of the earlier tune around which they built a lasting poetic tribute to their school. Several other colleges and many elementary and secondary schools have also borrowed the melody for their own alma maters. Originally a ballad named "Annie Lisle," the music was first published in 1858. Its composer was an obscure American, H. S. Thompson, whose ten fingers had written some other songs.

The compatible blend of smooth melody and well-crafted poetry have produced a dignified representative of Cornell, and by extension, of all the other universities and colleges in the United States. The much-borrowed "Far Above Cayuga's Waters" is far above most other musical creations that have evolved from American campuses. It is a soulful ongoing symbol of the positive enduring values of academic life.

Fight on for USC

The brilliant brothers George (1898-1937) and Ira (1896-1983) Gershwin wrote much sweet and lively music. Among their most rousing songs was "Strike Up the Band!," which first caught the attention of the public in the 1930 musical of the same title. A few years later, in 1936, wordsmith Ira adapted the march into a football song for the University of California at Los Angeles (UCLA).

Anyone who follows college athletics knows that UCLA's chief rival is the crosstown institution, the University of Southern California (USC). Perhaps as a reaction to the excellent song used by UCLA, a sweet and lively song was composed for USC by Milo Sweet and Glen Grant in 1948. Called simply "Fight On," or to give it more identity, "Fight On for USC," the song is one of the most innovative and sparkling college fight songs.

But this tale of Los Angeles doesn't end there. Ironically, among the other songs that have been written for UCLA, the fight song "Go On Bruins" lists none other than Milo Sweet as one of its creators, along with Gordon G. Holmquist and Gwen Sweet. It makes one wonder who Milo rooted for at UCLA-USC football games.

Iowa Corn Song

If you have heard the "Iowa Corn Song" and its unique line "Ioway, that's where the tall corn grows," you probably won't forget it easily. It is perhaps the best-known song associated with the state of Iowa, unless you count "Seventy-Six Trombones" from Meredith Willson's smash 1957 musical *The Music Man*, which was set in rural Iowa. (Incidentally, Iowan Willson (1902-1984) also wrote one of the songs of the University of Iowa, "Iowa Fight Song.")

The seeds of the corn song were planted in 1912 when George Hamilton wrote the first verse. Additional lyrics were penned by Ray W. Lockard, a musical setting was created by Edward Riley, and the complete song was published in 1921. While we are on the subject of Iowa songs, the official state song is "The Song of Iowa," written in 1897 by Samuel Hawkins Marshall. The music for Marshall's song is the same as that used for the anonymous sixteenth- or seventeenth-century German carol "O Tannebaum" ("O Christmas Tree") and for another state song, James Ryder Randall's "Maryland! My Maryland" (1861).

The Maine Stein Song

Starting in 1930, the world-famous entertainer Rudy Vallée (1901-1986) made an obscure college song, "The Maine Stein Song," part of his repertory. The composition soon became a big hit, and the music and the singer were closely intertwined in the public eye. Some persons even thought Vallée had written the rousing piece. But Vallée only made an arrangement of it in 1930, based on an arrangement made by Adelbert W. Sprague, a University of Maine student, in 1905.

Sprague had adapted some music by E. A. Fenstad, who in turn had based his composition on one of Johannes Brahms' Hungarian dances. So by the time Vallée crooned the song to millions, the fine melody could be described as the work of Brahms, Fenstad, Sprague, and Vallée.

The lyrics, however, were fashioned only by one person. That is, up to now, only one person has been involved with the lyrics. Lincoln Colcord (1883-1947), another Maine student, wrote some lyrics to accompany the Sprague arrangement of the music, and the completed song was published in 1910. Later on, Colcord was to become an author of some distinction.

But Colcord's well-known song lyrics may not last as long as his other writings. Starting in the late 1980s, various persons began to push for revision of the lyrics because of sexist terminology and obvious references to drinking. This author strongly supports this quest for change. The citizens of Maine would be better served by a more appropriate set of lyrics to go with the exceptional tune that over the years has garnered so much favorable publicity for that state.

Notre Dame Victory March

It's not the oldest, the biggest, or the academically best university in the United States, but throughout the world it may be the best-known American institution of higher learning. This reputation was not gained by the school's fine program or its striking gold dome, but by the autumn sport with which Notre Dame is semisynonymous. Largely through the talents of Knute Rockne (1888-1931), who played on the Notre Dame football team and coached it from 1918 to 1931, the rough, very physical simulation of war has made the college with the gentle name of "Our Lady" internationally famous. (Ironically, Rockne was Swedish, not Irish, and was not even a Catholic for most of his life.)

About a decade before Rockne's tenure as coach, two young men attending the college created a fight song for the "Fighting Irish." The brother team of Michael J. Shea and John F. Shea, appropriately Irish, wrote the "Notre Dame Victory March" or "Cheer, Cheer for Old Notre Dame" in 1908.

"Notre Dame Victory March" is undoubtedly the most famous piece associated with collegiate sport. The school's legendary football prowess is much of the reason, but the pulsating rhythms and rousing lines of the excellent composition might have made even a football nonpowerhouse a bit of an autumn legend. Parodies like "We never falter, We never fall, We sober up on the wood alcohol" do nothing to stop the march from going down the field to further victory. Instead, when hundreds of high schools around the nation playfully proclaim their toughness in such a manner, it just runs up the song's score even higher.

On Wisconsin

The game of football began to develop in the United States starting around 1869. By the turn of the century, football had progressed considerably from its parent sport rugby and had become a very popular activity at the collegiate level. In 1902, the first Rose Bowl game was played and around the same time, football fight songs became more and more prevalent.

One of the earliest and best fight songs was the 1909 classic, "On Wisconsin." With a fine tune by William Thomas Purdy (1883-1918) and good lyrics by Carl Beck, it has been a quite honorable symbol of the University of Wisconsin in Madison for the better part of a century. It also has been adapted as Wisconsin's state song, as a Boy Scout song, as a service club piece, and for other purposes. (There are some persons who claim that John Philip Sousa regarded "On Wisconsin" as the best college song he had ever heard. However, the claim is also made for the University of Michigan's "The Victors," and because "The Victors" is closer to Sousa's style, and because Sousa had closer ties to Michigan, the claims for "On Wisconsin" are probably in error.)

The melody has a rhythm that gives the impression of 11 men strongly and artistically moving across the gridiron toward victory. However, if you have ever seen Tchaikovsky's 1877 ballet masterpiece *Swan Lake* with a team of dancers strongly and artistically moving across the stage toward the production's culmination, you may have noticed a section whose notes and timing resemble the later composition. Even if Purdy partially borrowed his famous melody from an earlier source, he had the good taste to dip into a great classical piece and the intuition to select an art form which, like football, depends on a highly coordinated and athletic group of people to achieve a successful end product.

Rambling Wreck from Georgia Tech

College fight songs usually extol the superhuman virtues of their athletic teams. When such a piece takes a totally different course and actually pokes fun at the institution, you have to appreciate the sense of humor exhibited by the author and the school that adopted and perpetuated the less-than-perfect image.

In the situation of Georgia Institute of Technology, it's bad enough for its students to confess that "I'm a rambling wreck from Georgia Tech." But for a school that has deserved pride in its engineering programs, it requires a remarkably puckish confidence to even satirically admit being "a heck of an engineer."

The person who wrote the tongue-in-cheek lyrics of "Rambling Wreck from Georgia Tech" is unknown. One may suspect that it was a student or students at the school. When published in 1919, the entire song was credited to Frank Roman, who was a bandleader at Georgia Tech at the time. Roman definitely was not the creator of the melody, since it goes back to at least 1873, and he probably was not the lyricist either.

The actual composer of the tune is not known, but he/she apparently was an American. The tune's first publication (1873), in a collection of Yale songs, was under the title "Son of a Gambolier." ("Gambolier" seems to be an extension of the word "gambol," meaning "frolic," something that college students do frequently.) The line "I'm a rambling rake of poverty" appeared in this song, just waiting for a young Georgia Tech student to to twist it around. In 1894, the melody frolicked over to Princeton using the title "Dunderbeck," and in 1898, "Son of a Gun" pranced around Dartmouth. By the time the tune reached Atlanta, it could honestly claim "I'm a rambling song, I've traveled long, But I've finally gotten here!"

The Victors

The bold lyrics "Hail to the victors valiant, Hail to the conquering heroes" cannot be just tossed about without a lot of accomplishment to back it up. This is even more true when the boast "the champions of the West" is added. But the University of Michigan, which has fielded many triumphal football teams over a long span of time, does have the facts of the past to reinforce the claims of its famous and feisty fight song.

Written in 1898, during the golden pretelevision era of college football, "The Victors" is one of the very best compositions ever to be roared by thousands on a Saturday afternoon. Reportedly, the great march composer John Philip Sousa felt it was the finest college song then in existence. The lyrics and music of this Midwestern minimasterpiece were created by Louis Elbel, a University of Michigan student about whom little is known except that he was associated with South Bend, Indiana (the home of a rival university, Notre Dame).

But Elbel's song has become quite well known, not only among the over 100,000 fans who frequently fill the stadium in Ann Arbor, but among the millions who have heard the challenging beat of "The Victors" enthusiastically ring around the United States and elsewhere via the medium of TV. "The Victors" is a very rousing piece, just about perfect for its purpose. About the only flaw is the reference to "the West," which by any distortion of the atlas does not apply to Michigan. Elbel's choice of words, however, is defensible, for if he had instead used the geographically correct term "Midwest" the rhythm at that point would have changed, making for a less satisfactory musical mascot.

The Whiffenpoof Song

This book has been like the month of March. It started like a lion with a windy boast about "the world's greatest songwriter" and is ending now with the poor little lambs of "The Whiffenpoof Song."

There are enough persons associated with "The Whiffenpoof Song" to form a chorus to sing it. First there was Guy H. Scull (1876-1920), who was a Harvard man. You may ask why a graduate of *the* rival university happens to be involved in this traditional Yale curiosity. Although it is not certain, it appears that around 1893-1894 and prior to entering Harvard, Scull wrote the melody. It was composed to accompany Rudyard Kipling's poem "Gentlemen-Rankers" (That makes two persons for the chorus.)

In 1909, an obviously free-spirited Yale choral group decided to name themselves "The Whiffenpoofs." That strange word came from Victor Herbert's 1908 stage production *Little Nemo*. The whiffenpoof was an imaginary fish. Two of the group, Meade Minnigerode (1887-1967) and George S. Pomeroy (1888-?) changed the lyrics of Kipling's poems into a sort of parody, and cohort Tod B. Galloway (1863-1935) reworked Scull's tune to fit. (Now there are five chorus members, not counting the persons involved with *Little Nemo*.) It was nine years after the 1909 creation of "The Whiffenpoof Song" before it was published in *The New Yale Song-Book* (1918), thus making it more or less an official part of the university. The song became popular outside of the Yale community in 1935 when Yale graduate Rudy Vallée (1901-1986), the well-known entertainer, sang it into the hearts of the American public. (Now the choral sextet is complete and ready to harmonize our sentimental musical subject.)

With the background on "The Whiffenpoof Song" thus summarized, this book of essays is coming to a close. In the spirit of the Whiffenpoofs, may a few final lines partially characterizing this publication be hereby added:

We're poor little words that have lost our way,
Bah, bah, bah.
We're little black ink that has gone astray,
Bah, bah, bah.

Title Index

Person and Group Index

Order Your Own Copy of
This Important Book for Your Personal Library!

THE AMERICANA SONG READER

_____in hardbound at $19.95 (ISBN: 0-7890-0150-0)

COST OF BOOKS_____	☐ **BILL ME LATER:** ($5 service charge will be added) (Bill-me option is good on US/Canada/Mexico orders only; not good to jobbers, wholesalers, or subscription agencies.)
OUTSIDE USA/CANADA/ MEXICO: ADD 20%_____	
	☐ Check here if billing address is different from shipping address and attach purchase order and billing address information.
POSTAGE & HANDLING_____ _(US: $3.00 for first book & $1.25 for each additional book) Outside US: $4.75 for first book & $1.75 for each additional book)_	
	Signature_____
SUBTOTAL_____	☐ **PAYMENT ENCLOSED: $**_____
IN CANADA: ADD 7% GST_____	☐ **PLEASE CHARGE TO MY CREDIT CARD.**
STATE TAX_____ _(NY, OH & MN residents, please add appropriate local sales tax)_	☐ Visa ☐ MasterCard ☐ AmEx ☐ Discover Account # _____
FINAL TOTAL_____ _(If paying in Canadian funds, convert using the current exchange rate. UNESCO coupons welcome.)_	Exp. Date _____ Signature _____

Prices in US dollars and subject to change without notice.

NAME _____

INSTITUTION _____

ADDRESS _____

CITY _____

STATE/ZIP _____

COUNTRY _____ COUNTY (NY residents only) _____

TEL _____ FAX _____

E-MAIL_____
May we use your e-mail address for confirmations and other types of information? ☐ Yes ☐ No

Order From Your Local Bookstore or Directly From
The Haworth Press, Inc.
10 Alice Street, Binghamton, New York 13904-1580 • USA
TELEPHONE: 1-800-HAWORTH (1-800-429-6784) / Outside US/Canada: (607) 722-5857
FAX: 1-800-895-0582 / Outside US/Canada: (607) 772-6362
E-mail: getinfo@haworth.com
PLEASE PHOTOCOPY THIS FORM FOR YOUR PERSONAL USE.

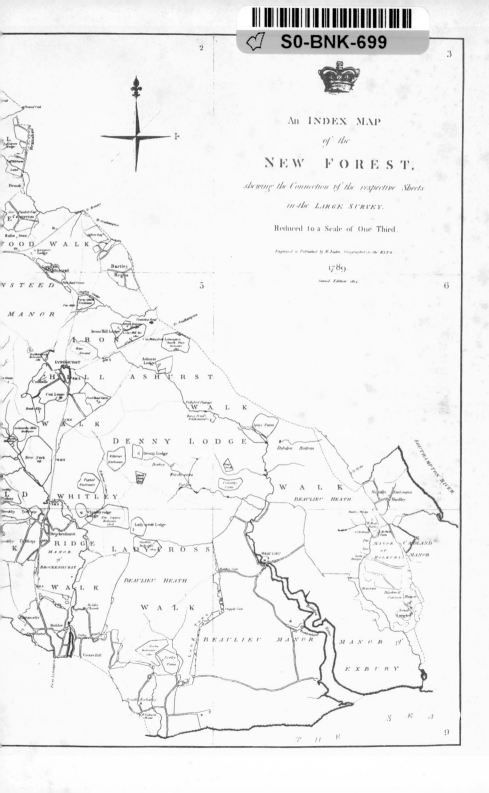

An INDEX MAP

of the

NEW FOREST,

shewing the Connection of the respective Sheets

in the LARGE SURVEY.

Reduced to a Scale of One Third.

Engraved & Published by Wm Faden, Geographer to the KING.

1789.

Second Edition 1814

This guide book is intended as a companion to
the Forestry Commission Guide *New Forest,*
also published by HMSO

London
Her Majesty's Stationery Office
1975

Explore the New Forest

An official guide by the Forestry Commission

Edited by Donn Small

Page 2 and 3:
Index to Drivers Map (see p. 46)

Page 4 and 5, left to right:
1 *Spring in oak plantations.* [HA]
2 *Summer in Holmsley Camp.* [RF]
3 *Autumn in Ancient and Ornamentals.* [HA]
4 *Winter on the heath.* [RF]

Contents

Foreword

Welcome to the New Forest

The Queen's House
Lyndhurst
Hampshire
SO4 7NH

There may be aspects of the management by the Forestry Commission of this unique national heritage which are not fully understood by the millions of visitors who come here each year. In order to sketch in the background and show something of how it works I have invited several authors with considerable local experience to describe the history and practical aspects of forest life.

We have protected the great open heaths and woodlands from trespassing cars and indiscriminate camping, so that the visitor may seek peace, solitude and a respite from modern pressures amidst varied undisturbed scenery and wildlife in natural surroundings.

The visitor is most welcome to walk on all paths and tracks, and, to help explore them, specially prepared maps are included in this guide. These give information on camp sites, selected historical locations and car parks from which different walks can be taken.

I hope the experience will be an enjoyable one and that it will further both knowledge and appreciation of how, despite increasing pressures, careful and sympathetic management will enable this ancient Forest to live on unscathed for future generations to enjoy.

Donn Small
Deputy Surveyor
of the New Forest

1

2

1 *Bolderwood fallow deer in velvet.* [RF]
2 *Ancient and Ornamental woodlands.* [RF]
3 *Tall Trees Walk, Rhinefield.* [DS]
4 *Eyeworth Pond car park.* [RF]
5 *Ponies on Avon Water bank.* [RF]

3

4

5

Introduction

DONN SMALL

Historical background

When, about AD 1079, William I created his "New" Forest in this corner between the Solent and the sea, the land consisted of relatively infertile woodland and furzy waste, sparsely scattered with farms and homesteads. The act of afforestation in Norman times transformed a whole neighbourhood into a royal hunting preserve, placing it under the hated forest law, which involved the curtailment of liberty and drastic punishment meted out for any interference with the beasts of the chase or their haunts.

Since the unfortunate peasants who dwelt in the Forest were forbidden to enclose their land lest any fence should interfere with the free run of the deer, their domestic animals were allowed to graze by common right and browse throughout the Forest and this grazing, reinforced by that of the deer themselves, severely diminished the ability of the sparse woodlands to perpetuate themselves. The dearth of new trees became a serious problem during the middle ages, which saw an enormous increase in the consumption of wood, the principal raw material of the time, and enactments were made to enable large areas in the New Forest to be enclosed for the purpose of establishing woodlands, later to be thrown open when the trees were past the danger of damage by grazing animals. This process became known as the rolling power of enclosure. The first tree-growing act was passed in 1483

and others followed. The act of 1698 allowed the enclosure of 6 000 acres and as the Crown assumed rolling powers, this meant that the area of woodland could increase beyond that, to the detriment of the commoners' grazing rights.

With time the royal hunting rights became less important and there is no record of any sovereign hunting in the Forest after James II. The way was thus clear for the passing of the Deer Removal Act of 1851, under which the deer were ordered to be destroyed and in return the Crown were authorised to enclose and plant a further 10 000 acres. It subsequently proved impossible to remove the deer, but these new Inclosures aroused considerable opposition from the commoners, whose cattle still grazed the Open Forest. Followed a Select Committee investigation, the Act of 1877 was passed, under which the Crown gave up its rolling powers and no more land could be enclosed beyond what had been enclosed in the reign of William II and subsequently up to the passing of this Act. This amounted to nearly 18 000 acres, but the total area enclosed at any one time (other than the enclosure of Crown freehold land) might not exceed 16 000 acres. The Forestry Commission took over the management of the Forest in 1924 and the Act of 1949 authorised the enclosure of a further 5 000 acres, with the authority of the Verderers, for the growing of timber; just over 2 000 acres of this additional land has been enclosed and planted.

The New Forest today reflects the history of its woodlands and commons. The Timber Inclosures, some of which have been open for decades, with the Crown freeholds, take up less than a third of its area. The larger part is Open Forest, consisting of over 65 000 acres of grasslands, heath, scrub and the Ancient and Ornamental Woodlands, the ragged descendants of ancient Inclosures now developing as natural oak and beechwoods; the whole roamed by the commoners' animals – ponies, cattle, pigs – and the deer who have survived both the sport of kings and an Act of Parliament to exterminate them. The New Forest made a major contribution to the 1939-45 war, providing enough timber to build a bridge nine feet wide by 1½ inches thick from Southampton to New York from twenty six sawmills scattered throughout the woodlands. Remnants can still be seen today at Anderwood, Ashurst and Hawkhill. It was one of the largest assembly areas for the troops embarking on the invasion of France in 1944. Today visitation by the public exerts additional and a more rapidly destructive pressure on the Forest.

Geology and soils

The New Forest lies in a broad shallow basin – the Hampshire Basin – surrounded by the low chalk downlands of Cranborne Chase, the Wiltshire and Hampshire Downs, Ballard Down and the spine of the Isle of Wight. The basin is filled with gravels, sands and clays laid down when the Forest area was occupied by a large river estuary or shallow sea; the gravel was apparently spread over the previously-deposited clays and sands by glacial drift, forming gravel cappings which have been extensively eroded by streams to expose the underlying deposits below.

There are three main types of surface form: infertile, flat-topped gravel plateaux, rich well-drained clays and loams, and low-lying ill-drained marshland. The water-logging which characterises so much of the Forest is caused by the existence of a hard pan at a depth of one to three feet, or impervious clay beds, which account for the poverty of many of the Forest soils.

Vegetation

Three distinct types of vegetation are linked with the surface forms: heathland with self-sown Scots pine and birch, gorse, heather and hardy grasses; woodland on the long gentle slopes separating the plateaux – beech, oak, yew, holly and thorn; and on the marshy ground alder thickets, willows, heath, bracken, sedge, bog moss and cotton grass.

Conservation

Because the Forest is the home of so many rare plants, animals, reptiles, birds and insects, the Forestry Commission has signed a Minute of Intent with the Nature Conservancy Council recognising the Forest to be of National Nature Reserve status, and agreeing to consult with the Council on general policy with regard to the management of the Forest. The Commission has a statutory duty to drain the Open Forest and clear coarse herbage to protect the grazing for the Commoners' animals, and all plans for such work are agreed by joint committees on which the Nature Conservancy Council is represented. The Commission is now embarked on a programme of conservation designed to protect the Forest against damage and penetration by tourists' cars with physical barriers to prevent car access, controlled camping areas, car parks, picnic places and other amenities which together will channel visitors to areas most able to accept them without major environmental degradation.

Page 10: *The Great Seal of William Rufus.*
Page 10 and 11: *The King Hunting.*

New Forest management plan

The overall management of the New Forest is the responsibility of the Forestry Commission, under the direction of the Deputy Surveyor of the New Forest, an ancient title for the officer in charge under the Surveyor General of all Crown forests. The latter appointment no longer exists. The agreed management plan for the period 1972–1981 is based on the Mandate presented at the Court of Verderers on 3 May 1971 by the Right Honourable James Prior MP, Minister of Agriculture, Fisheries and Food and has the following major objectives:

'The New Forest is to be regarded as a national heritage and priority given to the conservation of its traditional character.

The Ancient and Ornamental Woodlands are to be conserved without regard to timber production objectives.

In the Statutory Inclosures the existing balance between the conifers and broadleaves is to be maintained; the latter are to be managed with greater emphasis on visual amenity, on a rotation of at least 200 years and felling limited to single trees or small groups.'

The Statutory Inclosures, from which grazing animals are excluded by fences, contain a rich fauna and flora as well as mature trees, in contrast to the grazed open forest waste. By historical accident there is however an excess of mature broadleaved trees which if not regenerated would lead to an imbalance of age structure and their eventual decay. The objectives here are to achieve in the long term an even distribution of ages by regeneration treatments which will cause the minimum disturbance in the process, and in doing so to enrich the ecological diversity within each stand.

The Ancient and Ornamental Woodlands, which are not enclosed and are subject to deer browsing, grazing by commoners' animals and public recreation, consist chiefly of old oak and beech, probably the remnants of ancient plantings. A survey carried out in 1971 by the Forestry Commission has shown that 73 per cent of these woodlands contain an adequate naturally regenerated successor crop and that the total area of broadleaved forest has in fact increased since 1867 at an approximate rate of 12 acres per year. Artificial regeneration is therefore unnecessary but in some areas where the dominance of beech is likely to exclude future regeneration of oak, a continual and selective thinning of the beech to favour oak will be desirable to maintain an acceptable and enriched ecosystem.

The Open Forest Waste consists of natural heathland with gorse, areas artificially re-seeded with grass during the Second World War, self-seeded Scots pine, emerging Ancient and Ornamental Woodland and bog. An acceptable balance is to be kept between grazing for commoners' animals, biological diversity, stability of the surrounding woodland and peaceful enjoyment by the public. This will be achieved by rehabilitating heath and gorse for the purposes of rejuvenation, by not extending further artificially grass re-seeded areas and by carrying out drainage only to benefit the stability of surrounding woodland and the grazing, all without loss of biological diversity. Newly regenerating woodlands encroaching on the Forest Waste will be recruited to the Ancient Woodlands of the future. This will be done in consultation with

Open Forest
1 *Heathland, Latchmoor.* [DS]

Ancient and Ornamental
2 *Over mature and dying oak.* [DS]
3 *Beech natural regeneration.* [DS]

Statutory Inclosures
4 *Conifer artificial regeneration.* [DS]
5 *Oak artificial regeneration.* [DS]
6 *Beech natural regeneration.* [DS]

1

the Nature Conservancy Council and by agreement of the Verderers.

Recreational use of the Forest will be accommodated without allowing the Forest's fundamental character to change and with the minimum of conflict between the many diverse interests in the area. The provision of facilities designed and constructed by the Forestry Commission commenced in 1972 and is based upon the final recommendations of the Joint Steering Committee whose report was approved by the Minister of Agriculture in 1971.

These facilities consist of car parks and camping areas dispersed throughout the Forest in suitable locations, associated with areas protected from unofficial car access. The visitor is encouraged to walk into and learn from the Forest by the provision of waymarked walks and information services, including special facilities for educational use by schools; and there is co-ordination of specialised activities to avoid conflict with other uses of the Forest.

Involvement, understanding and encouragement by the visitor is essential if such major conservation measures are to be successfully completed. In 1971 the Forestry Commission formed the New Forest Consultative Panel, on which over 45 different users are represented and by which management and recreation proposals are discussed. This is in addition to the statutory agreement which must be obtained from the Verderers.

Constant monitoring is undertaken by the Forestry Commission to ensure that adequate measures can be embarked on to meet the enormous pressures that the Forest is subject to today.

The New Forest is probably unique in the world for its historical associations, its rare animals and plants and its living traditions. It lies within easy reach of millions of people and the Forestry Commission will ensure that in making the beauty of its wilderness freely available to them it also takes adequate precautions to see that it is not destroyed.

2

3

4

5

6

One

How the Forest has survived

DAVID J STAGG

"The forest law is hereby abrogated". These six words which are contained in the Wild Creatures and Forest Laws Act 1971 mark the formal ending of forest legislation dating back to at least the twelfth century. The majority of these laws had long become obsolescent, but at one time they were essential for the protection of the forest and the king's deer, and to a lesser extent to define and limit the duties and responsibilities of the inhabitants of the forest.

It is frequently stated that the forest laws were first introduced by King Canute, but this is untrue and the document upon which the claim is based has been proved to be a forgery. The forest laws were made by the Norman kings, the earliest surviving text being that known as the Assize of Woodstock and dated 1184, but this can be shown by documents of the period to be nothing more than a re-enactment and possible expansion of the then existing laws, and in fact the very first article refers to the more stringent penalties which had been exacted during the reign of Henry I.

The restrictions, which were intended to protect the game, included the possession of bows and arrows, the keeping of unlawed dogs – that is dogs not lamed so as to prevent them chasing the deer, the setting of traps for deer, and hunting at night. For the preservation of the woods it was an offence to cut timber except under the supervision of a forester, and far more serious was the offence of assarting – the conversion of woodland into arable land, and purprestures – the enclosing of forest land. More information is contained in a document known as "The Customs and Assise of the Forest". This details the customs and laws concerning trespasses to the vert and the venison, the procedure of the Courts, the duties of the inhabitants, and those of the foresters. For instance it gives such detail as the number of sureties in respect of various offences, these

being required to ensure the attendance of the offender at the next Forest Court. If a deer was found dead it was required that an inquest should be held among the four nearest villages.

The Charter of the Forest AD 1217, the forest's equivalent to Magna Carta, granted some relaxation of the forest laws. It was provided that certain recent extensions of the forests should be disafforested, an amnesty was granted to offenders who has been previously outlawed or exiled, fewer attendances were required at the Forest Courts, certain improvements to private lands within the forest would no longer be regarded as purprestures, rights of common were protected, there were to be safeguards against abuses and extortion by officials of the Crown, and no longer could offences be punished by mutilation or death.

The administration of justice within the forests was done in two stages, first by a local Court which determined whether an offence had been committed but was not empowered to pass sentence, the offenders being referred to the Forest Eyre, or Justice Seat, a Court presided over by the Lord Chief Justice in Eyre and held at irregular intervals around the various forests. The last such Court was held in the New Forest in 1669–70, and although the forest laws remained in force, the New Forest Act of 1698 specifically drawing at tention to this point – "the said Forest and every Part thereof shall be subject to and under the Laws of the Forests", the actual enforcement of these laws became virtually impossible.

The 1698 Act was primarily concerned with the establishment of timber Inclosures, but it did give the lesser Courts, held by the Verderers and known as the Court of Swainmote and the Court of Attachment, the power to impose fines for such offences as stealing timber, burning the heath, and destroying the covert. Further

ANNO NONO & DECIMO

GULIELMI III. REGIS.

C A P.   XXXVI.

An Act for the Increase and Preservation of Timber in the *New Forest* in the County of *Southampton*.

powers were given by the New Forest Act 1800 in respect of unlawful enclosures, purprestures, and encroachments, and an Act of 1819 gave powers over the exercise of common rights, and the right to enquire into the conduct of the under-officers employed in the forest. Throughout this period it was also possible, if less convenient, for more serious offences to be dealt with by the Court of Assize at Winchester.

The greatest threat to the New Forest did not arise from minor encroachments and the destruction of timber, but occurred in 1871 when the Treasury introduced into Parliament a Bill for the Disafforestation of the New Forest. This was a course that had been adopted for other royal forests, but fortunately on this occasion public opinion was aroused and the Bill was withdrawn. Reaction went even further in that a Resolution was passed in the House of Commons that no felling of timber should take place, and no further timber Inclosures be made, pending legislation on the New Forest. This took the form of the New Forest Act 1877, which is still largely in force and forms the basis of modern day management of the Forest. Under this Act the Crown's powers of Inclosure were greatly limited, and, equally important, amenity considerations were recognised in that regard was to be given to maintaining the picturesque character of the Forest, with attention being given to its ornamental value. The interpretation and implementation of this Act has from time to time aroused considerable controversy, especially so in the economic conflict between broadleaved trees and the more recently introduced conifers, but an acceptable compromise now appears to have been reached.

Other significant changes over the last 150 years have been more gradual and therefore less perceptible. What was once to all appearances an untouched wilderness has now been fragmented by railways and motor roads. There has been a vast increase in residential development, and around the margins of the Forest have been established an airfield and various industrial complexes. There are now very few areas of the Forest which remain unaffected by the sight or sound of modern technology, and it is this development that represents the present danger. Extreme care must be exercised if the beauty, character and uniqueness of the New Forest is to continue to survive.

Two

Buried relics of the past

ANTHONY PASMORE

The importance of the New Forest to the archaeologist lies in the fragile traces of ancient agriculture, forestry and industrial processes which have survived in this uncultivated region long after their destruction in more developed areas. The Forest can boast none of the spectacular stone circles, Roman villas or major defensive earthworks which are popular tourist attractions elsewhere, but the lesser sites which it does possess are rare and therefore of particular interest. Wherever man has lived or worked in the Forest he has left his mark in the form of earthworks – boundary banks and ditches, cattle pounds, coppice enclosures, burial mounds and industrial waste. There is little natural stone here, and local building materials were usually derived directly from the soil or what grew upon it. Earth being the most plentiful and durable of these resources has survived most widely.

The Bronze Age round barrows (of which there are well over one hundred in the Forest) are the best known of these earthworks. Large rounded mounds, sometimes forming a skyline feature as at Black Down, Map 8, or the Butt, Fritham, Map 3 are scattered throughout the district with the largest concentrations around Beaulieu. Many have been badly damaged by vandalism and uncontrolled excavation, but the rewards of this plundering have been fitting. Unlike the rich burials of surrounding counties, the Forest's barrows contained no more than patches of charcoal or an occasional decayed clay urn.

The defensive enclosures of the Forest are confined to one or two small hilltop forts, tentatively ascribed to the Iron Age. Of these, only Castle Hill at Burley, Map 9, and Castle Piece, Roe Inclosure, Map 5, are open to the public, although there are others on private land. Linear earthworks which appear to be of a defensive character may be seen to the

west of Hatchet Pond, Map 16, and at Red Hill, Map 11, but evidence as to the origin and purpose of these banks is lacking.

The Roman occupation has left little surviving trace within the Forest's boundaries. An important native pottery industry flourished here in the third and fourth centuries, and examples of its products may be seen in local museums. One reputed Roman road has been traced from Nursling to Stoney Cross, but the best preserved sections of this at Cadnam were destroyed by the construction of the M27 in 1974. Another earthwork claimed by some authorities as a Roman road may be seen in Fawley and Hardley Inclosures, Map 13. It seems that the Romans, like many of their successors, avoided major development of the poor land and difficult country presented by the New Forest.

In historic times the evidence for dating some of the Forest's sites is more plentiful. For example, the sites of six royal hunting lodges of the thirteenth to fifteenth centuries have recently been discovered. The most accessible of these is at Bolderwood, Map 6, where the present keeper's cottage is within a few yards of the original site. Five of these lodges occupied commanding positions overlooking the surrounding country for miles around, although they all now lie in densely wooded areas. They were in most cases probably little more than overnight camping places with a simple timber building roofed with thatch or slate and surrounded by a ditch, but we know from documentary sources that one at least (yet to be discovered) was a more elaborate structure with a chapel, stables and other buildings.

While the king was engaged in hunting, his subjects were probably more interested in the less exciting activity of pig keeping. The small pounds – earth banked inclosures once surmounted by a hedge or rails – survive in the more remote parts of the Forest. Some may date from as early as the eleventh century and due to their very slight construction they are difficult to locate on the ground. There are examples at Pinnick Wood and to the west of the Bishop's Dyke. These pounds were probably related to the commoners' rights of pannage, and they provided a comfortable and secure home for the pigs to return to at night.

Farming on a larger scale, often by illegal enclosure from the Open Forest, is represented by abandoned field systems in many parts of the district. The most extensive is at Crockford, Map 16 (355995) where the boundary banks cover nearly one hundred acres. This system may be medieval in origin, but encroachments continued well into the nineteenth century and were generally on a smaller scale. Tiny paddocks were taken in by cottagers during periods of agricultural prosperity, and were then abandoned in a subsequent depression or were re-possessed by the Crown. Good examples of these "Forest edge encroachments" may be seen at Beaulieu Rails (367990) and Hill Top, Map 13 (401040).

The Crown also made enclosures in the Open Forest, and among the earliest of these were extensive parks for the deer, constructed in order to facilitate hunting. The Park Pale at Lyndhurst is the best authenticated of these and dates from at least the late twelfth century. Its massive banks with their internal ditch are well preserved at Matley, The Ridge, Map 7. Other smaller deer enclosures of uncertain date survive at Denny, Map 7 (Stag Park) and Holm Hill, Map 6, the former being close to the road through the wood.

Later Crown enclosures were made for timber production, at first in small irregular shaped blocks for coppice wood, and then in large tracts of over 300 acres. Most of the latter date from 1700 onwards, and many still carry

fences on top of the old banks. Coppice enclosures are earlier (sixteenth and seventeenth centuries), and their remains can be seen in New Copse Inclosure and the Round Hill Camp Site, Map 11 (335020).

Apart from the pastoral activities of the Forest population, there were occasional related industrial processes which have left their mark. An abortive attempt at saltpetre production in Elizabethan times has left an abandoned factory site near Ashurst Lodge, and bricks were produced in many parts of the Forest. The old clay pits are clearly visible at Park Grounds where the remains of the kiln can be seen adjoining the main road. Charcoal burning by the old pit method died out here fifty years ago, but the slight charcoal circles up to 60 feet across survive for centuries, and can still be found with a little practice. There are many in the woods around Lyndhurst and Beaulieu.

1 *Pottery find, Sloden.* [RF]
2 *Black Down Barrow.* [RF]
3 *Castle Hill, Burley, from Picket – Burley road.* [RF]
4 *Roman Road, Fawley Inclosure.* [RF]

Three

The ecology of the Forest

COLIN TUBBS

Since the eighteenth century dramatic changes have occurred in the English countryside. Successive tides of reclamation from the wild, each lapping a higher shoreline than its predecessor, have left us today with little more than fragments of wilderness. Through a series of historical accidents the economic pressures for radical change were largely deflected from the New Forest so that it now embraces the most extensive tract of unsown, or semi-natural, vegetation in the lowlands of Britain – gently contoured mosaic of woodland, heathland and acid grassland with valley bogs and in places fertile alluvial "lawns" marking the drainage pattern. It is important to appreciate that this is not a "primeval" landscape. It has been shaped since prehistoric times by man and his animals. The heathlands and grasslands have arisen as a secondary condition to an early woodland cover, the clearance of the woodland commencing at least as early as the Middle Bronze Age and continuing into modern times, though checked after the eleventh century by the

Forest Law, which protected the woodland against exploitation if not from the depredations of deer and the commoners' animals. Indeed, the large numbers of deer maintained in the Royal Forest, together with the commoners' animals, limited the regeneration and expansion of the woodlands.

The age structure of the unenclosed woodlands today is closely related to the fluctuations which took place in the numbers of these herbivores over the past three centuries or more. The long centuries of grazing and browsing have also much modified the species composition of the woods, for example by eliminating palatable shrubs like hazel and by impoverishing the ground flora. The commoners' animals have aptly been described as the architects of the Forest's scenery.

It is thought that few of the remaining areas of heathland in lowland Britain are large enough to support indefinitely many of their characteristic plants and animals. The New Forest is thus ecologically important because it offers the best chance of conserving the most

1

2

1 *Beefsteak fungus*. [RF]
2 *Wild gladiolus*. [RF]
3 *Dartford warbler*. [NO]
3

complete spectrum of the heathland flora and fauna. The fauna includes such birds as the woodlark, stonechat, Dartford warbler and nightjar; reptiles like the sand lizard and smooth snake; and butterflies such as the attractive silver-studded blue and the grayling. All these species have declined in Britain and the most important contributory factor has been the loss of their habitats. All occur in the New Forest and for some it is now their main stronghold in this country.

The Forest's bogs comprise deposits of saturated peat, accumulated in hollows and valleys. Because they receive some of the products of leaching on the higher ground the bogs tend to be base-enriched in contrast to the acid environments of their catchments. The central watercourses are often marked by alder or willow carr and the flanking vegetation is generally dominated by tussocks of purple moor grass. The bogs are floristically the Forest's richest habitats and their flora includes many local and rare species, like the marsh gentian and bog orchid. They also support a rich invertebrate fauna, including such specialised and rare insects as the tiny damsel fly and the impressive large marsh grasshopper. In the spring they come alive with the calls of breeding lapwing, redshank, curlew, snipe and other marsh birds. For the naturalist they are among the Forest's gems. Scientifically they are some of the finest remaining examples of their kind in western Europe.

The unenclosed woodlands no longer have any strict parallel in Britain. Lowland woods in which man does not shorten the natural life-span of the trees by felling are now rare and, outside the Forest, survive only as small fragments. The Forest woods are the finest relics of relatively undisturbed deciduous forest in Britain and probably in the lowlands of western Europe. They are mainly of oak, beech and holly and their essential ecological characteristics are their varied age structure; the abundance of mature, senile and decaying trees; and a rich epiphytic lichen and moss flora and insect, bird and bat fauna. The large bird populations of the woods depend mainly on the rich invertebrate fauna, which in turn is associated mainly with the abundant old timber. Birds characteristic of the woods include many which are rather locally distributed elsewhere, such as the redstart and wood warbler. As to be expected, hole and crevice nesters including woodpeckers, the nuthatch, tree-creeper, stock dove and the tits (except, notably, the willow tit) are particularly numerous. The woodland edges and glades are the habitat of two New Forest "specialities" one an insect, the other a plant – the New Forest cicada and the wild gladiolus, neither of which occur elsewhere in Britain.

The Inclosures have their own special species, besides forming extensive refuges for the Forest's larger mammals – deer, badgers and foxes. Breeding birds include crossbills, goldcrests and firecrests, all of which are associated with conifers, whilst the old oak plantations possess a flora and fauna sometimes approaching that of the unenclosed woodlands in variety.

In addition to those already outlined, two further factors contribute to the variety and well-being of the Forest's wildlife. First, the area is largely free from the use of toxic chemicals in agriculture or forestry; and secondly, because it is not used for game-rearing it possesses large populations of pre-datory birds such as buzzards, kestrels, sparrowhawks, tawny owls and others, which despite legal protection are persecuted else-where because they are still regarded as vermin.

Diversity is the ecological keynote of the New Forest. It possesses great variety of soils, habitats, plants and animals. Moreover, it includes large and ecologically viable areas of habitats which elsewhere in lowland Britain have been largely lost to agricultural re-clamation, afforestation and development. It is a fair claim that today the New Forest is a unique reservoir of wildlife.

1

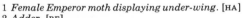

1 *Female Emperor moth displaying under-wing.* [HA]
2 *Adder.* [RF]
3 *Smooth snake.* [RF]
4 *Stag-headed oak tree near Queen's Bower.* [HA]
5 *Grass snake swallowing a mouse.* [RF]
6 *Heath Spotted orchid.* [RF]
7 *A Coral fungus.* [RF]

Four

Ships and Timber

New Forest timber and the Navy

David J Stagg

It is a mistake to regard a medieval forest as being nothing more than a royal game preserve, a place where the King could find amusement and relaxation. In practice the forests were of great economic significance, the deer being a necessary source of meat and their skins being used for a multitude of purposes from clothing to writing materials.

At the same time the Forest provided a source of building material for the royal houses. In 1250 the Keeper of the New Forest was ordered to prepare 20 000 shingles for roofing the King's Lodge at Clarendon and two years later a further 30 000 shingles were ordered for the same purpose. Revenue was obtained from the Forest in the form of fines imposed upon offenders against the Forest Laws, from the charging of rents in return for grazing privileges and also from the renting of Crown lands to private tenants.

Much wood and timber from the Forest was used for the construction of fortifications. As early as 1379 it is recorded that New Forest timber was supplied for Southampton defences and in later times timber was sent to Guernsey, the Isle of Wight, and Portsmouth, Southsea and Hurst Castles for use in fortifications. In the New Forest the first mentioned felling of timber for the Navy appears to be in 1611 when 1 800 oaks were supplied but supplies to the Navy remained intermittent until the latter half of the seventeenth century which saw the re-establishment of Portsmouth as one of the more important dockyards, also a rapid increase in the tonnage of the Navy.

1 *Buckler's Hard in 1805.*
H.M.S. Swiftsure *and H.M.S.* Euryalus *under construction, from a model at Beaulieu Maritime Museum.* [RF]

1

From about 1670 onwards a regular, if very small, supply of Navy timber was taken from the New Forest and on average this was 300 oak and 100 beech each year. It is impossible to know how many trees were actually felled as it would appear that a great quantity of timber was stolen. It is recorded in 1671 that much of the timber for a frigate then framing in the Forest has been embezzled by the carpenters and workmen. In the dockyard the small chips were by custom the carpenters' perquisites but under this pretence much good timber was stolen.

In 1670 some 300 acres had been planted as nurseries for timber and for this purpose the woodward was instructed to gather 1 000 bushels of acorns and 1 000 bushels of beech mast, also hawthorn berries and sloes. The hawthorn and sloes, also known as white-thorn and blackthorn, were planted to provide ground cover for the protection of the growing trees. At this time the Forest's stock of red deer had just been replenished by the gift of 60 stags from the King of France and both in planting and in felling the well-being of the deer was a first consideration. Objections were made to the use of Holm Hill as a nursery for timber, it being "a place very much delightful for the feeding and harbouring of His Majesty's deer" and when timber was cut it was not to be done "injurious to the beauty of the park or the shelter of the deer".

A survey of the timber made in 1707 reported that there were only 12 476 oaks suitable for the Navy. This has frequently been taken to mean a general depletion of the woodlands but in fact it was an indication of a serious failure in their administration as regards the production of Navy timber. Further surveys made in 1764 and 1782 show a steadily improving situation but the needs of the Navy were increasing at an even faster rate. A further 1 000 acres of oak had been planted in 1700, and a little more towards the end of the eighteenth century but finally, in 1808, an extensive programme was begun and 12 000 acres of oak were planted during the next sixty years. Of course it was too late.

New Forest oak today

David J Stagg

The oaks planted as a result of the New Forest Enclosure Act of 1808 were destined never to sail the seas, with one curious exception. Some New Forest oak timber was used in the 1939–45 war to build wooden mine sweepers. These ships were safe from an otherwise deadly weapon – the German magnetic mine. Wooden ships were replaced by ironclads and 1862 was the last year in which a considerable quantity of Navy timber was supplied from the New Forest. Oak is, however, regularly used on a large scale for Scottish fishing vessels. Today there remain some 5 000 acres of mature, even-aged oak plantations within the Statutory Inclosures. Eventually these will be replaced by woodland of mixed ages but it is the intention that they should be retained as long as possible as a most interesting example of eighteenth-nineteenth century silviculture and a unique memorial to the age of wooden ships.

The wooden walls of England

David Cobb

In the eyes of the British Shipwright, English Oak (*Quercus robur*) was the best ship timber in the world and at the time of the Tudors the country was well-supplied with oak on a scale to meet all foreseeable needs. Yet over the next two centuries massive depletions took place, the greatest devourer being the iron industry which needed charcoal for smelting; ships of war and merchant ships also consumed large quantities; domestic buildings, casks for beer and wine competed for the available supplies. The land was scoured for its trees without regard to their replacement.

The oak shortage struck the Navy towards

the end of the seventeenth century, when the hasty use of unseasoned wood to meet demands for new ships wasted England's available ship timber with nothing more to show for it than some rotting hulks.

Urgent action was overdue, as an oak must grow for a hundred years before it can be used in a ship. Parliament's eyes fell upon the Royal Forests: the Dean, the New Forest and Alice Holt. In 1698 a New Forest Act provided for 2 000 acres of trees to be planted and 200 acres a year for twenty years. By 1725, however, these policies has fallen into complete neglect and during 57 years in the eighteenth century the total output of all the Royal Forests amounted to no more than four years' naval supply, the balance being made up from provident private estates and increasingly from abroad.

Between 1745 and 1818 some fifty vessels were built by contract at Buckler's Hard, Beaulieu, including the famous warships *Agamemnon (64 guns)*, *Swiftsure (74 guns)* and *Euryalus (36 guns)*. From such a small yard over a short period this is a fine record; the Royal dockyards took longer to build a ship and their costs of construction were greater.

The *Agamemnon*, which was the smallest type of ship fit to fight in line of battle, required 2 000 mature oak trees in its construction in 1781, apart from other timber such as elm and beech for planking.

Ship-building timber was classified into mast, plank and compass. The latter came from the curved branches whose shape adapted easily to the frames or ribs of the hull. New Forest oak was more productive of compass timber than of plank, which had to be in long straight runs.

Timber accounted for half the cost of construction of a wooden ship, which in the Napoleonic period was reckoned to be about £1 000 per gun. Thus the *Agamemnon* would have cost some £65 000 without ordnance. Durability had a marked effect on overall costs: Nelson's Victory cost only £63 174 when she was launched in 1765, by the time she fought at Trafalgar repairs had swelled this to £251 981 and by 1815 she had cost the country some £371 922. Even more astronomical sums would no doubt have been expended on the Queen Charlotte had not the Navy sensibly cut its losses when she rotted away almost completely within two years of her launch, without ever putting to sea. Yet the *Royal*

William, built in 1719, lasted for nearly a century without expensive repairs.

Properly seasoned, oak, as Evelyn wrote, is "tough, bending well, strong and not too heavy, nor easily admitting water". In 1805 some one and a half million oak trees were at sea in the shape of the British Navy. Today the oceans carry steel and fibreglass; the hearts of oak are no more.

1

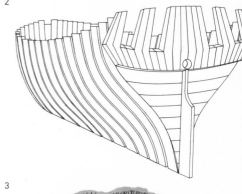

2

3

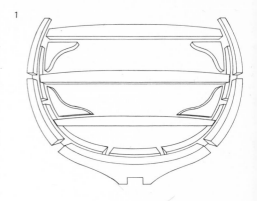

1 *A detail of the midship section of a wooden ship.*
2 *An indication of the volume of framing timber required for a wooden ship (nineteenth century) before the planking is in place.*
3 *Some typical shapes of shipwright timber provided by the oak.*
4 *Blackwood's frigate* Euryalus *(launched at Buckler's Hard in 1803) which brought about the interception of the Combined Fleet by Nelson at Trafalgar.* [DAVID COBB]
5 *Frontispiece of* New Forest *by Percival Lewis, 1811. Engraving by C. Sheringham.* [RF]

Five

Place names and personalities

ARTHUR T LLOYD

To an historian the names on a map summon up the past and supply vital clues to events which might otherwise be lost. They are living signposts, but caution is needed, as frequently the obvious meaning is not the correct one.

The oldest place names in this area are those of the waterways that bound the Forest, namely the Avon (Celtic word for "river") and Solent (origin uncertain). Flowing through the Forest is the Lymington river; the prefix means "elm".

Iron Age hill forts were usually called in Saxon times "bury". South west Hampshire has several, such as Burley, Tatchbury and Exbury. The name "Rings" at Buckland also indicates such a fort. But in the case of Holbury the suffix may refer to a Roman building, and the prefix show is ruined state (in holes). "Drakenhorde" in Rockbourne probably points to the discovery of a Roman treasure; it is close to the fine villa found in 1942. Similarly, Hordle, south of the Forest, means "treasure hill".

One reference in Domesday shows that as late as William I's reign people remembered the Celtic name "Andret" for this stretch of woodland along the south east coast. On the death in 1100 of William Rufus a chronicler wrote that the old name for the New Forest was "Ytene". Philologists have known for eighty years that this means "(land) of the Jutes", proving Bede's assertion about 730 that the Jutes had settled in southern Hampshire as well as the Isle of Wight and Kent.

The Forest has interesting links with the Saxon Royal House, for the Chronicler stated that Cerdic landed in 495 at "Cerdicesora", which might be Ower, Calshot. Cerdic's battle in 508 against the Britons led by Natanleod may have taken place at Nateley; if so, the name is derived from that of the chief. These are surmises, but with Charford we have a name that is definitely derived from Cerdic's battle in 519 at "Cerdicesford".

Eling is the next oldest name of Saxon origin in this area, meaning "Edla's followers". Ellingham, far to the west, means "homestead of Eling men". Keeping, in the Beaulieu area, may be a Jutish type of -ing name. Canterton near Brook, "farm of men from Kent", shows a link with the earlier Jutish settlements there.

South-west Hampshire may have been the last English area to retain its Germanic heathenism. Here two heathen Jutish princes fled in 680 from the Island. Nearby, in the bounds of Millbrook, Thunor was worshipped – the god who gave his name to Thursday. On the Forest's western bounds are Godshill and Devilsden, named in 1300.

Place names prove the area was well-wooded in early times. Six incorporate the word "wood", besides another five on the Forest edge like Arne- ("Eagle"), Ring- ("edge") and Wootton ("farm in the wood"). Lyndhurst ("lime tree wooded hill"), Brockenhurst (possibly "badger hill wood") and Bramshaw ("bramble copse") tell the same story. So do the 36 examples in the Forest and 25 nearby of the ending -ley, meaning "wood" or "clearing". Oakley, Bartley ("birch") and Ashley specify the tree species; others give each owner's name, as Sopley and Woodfidley: the latter's owner was probably a lady, Wulfgyth. Apple and Alder also appear as prefixes, as does Maple in the lost Domesday name "Mapleham".

The Danes, of course, made little impact. Only "Colgrimesmore" on the Beaulieu bounds in John's reign is definitely Danish, whereas the name Dane Stream arising near Wootton is derived from the Saxon "denu" (valley). A few Norman names survive, especially in the area of Beaulieu, itself of course French, from the Latin "Bellus locus regis", where kings had owned a hunting lodge before the Abbey was founded. On Abbey lands are Beufre and Bergerie (beef and sheep farms). The word "Purlieu" is used, associated with Dibden and Ogden, and close to the Forest edge are Hinton Admiral, reminding us of the Albamarlia family, and Tiptoe, the name a family brought with them from their Norman village.

Of course, the name New Forest derives from William I's afforestation. Domesday named 45 manors reduced to little value once the King's

2

3

1 *Avon River viewed from Castle Hill.* [RF]
2 *Bolton's Bench, Lyndhurst at sunset.* [RF]
3 *Boldre Church, associated with Gilpin.* [RF]

hunting took precedence. Of those identified only recently, the most important historically is "Thorougham", wrongly linked with Fritham (homestead in woodland) since the eighteenth century. It is definitely the area now Park Farm, on the Beaulieu Estate. Its significance comes from it being the site identified earlier than any other with the death of Rufus.

When William I created the Forest his officials and local people had to know its bounds. Named tumuli, for example Lugden's Barrow and Knave's Ash on West boundary, were used; more interesting is "Rodedic" on the bounds, for this was a meeting place for the local Hundred. Within the Forest is Bishop's Dyke, which is said to demarcate an area round which the Bishop of Winchester crawled in one day to secure land for his church. Queen's Bower must be the medieval hunting lodge called "Queneboure" (named after Eleanor, wife of Edward I).

At the end of the Middle Ages, both the widow of Warwick the Kingmaker and Perkin Warbeck claimed sanctuary at Beaulieu, but soon all such monastic property fell into lay hands. The Forest saw many armed horsemen again in the Civil War, but it must be remembered that Marryat's children's story is all fiction.

It was Charles II who enclosed New Park near Brockenhurst, and it was his brother's judge (Jeffreys) who dealt so harshly with Dame Alice Lisle of Moyles Court, after Monmouth failed to reach Lymington and escape by boat.

Bolton's Bench commemorates a member of that Ducal family which held the office of Groom Keeper of Burley Bailiwick throughout the eighteenth century.

In Boldre churchyard lies asleep the Reverend William Gilpin, lover of the Forest scene; the historian John Wise is buried in the new cemetery at Lyndhurst, the grave of Sir Arthur Conan Doyle is at Minstead, Brusher Mills the snake catcher is buried in Brockenhurst churchyard, and in the family vault at Lyndhurst parish church lies Alice Hargreaves, who as a little girl was given immortality as Lewis Carroll's Alice.

Where the Forest begins to slope towards the sea, Peterson's Sway Tower built in 1884 stands as a curious memorial to one man's faith in reinforced concrete as a material for building.

Six

William Rufus

The strange death of William Rufus

John Chapman

"On the morrow of Lammas, King William was killed with an arrow while hunting by one of his men". Thus ended, according to the Anglo-Saxon Chronicle, on 2 August 1100 in its thirteenth year, the reign of William II of England, third son of William the Conqueror, done to death in his father's New Forest, which had already claimed two of his kinsmen.

Nothing else is known for certain about the King's death and it is partly because of the mystery surrounding it that the tragedy today still casts a lurid glow out of England's savage past like those fires of hell to which so many of the King's subjects thought his soul had descended.

Some twenty years later two men who had been living at the time wrote more circumstantial accounts and although they differ in detail both agree that an arrow loosed by one Walter Tirel at a stag by mischance entered the body of his sovereign. Tirel apparently fled immediately to France and the fact that no attempt seems to have been made to investigate the matter in any way supports the common assumption of the time that the King's death was an accident.

Rufus was a cynical, greedy and determined ruler, small, thickset, ill-shaped, his face redder than his hair, his eyes of two different colours, and his oppression of the Church and dissolute ways had made him many enemies amongst his subjects. Small wonder then that stories of dreadful portents began to circulate which with hindsight seemed to suggest that he was destined for calamity in retribution for his sins.

He is said to have dreamed the night before he died of a gout of blood spurting up from his breast to obscure the sun. The Earl of Cornwall, hunting in a distant wood, met a black goat with the body of a naked man wounded on its back and crying "I bear to judgment your King, or rather your tyrant, William Rufus. For I am a malevolent spirit and the avenger of his wickedness which raged against the Church of Christ and so I have procured his death".

Some later anthropologists have gone further and suggested that the King went voluntarily to his death as a scapegoat for the sins of his people, the sacrificial victim of an ancient fertility cult surviving in Europe under the veneer of Christianity, but this can be no more than supposition.

The possibility that the Red King was murdered is a much more tenable theory and is consistent with the evidence. His younger brother, Henry, was a member of the fatal hunting party and as soon as he learned of his brother's death he left for Winchester where he demanded the keys to the King's treasury as the lawful heir. He then rode to London and procured his own coronation as Henry I on 5 August, only three days later. This was a remarkable feat by any standards and would have been difficult enough if planned in advance. Perhaps it was. Certainly the timing was favourable: the rightful heir, Robert, Duke of Normandy, was conveniently out of the country on a Crusade.

Tirel made good his escape and no action was ever taken against him; indeed he kept possession of lands he held in England and his brothers-in-law, the Clares, who were also members of the hunting party, prospered under the new King. Possibly there were compelling reasons for leaving him alone. He is said in later years to have asserted that he was not with Rufus when he was slain but if he agreed to act the fugitive to protect someone else there is no record of any reward given to him save immunity from reprisals.

Unfortunately we shall never know. If there were a conspiracy to kill the King, it was most effectively concealed, as well it might be since the prize was the crown of England itself. And perhaps something more: a local historian, Marjorie Triggs, has pieced together from the records an intriguing theory about which she writes here for the first time.

Yet one more mystery remains to discuss: the exact place of Rufus's death. Much research on this subject has been done by Arthur Lloyd, who is now convinced that the generally accepted location in Canterton Glen is in fact the wrong one and that the King died near the present farm buildings at Park Farm on the Beaulieu Estate.

The earliest writer to mention the place where the death occurred is Leland, who stated, some 440 years after the event, that it was at Thorougham. That place name became lost but the chief oral tradition indicated a tree in Canterton Glen and it was there that John, Lord Delaware, erected a stone on the site in 1745. The Reverend William Gilpin of Boldre, writing in 1790, suggested that Thorougham might have been what is now called Fritham, which is near Canterton.

Lloyd points out that Park Farm was originally called Thorougham and translates from the latin of the Annals of Waverley Abbey: "In the year 1204 King John once built a Cistercian Abbey which he named Bellus Locus near the spot where William Rufus the King was killed". Park Farm is only three and a half miles from Beaulieu whereas Canterton is about ten miles from the Abbey.

Again, Leland mentions a chapel at his Thorougham, of which there is no trace at Canterton whilst there are references to a

1 *The original Rufus Stone from Drivers Map, 1789.*
2 *Death of William for Barnard's* History of England.

chapel at Park Farm. The earliest known Royal hunting lodge in the Forest was at Beaulieu.

Arthur Lloyd's arguments, which he set out in full in Hampshire Magazine for September 1962, are persuasive but prompt one final doubt: if Leland's reference to Thorougham was mistaken, then the main link with Park Farm is broken. Again we shall probably never know.

"Did Rufus die for love of a lady?"

Marjorie Triggs

One version of the death of King William II tells us that, killed by an arrow, his body lay forlorn in the New Forest, forsaken by his hunting companions, who had fled in confusion, except for William de Breteuile who rode to Winchester to claim the throne for Robert, Duke of Normandy. The shot, through the heart, was a bulls-eye, the hallmark of the professional marksman. Was this then no mischance, but contrived accident . . . treason?

Rufus had no legal heir but a reciprocal treaty between him and his elder brother made Robert his heir.

Yet after the hasty interment of Rufus's body the next day Henry, the youngest of William the Conqueror's sons, claimed the Throne. Robert at this crucial time was far away Crusading and in spite of vigorous protest by William de Breteuile on his behalf, Henry became King-elect, being crowned on 5 August.

Although already the father of several children by various mistresses Henry was also without legal heir and his counsellors urged him to marry. His choice was Eadgyth, daughter of Malcolm Canmore, King of Scotland and of his Queen, Margaret, granddaughter of Edmund Ironside, an early king of the English.

An intriguing story tells how, some years before, Rufus was so impressed by reports of the beauty and charms of youthful Eadgyth then staying with her aunt, the Abbess Christian, at Romsey, that he went to see her. Neither his dissolute reputation nor his appearance, described as repulsive, were likely to commend him to the Abbess or her niece. Fearful of his intentions Christina hastily dressed her ward in nun's habit and veil, sending her into the garden with other nuns. Greeting Rufus, she invited him into the garden to see her roses. Here he saw Eadgyth garbed as a nun, seemingly a novitiate, whereupon he left.

The fair Eadgyth came into the care of her aunt again at the death of her parents; perhaps she was living as a nun at Romsey when Henry became King. Wherever she was Henry put the case of their marriage before the newly returned and reinstated Archbishop Anselm. She was willing and eager to marry Henry; his plea spoke of his long-standing love for her, so this was no new or sudden desire.

Anselm convened an Assembly of dignitaries after whose deliberations he declared Eadgyth no nun and therefore free to marry Henry. On 11 November 1100 Eadgyth (or Edith) became his Queen Matilda, amidst public acclaim, for her Royal Saxon ancestry assured Henry's acceptance by the English as their king, firmly establishing his sovereignty.

While Rufus lived what hope did Henry have of achieving this marriage? For it has been said that when the question of Matilda leaving the Abbey had been raised, Rufus told Anselm that he wished her to remain there. If that was so Henry could hardly overcome his opposition, for Rufus was omnipotent.

Was this long-standing love for Matilda the deciding factor in Henry's unsurping the Throne, so that he could gain the power to release her from the cloistered life? Did then Rufus die for Henry's love of a lady, the desirable Matilda?

But how can we know what really happened, who can we truly believe when one of the early chroniclers has said how difficult it was to tell the exact truth "especially when Kings are concerned"? And . . . a certain Queen?

Seven

Smugglers and their ways

K MERLE CHACKSFIELD

"I have myself seen a procession of twenty or thirty waggons loaded with kegs of spirits; an armed man sitting at the front and tail of each; and surrounded by a troop of two or three hundred horsemen, every one carrying on his enormous saddle from two to four tubs of spirits; winding deliberately and with the most picturesque and imposing effect along the skirts of Hengistbury Head on their way towards the wild country north-west of Christchurch".

So wrote Richard Warner in his "Literary Recollections" published in 1830, and there is no doubt that during the eighteenth and nineteenth centuries such a scene might have been common on almost any part of the coast where the New Forest comes down to the sea and where the beaches and chines, or small ravines, running seawards, provided conditions ideal for smuggling.

This was a time when severe taxation, combined with the general poverty of the working people, led to smuggling on a very large scale. The operation consisted essentially of buying a shipload of dutiable goods across the Channel, shipping them to a lonely English beach, preferably by night, to be hidden away locally

if necessary and eventually distributed into the country.

"Free trading", as it was called, became big business, and played an important part in the economic life of the people. Capital was invested, perhaps by the squire and local traders, doctors, farmers and even the parson, and at the other end of the scale it provided an extra source of income for farm labourers, fishermen and small tradesmen in those poverty-stricken times when a labourer's wage was seven shillings a week.

Tea, tobacco, brandy, silks, laces, pearls, spices and wines, even aristocrats escaping the French Revolution and gold and spies during the Napoleonic wars, all passed through the smugglers' hands.

Against this widespread activity was pitted on land the small forces of law in the shape of a Riding Officer of Customs and Excise with a handful of men, who could call upon the assistance of the Dragoons if there were any in the locality. The area patrolled by one such Officer extended from Poole to Hurst Castle. The Revenue Cutters did what they could to intercept the cargoes at sea, but as a naval commander reported in 1815, to order a

1 *Naked Man, Wilverley.* [KMC]

2 *Cat and Fiddle Inn.* [KMC]

Revenue Cutter to pursue a smuggling lugger was "like sending a cow after a hare".

The New Forest offered excellent cover for smuggling and its leafy ways and secret In the were well known to the "free traders". places Queen's Head, a seventeenth century inn at Burley, the smugglers would make their plans for handling cargoes expected at Chewton Bunny, a miniature gorge where a stream runs down from the Forest to the sea at Highcliffe. This was a most convenient landing place for goods destined for Burley, Ringwood, Fordingbridge and Salisbury. The contraband was brought up in waggons or on horseback along the track from the head of the Bunny over Chewton Common to the Cat and Fiddle Inn at Hinton, where the men would unload some of the tubs.

Smuggling was an activity usually carried on by men, but there were some women who delighted in taking part in the excitement and profit of the illicit trade. One such was Lovey Warne, a high-spirited girl who, with her brothers, Peter and John, occupied a cottage by the smugglers' path at Knave's Ash, between Crow and Burley. Her chief task was to warn the free-traders during the daytime of the presence of the Riding Officer. Dressed in a cloak of the brightest scarlet, she would stand whenever danger threatened at the top of Vereley Hill, close to Picket Post, from where she was clearly visible to the smugglers at almost every approach to Burley.

John King of Burley was a man who remembered smuggling days. He was "a big man like a gnarled oak, hard as iron", and he had many times taken "a couple of forest ponies with sacks on their backs and had gone down to the sea". He said that the smugglers' route was "across Crane's Moor, up the smugglers' path, through Vereley and Ridley up to Smugglers' Road there and on to Fritham".

It would seem that John King, even as an old man, was still active with "the Gentlemen" and he would bring kegs of brandy all the way from Barton Cliffs to a hiding place cleverly concealed under the hearth. The smugglers' would say:

"Keystone under the hearth" and

"Keystone under the horse's belly",

meaning that the contraband was hidden either under flagstones by the fire or under the stable floor.

It is probable that there was a smugglers' walk over Poor Man's Common to Picket Post

1 *Smuggler's spout lantern.* [KMC]

and it is suggested that there is still a bricked-up cellar somewhere beneath the bracken where contraband was hidden.

A difficult area to cover when being pursued by the preventive men was the open heathland at Thorney Hill. During one hot chase, the horses and a waggon-load of goods were driven straight into the great barn at Chubb's or possibly Atkin's Farm. The farmer there, when questioned by the preventive men as to the whereabouts of the free-traders, pretended that he had been bowled over by the waggon and that his leg was broken. He said that if they rode hard they might catch up with them further on in the village of Burley.

Cargoes landed at Lymington, Milford and Milton were often taken up the Boldre River into the Forest, and further east the Beaulieu River formed another route from the coast.

Punishment for convicted smugglers was harsh and included transportation and even hanging. By the roadside at Mark Way, near Wilverley Post on the A35, stands on the lonely heath, surrounded by a protective fence, the insignificant remains of what was once a great tree known as the Naked Man. From its stout boughs many malefactors, highwaymen as well as smugglers, paid the penalty of their wrongdoings at the end of the hangman's rope.

When you see ponies cropping the green sward of the Forest, or stumble upon a sunken track half hidden in the young bracken; or perhaps when you sail the tidal waters of the Beaulieu River along Fiddler's Reach to Buckler's Hard, you may remember the "Gentlemen of the Night", who used these ways over two hundred years ago and risked transportation or hanging for two shillings and sixpence a keg, or five shillings for a night's smuggling.

Eight

The Commoner

HUGH C PASMORE

A New Forest commoner is a person who, by virtue of occupying land to which attaches a Right of Common, as registered in 1858, is entitled to certain privileges, all of which originate from the distant past.

The farming commoner is much influenced by his use of these rights for though he may himself occupy only a few acres, his ability to take advantage of the forest enables him to farm on a comparatively large scale. On the other hand there are many modern commoners who do not actually farm but have a full time job in the district, for even a garden plot to which attaches the appropriate right entitles the occupier to "farm" the forest.

There are five Rights of Common in the Forest and these are described below:

COMMON OF PASTURE is the most valuable right and enables the commoner to depasture animals on some 45 000 acres of open forest. This right of grazing is believed to date from the days of William the Conqueror when the New Forest was a hunting preserve and local husbandmen were prohibited from fencing any of their land lest it interfere with the Monarch's sport. It was recognised that this imposed on the farmer a very great hardship and he was therefore permitted to allow his beasts to wander over the forest for five summer months (excluding four weeks in June/July – Fench month (20 June to 20 July – when the does normally dropped their fawns). During the winter months (Winter Heyning – 22 November to 4 May) when keep was scarce the right was withdrawn so that the deer would not go short.

Over the years extensive changes have taken place and in 1851 an Act of Parliament decreed that all deer should be destroyed or removed from the forest in return for the commoners' agreement that 10 000 acres of open land should be fenced and used for timber production. Thus today commonable animals have a legal right to remain on the forest for the whole of the year, though in fact deer have re-established themselves throughout the forest.

It has become a fairly constant pattern that about 5 000 commonable animals run on the forest and in recent times the number of ponies has exceeded the cattle by three to two. Donkeys will be found mainly in the north and west on light or sandy soils but seldom number more than fifty.

The number of commoners actually using

1 *Cattle and ponies grazing on Broomy Plain.* [RF]

1

their rights of turning animals on to the forest is in the region of 350 but this is only a fraction of those entitled to do so. In the office of the Clerk to the Verderers are maps prepared by the Forestry Commission showing all the land to which common rights attach and these may be inspected on payment of a nominal fee. Lands bearing rights stretch well outside the forest boundary, even as far away as Bournemouth and Cranborne.

The right to run cattle on the forest is of inestimable value to farmers whose land adjoins the forest, for during wet weather instead of his land being "poached" or cut up by his herd the animals are fed and remain outside, only coming in for milking or veterinary attention. Ponies on the other hand remain permanently on the forest and may well "haunt" (the foresters' name for the district a pony inhabits) an area many miles from its owner's farm, where fortunately for the owner it usually remains within a radius of two or three miles throughout its life.

Though commonable animals (ponies, cattle, pigs and a few sheep) run on the forest as of legal right, they are subject to Byelaws imposed by the Court of Verderers under statutory powers and the owner pays to the Court a grazing fee in respect of each one. Currently

(1974) this amounts to £3 per head per annum and is collected by the Agisters for the Court to use to defray the cost of supervising and controlling the animals.

No commonable animal may graze upon the forest unless it is branded with its owner's mark and the Verderers maintain a complete register of these identification brands. Traditionally, ponies are branded on the left or near side in one of three places: on the back where the saddle normally sits, on the shoulder or on the hip. Cattle on the other hand are branded on the right or off side flank. Branding is carried out by clipping the hair as short as possible and then "touching" the hide with a red hot branding iron. Many forest farmers use brand designs which have been handed down through generations of their families. Recently a few animals have been branded with a chemical freeze process which turns the hair permanently white in colour but this is not popular with commoners.

In addition to the forest Right of Pasture there are others less widely used today, though in the past they also were much prized by the commoner.

COMMON OF MAST is the right to turn pigs on to the forest during what is known as the

Pannage Season when acorns and beech-mast have fallen and provide excellent feed for pigs, though when green are poisonous to cattle and ponies when taken to excess. Until the New Forest Act of 1964 Pannage dates were fixed from 25 September to 22 November but in those seasons when the acorn fall was late, pigs in search of food invaded local gardens, hence the Act provided for the Forestry Commission after consultation with the Verderers to fix any suitable term of not less than sixty days. The commoner pays a small fee per animal to the Verderers. On the 3 500 acres of private commons which march with the true forest, local commoners are not subject to the Pannage dates and there pigs roam throughout the year.

COMMON OF TURBARY entitled the commoner to cut turf for burning in his dwelling, the rule being that for every turf cut the two adjoining ones must be left, thereby avoiding stripping the area completely. Only one or two commoners avail themselves of this right today.

COMMON OF FUELWOOD, sometimes referred to as Estovers or Assignment Wood. The Forestry Commission allocates one or more cords of burning wood to certain tenements to which this registered right attaches and as in the case of Turbary the wood has to be burnt in the house. Over the years these rights have diminished in number and today only some eighty commoners enjoy allocations. The Forestry Commission cuts and stacks the wood, usually reasonably close to the commoner's holding, and assigns the correct cordage to the rightholder who has to collect it.

1 *Pigs at pannage in Rhinefield.* [RF]
2 *Assignment fuelwood.* [HA]
3 *Mare and foal.* [RF]
4 *Sample of commoners' brands for ponies, Green Dragon Brook.* [HI]

COMMON OF MARL. This is a right to take Marl from the twenty-three forest pits for spreading on the commoner's land as a form of manuring. Modern agricultural methods have now rendered this right more or less obsolete.

In 1909 the New Forest commoners formed an Association known as the New Forest Commoners' Defence Association and today with over 500 members the Association still fulfills its original function of safeguarding the members' rights, whilst at the same time forming a valuable link with the Forestry Commission and the Court of Verderers whereby many difficult forest problems are solved.

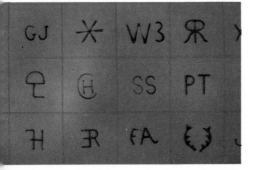

Nine

The Verderers

MALDWIN DRUMMOND

The title Verderer comes from the Norman word "vert" meaning green and referring to woodland. William the Conqueror set aside vast areas for hunting, creating "forests" protected by new laws and officials. In these, the "vert" and the "venison" (the flesh of beasts of the Forest: red, fallow and roe deer and wild boar) were for the benefit of the King.

The Verderers were part of the judicial and administrative hierarchy of the Forest. This system was modified in 1238, when the Forests of England were divided into two provinces, one north and the other south of the River Trent. A Chief Justice was appointed for each province and he travelled around on circuit, hence the name of his Court, that of the Chief Justice in Eyre (errer – old French for journey). This was the senior Forest Court, being dependent on the lesser court of "Attachment" and on "Inquisitions" for its clients.

The duty of the court of "Attachment", on which Verderers sat, was to investigate and record "attachments" made by officials of the Forest. It could only deal with minor vert offences and had a limit of 4d on the fines it could impose. In addition, the Court administered such things as wood rights and swore in Forest officials.

More serious offences, such as venison, were "attached" to the Court of the Chief Justice in Eyre.

"Inquisitions" investigated the death of one of the King's deer in much the same way as a coroner's court today, though the carcase was sent to "the spittal house or given to the sick and poor", while the head went to the freemen of the nearest town and the arrow was presented to a Verderer as evidence; the poor accused, if found, languished in jail to await the coming of the Court of the Chief Justice in Eyre.

"Assarts" or the illegal cultivation of land, "purpresture" or illegally erecting structures or digging fish ponds, were reported to the court by the "Regarders", an independent team of watchdogs who visited every three years. They also had charge of the "lawing of dogs". This was the multilation of three toes of the fore feet to prevent their harming the deer, if they were of the size to do so. The "Stirrup of Rufus" (actually a Tudor relic) in the Verderers' Hall was said to have been such a measure, for if the dog could pass through it he need not be so cruelly treated. The necessity though was usually overcome through payment of a fine or a bribe. It is said that the Regarders used to go through the towns blowing their horns to cause concealed and potentially deer-hungry dogs to bark and so reveal themselves.

The Assembly or Court of Swainmote, through which the Verderers superintended the pannage of pigs and the removal of cattle during the summer fence month and winter heyning (periods when the open waste of the Forest was reserved strictly for the King's deer), was sometimes allied to the Court of Attachment. Presentments could be made to this Court by the aggrieved. The distinction between the two "courts" became blurred and they exist as one today.

Then, as now, they were held in the Verderers' Hall at Lyndhurst. This was built within or beside the manor house of the Royal Manor of Lyndhurst in 1388. The old entrance used to be through the Tudor porch and was altered during the substantial changes to the Hall and the Queen's House in 1851. The panelling that lines the walls of the present court came from the upper rooms destroyed in the Victorian change. The Honourable Gerald Lascelles, however, built his offices above the Hall and restored the outside appearance of the old building to roughly what it was before 1851 and is again today.

Before the final demise of the supreme

"Forest" Court of the Chief Justice in Eyre in 1817, after long redundancy, attempts had been made to strengthen the Courts of Swainmote and Attachment in Acts of 1698 and 1800, but the real change did not take place until the passing of the New Forest Act 1877, or "Commoners' Charter" as it came to be called.

Under this Act, the number of Verderers was increased to seven, the Official Verderer being appointed by the Crown. They were to be elected by registered commoners and those who were parliamentary voters of any parish or township wholly or partly within the perambulation. To be elected, a candidate for a Verderer must own not less than seventy five acres to which common rights attached. This and the method of election, which was not secret, the voter having to declare his choice openly to the polling clerk, ensured that few contested elections were held in seventy years.

The Act also gave the Verderers administrative duties to control the grazing and health of animals depastured on the Forest and to make byelaws and to regulate the exercise of the rights of common. The re-organised Court of Swainmote was given the status of petty sessions and the sitting Swainmote Verderers, powers of a Justice of the Peace.

In 1947 the Baker committee produced a report which reflected the changing role of the Forest.

The 1949 Act reconstituted this court. A register of those entitled to vote was to be maintained by the Verderers and polling stations designated where a secret ballot could take place in order to choose the five elective Verderers. One Verderer each was nominated by the following four authorities: the Forestry Commission, Ministry of Agriculture, Hampshire County Council and Countryside Commission.

The Verderers' Court, Queen's House, Lyndhurst. [RF]

This new Act strengthened the powers of the Verderers' Court to control the health of animals, grazing and rights of common. The Verderers' Agisters carry out this day-to-day work on behalf of the Court. The Verderers were also given power to grant the Forestry Commission new Inclosures for timber production and for the regeneration of the Ancient and Ornamental Woodland. Ability was also given on presentment by the Minister to fence the Cadnam–Ringwood trunk road (A31). This was to lead, through the medium of the 1964 and 1970 Acts, to the fencing of the A35 and the fencing and gridding of the New Forest itself, embracing at the same time the outlying commons.

The Verderers' duties had passed from mainly judicial to administrative, encouraging and implementing advances in animal health, such as making the Forest the first unenclosed tuberculin tested (TT) area and the encouragement of conservation measures as embodied in the study "Conservation of the New Forest".

In 1877 the Court's time was taken up for the most part by the demands of the commoners and their animals. Today, although this is still a principal concern, the Court is increasingly involved in ensuring that the traditional life, beauty and unique natural history of the Forest is not spoilt by and for the hundreds of thousands that come to enjoy it, whether for the day or to camp and caravan.

The Verderers sit in "open" Court every two months on a Monday at 11.00 am. Any member of the public can make a "presentment", an ancient custom carried on from the Court of Swainmote. The senior Agister standing in the Court's old wooden dock and raising his right hand, invites this participation with the ancient message:

"Oyez, oyez, oyez!
All manner of persons who have any presentment or matter or thing to do at this Court of Swainmote, let him come forward and he shall be heard!
God Save The Queen!"

The relationship between the Forestry Commission and the Verderers has not always been happy because of the divergent interests of those who depasture cattle and those who are responsible for the production of timber. Perhaps it is because of the strong intervention of a third party, the public, that the Court and Commission now work in harmony for the benefit of all three. It is perhaps the happiest development from the Laws of William.

Ten

The Agisters

HUGH C PASMORE

It will be evident that with more than 5 000 commonable animals roaming over a hundred square miles of open forest, some form of supervision and control is essential. This control is provided by the Court of Verderers, whose constitution and powers have been described earlier. The Court appoints three men known as Agisters (derived from Norman "to receive payment"), whose duty it is to supervise all the commonable animals in that third of the forest which is allocated as their area. In direct control of these Agisters is a Steward to whom falls most of the clerical work involved and the public relations contacts with residents and others affected by movements of the animals. In addition he acts as a stand-in when any Agister is unavailable.

An obvious necessity for an Agister is that he should ride the forest to keep in touch with animals in the more remote parts, and he receives from the Verderers an allowance for the maintenance of a pony. Each man must be an accomplished horseman for much of his time is spent rounding up forest ponies which may well involve galloping across very rough country. He must also have an intimate knowledge of the very extensive area of woodland, moor and bog which constitutes his beat.

In addition, the Verderers have an arrangement with the Hampshire Police Authority whereby each Agister and the Steward have installed in their cars a two-way radio, enabling them to pass and receive messages from Police Control and also to communicate direct with each other. This is of tremendous benefit when an animal is injured in a road accident or is otherwise in trouble. The Police call up the Agister on the radio and within minutes he will be on the scene of the mishap.

Accidents on the road have decreased from 378 in 1962 to less than half that number today, due mainly to the fencing of some forest roads, but even so a considerable part of the Agisters' time is absorbed in dealing with these emergencies. Since the majority of road accidents occur after dark he frequently works under conditions of great difficulty. Of necessity each Agister is issued with a humane killer and when dealing with an injured animal he is authorised by the Verderers to use his own judgment in deciding whether or not to put the animal down.

During the summer months, when the animals have a smooth coat, the owners brands are clearly visible but in winter the hair grows long and thick and brands can

1

seldom be seen. The Agister knows a great many of the ponies and cattle by sight and no problem arises in communicating with the owner in the event of trouble, but in other cases he has to round up the affected beast and, with special branding scissors, he clips the long hair over the brand thereby exposing it for recognition.

A further aid to identification is known as tail-marking. On the autumn drifts (round-ups) the tail is cut to a special shape; in the case of two of the Agisters one or two notches out of the right side and in the case of the third an all round cut near the top. These marks

Pony drifting. [RF]
Ponies in pound. [RF]
Clipping "out" for branding. [RF]
Agister branding a New Forest yearling. [RF]

indicate that the owner of that particular animal lives in or adjacent to the area controlled by that Agister.

In addition to ensuring the welfare of animals under his control, each Agister has to collect for the Verderers the marking or grazing fees (as explained in a previous chapter). On receipt of the appropriate payment for cattle the Agister clips into the ear of the animal a plastic ear tag coloured according to the current year and this enables him, when seeing cattle in the Forest, to determine immediately whether the fee for the year has been paid. The same procedure cannot be followed for ponies because this causes unacceptable festering and no alternative visual mark has yet been found.

During the winter the amount of food available in the forest is necessarily restricted and the animals use their reserves of fat stored up in the summer. Nevertheless in the late winter many animals, both ponies and cattle, lose condition to an extent which renders it advisable for them to be returned to their owners' holdings. Local veterinary surgeons have formed an Advisory Panel and each winter month a veterinary surgeon, a Verderer and the Agister concerned examine all animals with a view to laying down a standard of condition to be adopted by the Agister during the ensuing month. The Agister causes any animal falling below this standard to be removed.

At all sittings of the Court of Verderers and on other special occasions such as the Stallion Show, the Agisters wear a most distinctive livery consisting of green jackets, riding breeches and leather gaiters, together with hard hats bearing the insignia of the Verderers' Stirrup.

An Agister's job demands not only toughness but also the ability to improvise, for he is constantly faced with new and unexpected emergencies requiring immediate action. An animal trapped in a bog is not unusual and rescue methods are fairly standardised but ponies have been found with their heads wedged between branches, legs entangled in wire, tins embedded over hooves, etc. all of which call upon resourcefulness of the man.

Agisters are almost invariably recruited from commoners who have spent their lives working with forest animals for theirs is not a job which could be picked up by a newcomer in a few months.

Eleven

The Foresters

HUGH INSLEY

Although the New Forest was not afforested (placed under forest laws) until 1079 there are records to show that as early as the reign of King Canute the area was hunted and that forest officers were appointed to look after it. The Foresters at that time were referred to as Lespegend and later Regarders.

Because the emphasis was upon the forest as a place in which to hunt rather than to grow trees, the records made during the early history of the Forest nearly always refer to the Keepers, whose job it was to safeguard the King's deer. The existence of Foresters at that time was recorded more by their transgressions against the King's deer than their activities in forestry. For instance, in 1271 a Steward of the Forest, Walter de Kanc, was reported to have taken one hart (red deer stag) and six bucks (male fallow deer). When the Verderers and Foresters who had obviously known of these activities were asked to report, they admitted that Walter and his friends had in fact taken over 500 deer. The Verderers and Foresters received reprimands but Walter, who was held to blame for all, received severe treatment. For the 500 deer he was fined £5 000 and for the other deer taken and destruction done to his bailiwick, he and his family were placed at the will of the King and Queen; in effect their lives and property were at the court's mercy.

Whatever woodland existed on the Forest during the eleventh century would have been natural woodland surviving from the effects of the Bronze Age and later inhabitants of the area. Before it became necessary to preserve and deliberately grow trees for timber, the job of the early Forester was probably one of guarding the natural timber against thieves and cutting what was required for the Crown's purposes.

The first record of enclosure for growing timber in the Forest is in a return made in 1438 by Henry Carter of Walhampton and Thomas Coke of Menestede (Minstead) to account for: 'money paid for enclosing 720 perches of wood and underwood at 4d the perch, and in making 3 gates to the said enclosure, with hinges, hooks, hasps, staples, locks and keys bought for the said gates'.

In 1535 during Henry VIII's reign, Godshill Coppice was recorded as a one hundred year old plantation of oak, thus showing that the Foresters had been actively growing oak since at least 1435.

Towards the end of the sixteenth century the use of the Forest as a royal hunting preserve began to decline but it was not until the importance of the Forest as a source of timber for the Royal Navy became realised that the Foresters for the first time began to share a place of equal importance with the Keepers. This was emphasised by the 1698 Act of William III, which begins:

'Forasmuch as the Woods and Timber, not only in the said New Forest, but in this Kingdom in general hath of late Years been much wasted and impaired and the said Forest, that might be of great use and conveniency for the Supply of His Majesty's Royal Navy, is in Danger of being destroyed, if some speedy course be not taken, to restore and preserve the Growth of Timber there;'

This provided for the immediate enclosure and planting of 2 000 acres and 200 acres more to be enclosed yearly for twenty years. The Crown also took the power of rolling enclosure which was not ended until 1877.

The method of planting the oak woods after the 1698 Act is interesting in that they were sown, not planted as is the practice now. Three acorns were sown in each bed or spit and the spits were spaced a yard apart. Half a bushel of acorns was allotted for each forest worker to plant in a day by the Regarders, two of whom stayed on site to ensure that the work was done properly. After the acorns had been planted hawes, holly berries, sloes and hazel nuts were planted throughout the area and traps were set by the Keepers to catch mice which would eat the acorns.

The Foresters and Keepers were the main people towards whom the penalties for abusing the Act were directed. A fine of £10 and being declared unemployable for life on Crown Estates was the penalty for cutting beech or oak trees, whilst for allowing a charcoal hearth within 1 000 paces of any Inclosure made under the Act, a Forester could be fined £100.

Despite these severe penalties the Foresters appear to have avoided their responsibilities. In 1789 their neglect "allowing constant thieving" is blamed for a lack of suitable oak trees for Royal Navy timber.

Following the Forestry (Transfer of Woods) Act 1923, the Forest was transferred to the Minister of Agriculture along with the Forest of Dean and the newly formed Forestry Commission was made responsible for their care and management. Forestry and the growing of timber tempered by the consideration for amenity – for the Forest was becoming a resort even then – remained the primary objective of the Foresters.

The New Forest Act 1949 made them responsible for a certain amount of open forest work also; this required the Forestry Commission to control scrub by cutting and burning and to carry out some drainage if considered reasonable and necessary and with the agreement of the Verderers.

The Foresters are responsible for the day to day management of the Forest. Today there are nineteen Foresters headed by three Chief Foresters, each of whom controls a section of the Forest's economy. One section deals with all the felling, thinning, preparation and sale of timber whilst another controls the establishment and maintenance of new plantations as well as the open forest work. The third section is responsible for the recreation facilities in the Forest and the conservation of its fauna and flora. As such they are the first group of Foresters in Britain to work as a specialist recreation and conservation section. To assist them there are mechanical engineers who maintain the machinery all-important in modern forestry, and civil engineers who construct the forest roads and forest drains, as well as designing and constructing the car parks which are provided around all the car-free areas.

Through almost one thousand years of the New Forest's history the role of the Foresters has changed three times, from guardians of a forest important only for its deer, to the true role of Foresters as growers of timber. This second role as tree growers must always remain to conserve the forest as we now know it; but recently the third role of Foresters as recreation land managers has developed and will undoubtedly assume increasing importance. Never before in the Forest's history have Foresters held such a responsible role as they do now and this is emphasised by the fact that there are now more Foresters working in the Forest than ever before.

Felling a mature Douglas fir. [RF]
Group felling in mature oak for replanting. [RF]
Careful thinning promotes growth and produces revenue. [RF]

Twelve

The Forest Keepers

MICHAEL CLARKE

"You shall truly execute the Office of a Keeper of the King's wild beasts. You shall be of good behaviour yourself towards the King's wild beasts and the vert of the same Forest. You shall not conceal the office (offence) of any other person, either in vert or venison that shall be done within your charge . . ."

This oath of a forest keeper was recorded by Manwood in 1598. Nearly five hundred years earlier King Canute had created the office of Tineman, who had much the same job.

Between the eleventh and seventeenth centuries the New Forest remained the hunting preserve of the Sovereigns of the day with the forest keepers tending the deer and enforcing the rigid forest laws.

Manwood records a law passed by King Edward the First . . . 'that if a man be apprehended hunting in the forest without warrant (permission) though he hath not taken a wild beast he shall be punished as if he hath taken and killed one.' Even so – according to Manwood – a poacher could only be im-

prisoned pending trial if he was 'Taken in the Manner' or caught red-handed as we would say today. He records four degrees of being Taken in the Manner:

Dog draw: Where a man has wounded a deer and followed it with hound or dog, drawing after it to recover it.
Stable stand: Found by a 'standing' ready to shoot deer, or with hounds ready to slip them after deer.
Back bare: Having killed a deer was found carrying it away.
Bloody hand: Found in suspicious circumstances with blood on him.

Unless taken in the manner and arrested the Court of Attachment, if the offence was discovered by other means, could 'attach 'or distrain on an offender's goods or chattels to ensure his attendance at the next Forest Eyre Hence the term Court of Attachment – the first Court before which offenders against the forest laws appeared.

1

During 1848 and 1849 much evidence was given before the Duncan Committee of the predations of deer onto the commoners' holdings. It was alleged that the numbers of deer in the forest had been as high as 7 000 or 8 000 but the actual numbers found by census were:

1845 – 4 582
1846 – 3 552
1847 – 3 196

from which it would appear that the numbers were already being reduced heavily. In 1850 a Royal Commission (the Portman Commission) was appointed and the Deer Removal Act of 1851 followed very closely the recommendations of that Commission. Its effect was to:

provide for the removal of the deer;
empower the Crown to enclose a further 10 000 acres for the growth of timber.

The Keepers made considerable efforts to implement this 'deer removal', but there was violent agitation by the commoners against the powers of enclosure given to the Deputy Surveyor and this resulted in the appointment of a Select Committee which made recommendations resulting in the passing of the New Forest Act 1877, laying the basis for the administration of the forest as we know it today. Evidence was given before the Select Committee proving that the unenclosed pastures of the forest had suffered by the drastic reduction in the numbers of deer. In 1883

1 *Young fallow deer.* [RF]   2 *New Forest Keepers.* [HI]
2

G E Briscoe Eyre, a Verderer, records '. . . the value and extent of such pasture depends largely upon the number of species by which it is depastured'. Thus it was quickly recognised that the deer were important to the survival of the open forest lawns and though the Deer Removal Act remained in force until 1971 it ceased to be observed and the deer were saved from possible extermination.

The Keepers' duties today bring them more into contact with the many visitors to the Forest although the deer remain the focal point around which their year revolves.

The Forest is divided into two ranges, each in the charge of a Head Keeper who supervises the work of six beat Keepers. During April a census is taken of the deer on each beat, involving the Keepers in hours of patient observation. From this census a shooting plan is made, for the deer must be controlled to prevent numbers rising beyond the capacity of their winter food supply on the Forest; other factors to be considered include the vulnerable state of the young plantations and the likelihood of damage to neighbours' crops. Using high velocity rifles from specially-sited high seats the Keepers cull the deer in due season. During summer when roe buck are in season this can mean a working day starting at dawn and lasting into the late evening, since the deer lie up during the heat of the day and are most easily seen on their feeding grounds at dawn or dusk. Poaching continues to be a problem with deer grazing near the forest roads providing an easy target for the poacher using a car at night.

Regrettably animals other than deer have to be controlled, for the hare, rabbit and grey squirrel all damage the trees and if the Foresters' work is to succeed then the Keeper must keep their numbers in check.

The Keepers carry out normal patrols in daytime, policing their beats not only for infringements of the byelaws but to check on the many activities which take place. In the summer months the Keepers also have a heavy commitment patrolling camp sites and the many parking and picnic places, where they are available to the public to give information. Many other duties are involved with these patrols throughout the year.

The New Forest Keeper is a man who lives with the forest throughout the year, carrying on the tradition of caring for it as did the Tineman nearly a thousand years ago.

Thirteen

New Forest ponies

DIONIS MACNAIR

In early times ponies roamed all over Britain but as farming and the population increased they were confined to small areas where they evolved slightly differently to suit local conditions and usages. In the New Forest they did all the work of the smallholdings, pulled the trap to market, carried the man to his work, and, within living memory, the children to school. Long ago they acquired a reputation as good children's ponies since James I is reputed to have had one for his children. They were always used to round up the cattle and ponies on the Forest and "colt hunting" is still not only a necessary part of the commoners' way of life but, along with pony racing, his traditional sport. This has encouraged the faster, sure-footed type of pony. When the New Forest Scouts were raised they were unusual among Yeomanry Regiments in being mounted on their own ponies who although small and rough had no difficulty in carrying the men and all their equipment Indeed, two of them managed to win the Auxiliary Services Jumping Competition at Tidworth Tattoo in 1902.

The earliest recorded attempt to improve the breed and get a larger faster pony was by the use of the thoroughbred "Masque", 1765–69. Thoroughbreds were also used on Forest mares by the Duke of York in attempting to breed for the Army. Some cart blood was doubtless used to get a heavier pony to haul timber and in 1852 the Office of Woods, thinking poorly of the ponies of the time, borrowed an Arab stallion from Prince Albert but he was not well patronised.

A persistent criticism has been that there were excellent mares who moved extraordinarily well but the standard of stallion was poor, so in 1891 the Society for the Improvement of New Forest Ponies was formed to award stallion premiums and hold annual races on Balmer Lawn. Lord Arthur Cecil considered the ponies inbred but decided that as all British

ponies had a common derivation the thing to do was to bring stallions from another area and so breed a British pony. He brought to the Forest Welsh stallions with very Arab characteristics still seen particularly in the "Denny Danny" line, a black Highland pony with yellow eyes (witch eyes and the dun coat he also brought are found in the "Spitfire" line), some Fells and an Exmoor. A Polo Pony "Field Marshall" is the ancestor of many of today's best ponies; the last outcross allowed was a Dartmoor.

In 1938 the above-mentioned Society amalgamated with the Burley and District New Forest Pony and Cattle Society to form the New Forest Pony Breeding and Cattle Society and since then no outside blood has been permitted in Registered ponies. This has been possible because the New Forest Verderers can control which stallions run and will only allow suitable sound registered stallions onto the Forest. Since 1970 all stallions must hold a Veterinary Certificate. So although a commoner may turn out any mare, provided her colts are removed before they are old enough to breed (many do this: piebalds and skewbalds are never pure bred Foresters), it is possible to breed pedigree stock on the Open Forest, unlike common land elsewhere where there are no Verderers.

The environment, aided by efforts to supply the current market, has a decisive effect in producing a type. For example the small carthorse is no longer needed so the heavy, hairy-heeled pony has practically disappeared. Nowadays the ponies are used mainly as children's or family ponies; they are very versatile, fast for their size, hardy and good tempered. They usually jump and several have achieved British Show Jumping Association standard. Many are to be found in various Pony Club teams around the country. Whilst narrow and docile enough for small or disabled children, they are strong enough for mother to ride. Few are afraid of traffic, often their undoing on the unfenced Forest roads but essential when ridden or driven. Now that as many New Forest ponies are bred on private studs as in the Forest, owners who favour a particular type can usually find it among the mixed ancestry and by selective breeding accentuate it again to diversify the type.

Colt hunting has two forms: one where perhaps two people ride out to catch an individual pony and secondly "drifts" held in late summer and autumn and organised by the Verderers' Agisters. A number of commoners ride over an area and drive as many ponies as possible into a pound. Here, the pounded ponies are wormed to free them from parasites and those to be sold or wintered on the holdings are loaded into lorries and trailers.

The original pony sale was at Lyndhurst Fair on Swan Green but as road traffic increased it moved to its present site near Beaulieu Road Station. Sales are held in April, August, September, October and November. From September the sales are predominately of foals, mainly colts. First to be sold are those ponies eligible for registration as New Forest ponies, then the registered ones and finally those not eligible. Riding horses and ponies are sold in a separate ring in the afternoon. The Fair atmosphere still prevails and there is always the chance of a bargain: one colt foal sold for 15 gns to a gentleman as a present for his granddaughter turned out a top class jumper and was eventually sold for £1 500! In the first year of the Pony Society's Performance Competition four of the ten prize winners were bought as foals at these sales.

To buy a wild sucker and turn it, four years later, into a satisfactory child's pony can be most rewarding but it can also be frustrating and time-consuming. Taken from its dam and familiar surroundings the foal will at first do all it can to get back to the Forest, so it must be securely shut in where it cannot hurt itself until it gets to know and trust its new owners. Often it will not eat, or only eat soft hay and long grass laboriously cut for it; teaching it will require much patience. As ponies are herd animals who hate being alone two foals usually do better than one.

The Forest as it appears today has been made and kept by the browsing and grazing of the ponies, cattle and deer. The pony's role is vital, as it lives not only on grass but on gorse, which has great food value but requires horny tongues and hairy faces to cope with it, brambles, holly, ivy and heather. He stores fat in the summer to use in the lean early months of the year. He is part of an ancient heritage but has adapted to all the various uses man has found for him and is now being exported to the continent where riding for children is becoming popular. Formerly continental children only started to ride when big enough to manage a horse but now there are over 5 000 New Forest ponies in Holland and many more in France, Germany and Scandinavia. Everywhere they have proved good tempered and teachable and so have made themselves new friends.

When you come to the Forest please do not feed the ponies, this draws them to the roads where they cause accidents to themselves and others.

1 *Beaulieu Road pony sales.* [RF]

1

Fourteen

Explore the Forest with maps

DONN SMALL

Under the early administration, the Forest was divided into ten bailiwicks, and these were under the charge of Lord Wardens up to 1856. They were sub-divided into fifteen keepers' Walks and these original divisions still remain by name only on modern maps. A reproduction of Driver's map of 1789 is included on pages 2 and 3 as it was the first record of their boundaries.

To present the reader with maps of a sufficiently large scale in a guide that can be placed in a field coat pocket, the two and a half inches to one mile 1:25 000 Ordnance Survey series has been chosen, and has been added to by the Forestry Commission in respect of land in its charge.

This Forest is well endowed with both major and minor county roads from which all the forest car parks are easily accessible, as are the camping sites. The Commission has usually named the car parks after a local place name which is generally recorded on the map.

The reader is invited to choose from the small key map the particular Walk he wishes to visit, travel there by the appropriate county road, select a car park and from there, using the two and a half inch maps, follow the tracks of his choice. Long or short walks are possible within a particular Walk and some guidance is given below on the interpretation of the map symbols.

Private land within the Forest is clearly designated and walkers are advised to remain on the public footpaths as shown. All Statutory Inclosures are named, with boundaries shown as a solid grey line, usually indicating a bank and ditch. All tracks are either depicted by a single dotted line, or a double dotted line where vehicles have used them in the past. Within the Inclosures certain forest rides are gravelled for the purpose of timber haulage and emergency access to fires. They have been added to the Ordnance Survey maps to offer the walker a dry surface and a well-identified route to

1

follow. Unofficial access by cars is not permitted. The wide gates to Inclosures are often locked for security reasons but a wicket gate is usually provided alongside for man and horse. On the Open Forest Waste access is either by a path shown as a single dotted line often labelled FP: footpath or a track shown as double dotted lines, sometimes gravelled by the Forestry Commission.

Most forest bogs are impassable and they should be avoided. They are often named Bog, Flash or Bottom. There are sometimes prepared crossings often depicted as "FB", ie footbridge; "passage", ie a culverted gravel ridge; and "ford" usually crossable in summer but not in the winter unless the walker is adequately shod.

Unfenced highways are not often distinguishable from forest tracks, but an additional colour has been used to denote them. The railway can be crossed by bridge at points indicated. There are also cattle creeps under the A31, A35 and A337 and these can be used by walkers to avoid the risk of crossing major traffic routes. They have been specially added to the maps.

A full legend to all Ordnance Survey details on these maps is included on page 116.

2

1 By Car *Blackwater car park.* [DS]
2 By Car *Whitefield Moor car park.* [RF]
3 Walking *Tall Trees walk.* [RF]
4 Walking *Rest and picnic.* [RF]
5 Camping *Hollands Wood camp site.* [DS]
6 Riding *Pony trekking on the heath.* [RF]

3

4

5

6

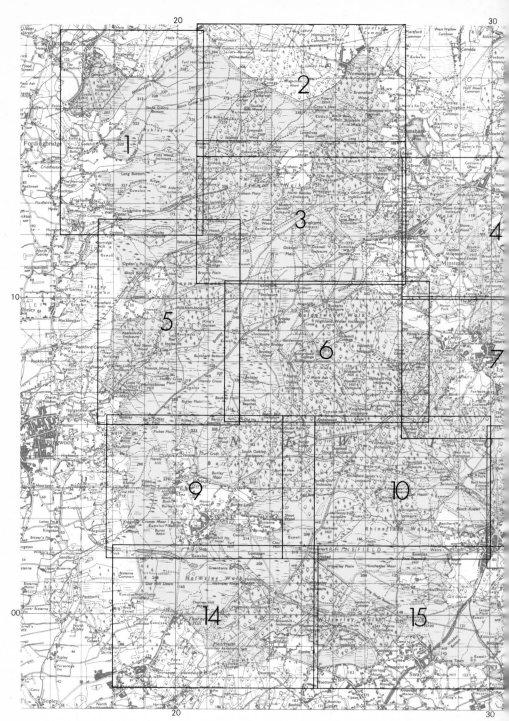

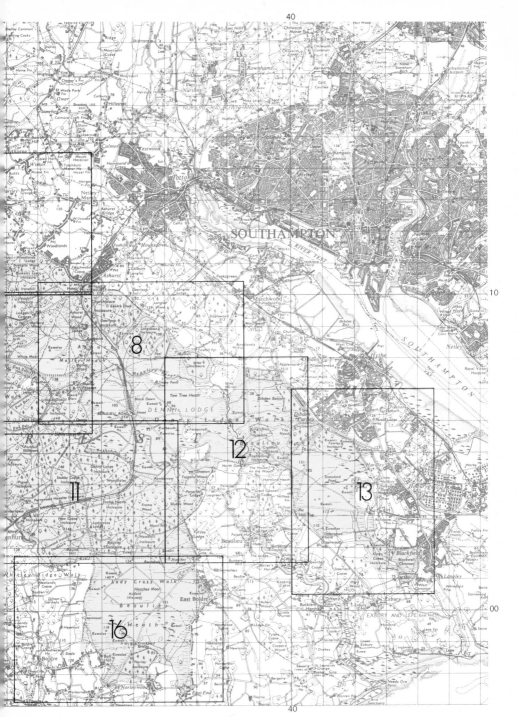

1
ASHLEY WALK

Named after the ash trees located around an old keeper's lodge at Lodge Hill this Walk covers the north west limits of the Forest, overlooking the River Avon. Large tracts of heathland are found in Stone Quarry Bottom, Hampton Ridge and Black Gutter Bottom. Two island Inclosures, Hasley and Pittswood, intrude into this otherwise treeless open space. Pittswood Inclosure was named after John Pitt, a Surveyor General of the Forest in 1773.

A notable feature of the stream banks in these valleys is the soil profile, valued by geologists in determining the past history of these deposits. Castle Hill near Godshill is said to be the only likely relic of a Norman fortification in the Forest.

Car parks will be found at Godshill, Castle Hill, Millersford, Godshill Cricket Pitch, Abbotswell, Ogdens, Dead Man's Hill, some affording fine views and others access on to foot tracks into the interior of the largest area in the Forest freed from cars and camping.

Interesting long walks using the map as a guide are from Cockley car park up to Lodge Hill via Pittswood across Ditchend Brook via Godshill Ridge. And from Abbotswell car park via Hampton Ridge to the Ashley Cross tumulus thence westwards to Alderhill Inclosure and Ogdens Farm. These Walks will depict some of the range of wildlife activity of these open heathlands. The forest gravelled roads in Godshill Inclosure are linked by grass rides, offering the walker a complete change of scenery.

The adjoining commons such as Hyde and Gorley, to the west, are not administered by the Forestry Commission.

1

2

1 *Black Gutter Bottom.* [HA]
2 *View through pine across Millersford Bottom.* [HA]
3 *Hover-fly.* [RF]
4 *Ling on Hampton Ridge heath.* [HA]
5 *Pitts Wood from Hampton Ridge.* [RF]
6 *Common gorse.* [RF]
7 *Fairy Shrimps – a forest rarity.* [HA]

3

4

6

5

7

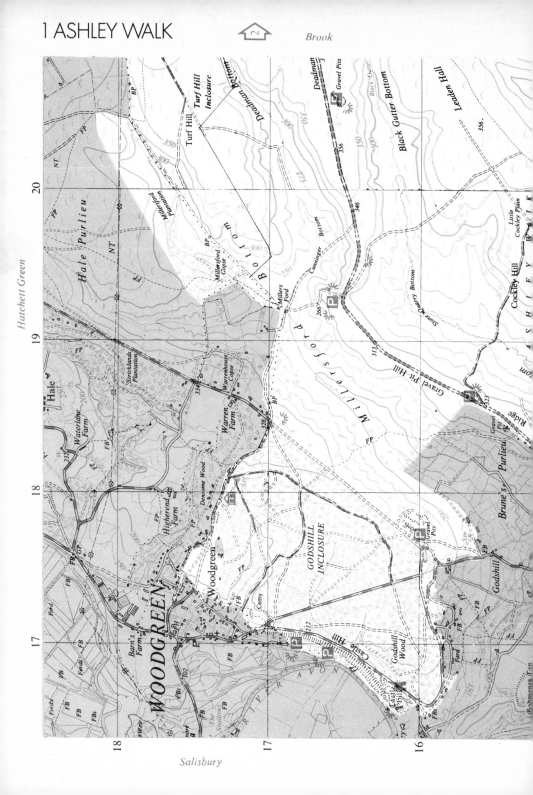

Brook

2

Salisbury

5

Coopers

Ashley Ho

Tumulus
Ashley Cross

Ashley Bottom

Ashleycross
Hill

Ashleycross Hill

Tumulus

Gaze Hill

Alderhill Bottom

Ford

Row Hill

ROMAN POTTERY
KILN
(site of)

Earthw

Alder Hill
300

Alder Hill
Inclosure

Deadbuck
Hill

Watergreen
Bottom

Hallickshole
Hill

252

Lodge
Hill

Pitts Wood
Inclosure

265

Pitchers
Knowle

180

Ford

227

Hive Garn Bottom

350

Little
Witch

Tickets Bury

Great Cockham Plain

212

250

Ridge

Hasley Inclosure

Great
Witch

Must Thorns Bottom

Ford

340

Latchmore Bottom

Ford

166

FB

19

Ditchend Brook

Ford

200

185

Forest Brook
Farm

Long Bottom

Burnt Balls

F O R D I N G B R I D G E

Hampton

Tumulus

Thompson's Castle

Lay Gutter Valley

Latchmore Sheath

Hasley Hole

Godshill

300

320

Rookham
Bottom

288

Hart
Hill

227

Rifle Range
(Disused)

FP

320

300

350

Windmill
Hill

P

Ogdens
135

Ford

18

Blissford
Hill

Blissford

Chilly Hill

Gravel
Pit

Ogden's
Farm

Ogdens

Arniss
Farm

FP

All Fords

172

Frogham Hill

Frogham

BH

255

137

HYDE COMMON

Hungerford

Bottom

134

Street
Farm

Sch

242

215

The
Merrie Thought

Newfoundland

High View

Broadhill
Wood

Grave Pits

Gravel Pits

FB

Sandy Balls

FB

(Camp)

20

17

2
BRAMBLE HILL WALK

Named after the small bramble covered woodland west of Bramshaw this most northerly part of the Forest is one of contrasts between the beautiful old Bramshaw Wood, the wet Howen Bottom and the oak plantations in Islands Thorn Inclosure. The original Groom Keeper's Lodge was at Bramble Hill which is now a private hotel. Here the Groom Keeper fed the wild deer with holly, ash and hay. It was said that, before the woodlands matured, from the hill one could see Southampton and the Isle of Wight on a clear day. At Bramshaw Telegraph during the Napoleonic Wars, semaphore was used in a link of communications from London to Plymouth.

Car parks will be found at Bramshaw Telegraph, Turf Hill, Longcross Pond, Coppice of Linwood, and in the winter Piper's Wait which is the highest point in the Forest being 420 feet above sea level; this is a small caravan site from April until September. An interesting long walk from Bramshaw Telegraph southwards into Islands Thorns Inclosure will lead the walker to an early earth castle at Studley and via the many grass rides to the solitude within the oak and beech plantations. Bramshaw Wood, a very mature ancient and ornamental wood, affords the walker some of the sylvan splendours of beechwoods sloping down to Judds Hill, as does Eyeworth Wood which is dealt with separately in the Eyeworth Walk. Longcross Pond is a fine representative of the Forest manmade dewponds which are seldom dry and provide valuable watering places for forest animals and birds. Access into Coppice of Linwood Inclosure can be gained from the car park south east of Longcross Pond.

1

2

1 *Crow's Nest Bottom.* [HA]
2 *Wood mouse.* [HA]
3 *Sulphur fungus.* [HA]
4 *Nomansland village green.* [RF]
5 *Hard fern.* [HA]

3

4

5

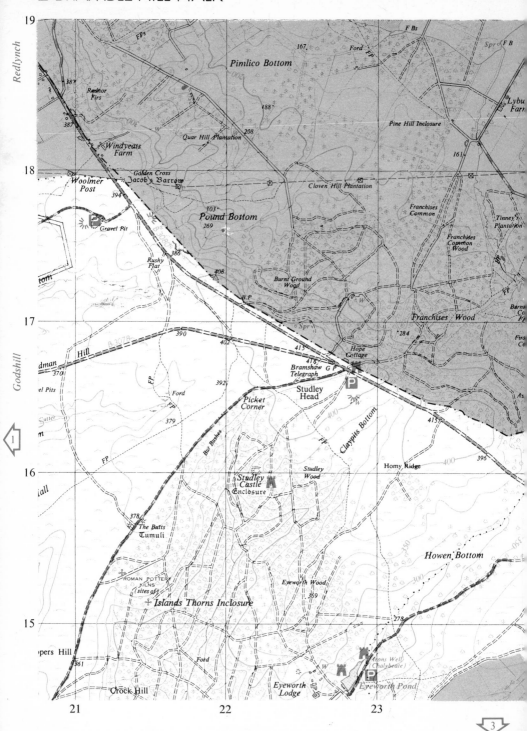

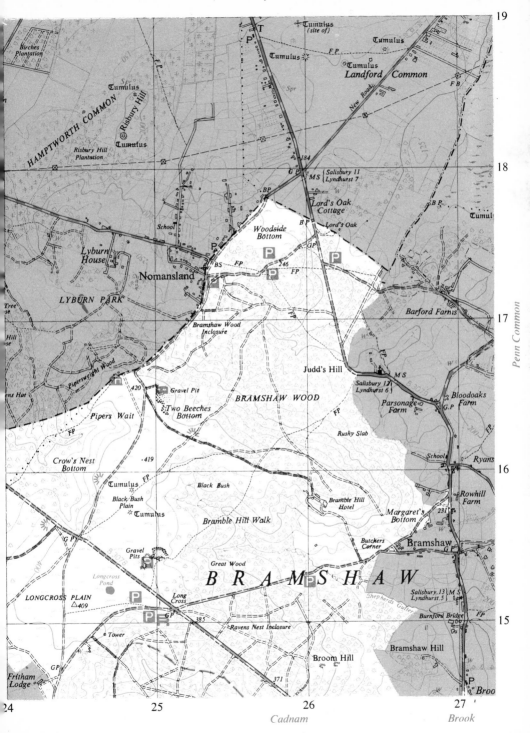

19

Birches
Plantation

Tumulus
(site of)

P T

Tumulus

Tumulus

Landford Common

F B

HAMPTWORTH COMMON

Tumulus

Risbury Hill

Tumulus

New Road

Risbury Hill
Plantation

Spr

184

18

G P

MS

Salisbury 11
Lyndhurst 7

B P

Tumul

School

BP

Lord's Oak
Cottage

Lord's Oak

Lyburn
House

P

Woodside
Bottom

P

GP

P

LYBURN PARK

Nomansland

BS

FP

246

FP

P

Barford Farms

17

Bramshaw Wood
Inclosure

Tree

Hill

Pipersweight Wood

420

Gravel Pit

BRAMSHAW WOOD

Judd's Hill

MS

Salisbury 12
Lyndhurst 6

Bloodoaks
Farm

ens Hat

Pipers Wait

Two Beeches
Bottom

FP

Parsonage
Farm

G.P

FP

Rushy Slab

Crow's Nest
Bottom

.419

FP

School

Ryans

16

Tumulus

FP

Black Bush

Black Bush
Plain

Tumulus

Bramble Hill
Hotel

Bramble Hill Walk

Margaret's
Bottom

231

Rowhill
Farm

G P

Butchers
Corner

Bramshaw

Gravel
Pits

Great Wood

B R A M S H A W

G P

Longcross
Pond

P

LONGCROSS PLAIN
△409

Long
Cross

Shepherds Gulley

Salisbury 13
Lyndhurst 5

MS

P

GP

385

Burnford Bridge

FP

15

Tower

Ravens Nest Inclosure

Bramshaw Hill

Fritham
Lodge

GP

371

Broom Hill

P

Broo

24

25

26

27

3
EYEWORTH WALK

One of the pleasant features of this Walk is the Pond which was created for the storage of water to assist in the manufacture of gunpowder near to the former Groom's Lodge which is now a private residence. This Walk covers a great variety of forest assets from Ancient and Ornamental Woodlands such as Eyeworth, Anses and White Shoot Bottom Woods, to the beautiful Inclosures of Amberwood, Slodens, Ocknell, the Bentleys, Broomy, Hollyhatch, Longbeech, Kings Garn Gutter and the great open level ground of Stoney Cross Plain resulting from the 1939–45 wartime airfield. The origin of the word "Garn" or Garden is understood to be where the Royal beehives were placed in the early days. Streams in the north of the forest are termed "gutters" or "brooks", and in the south they are called "waters".

Notable historical features are the Butt – a fine bronze age burial tumulus; Ocknell Clump – where in 1775 Scots Pine was reintroduced

to the Forest and especially used for demarcating Inclosure boundaries. Today can be seen how profusion of natural seedlings from these trees changes the open nature of the forest scenery and examples of complete clearance will be seen where the Forestry Commission is attempting to re-establish the open forest character. Certain clumps of pine are retained as natural landscape features.

Car parks will be found at Eyeworth Pond, Fritham Oak, Janesmoor Pond, Longbeech, Stoney Cross, South Bentley, Anses Wood, Cadmans, Ocknell and Foxhill Ponds, each giving access to Inclosures, or heathland or restful waterside picnic places, or open spaces over which to play cricket, fly kites, etc. Toilets are provided at Stoney Cross car park.

Camping is available at Longbeech and Ocknell from April to September with special overflow provisions during Bank Holiday weekends at Ocknell Pond and North Bentley.

1

2

1 *Eyeworth Pond.* [HA]
2 *Oak for the future – South Bentley Inclosure.* [RF]
3 *Eyeworth Wood.* [HA]
4 *Common frog.* [HA]
5 *Longbeech camp site.* [RF]
6 *Bogbean.* [HA]
7 *Eyeworth Pond car park.* [RF]
8 *King's Garn Gutter Inclosure from the air, 1971.*
 [FC]

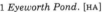

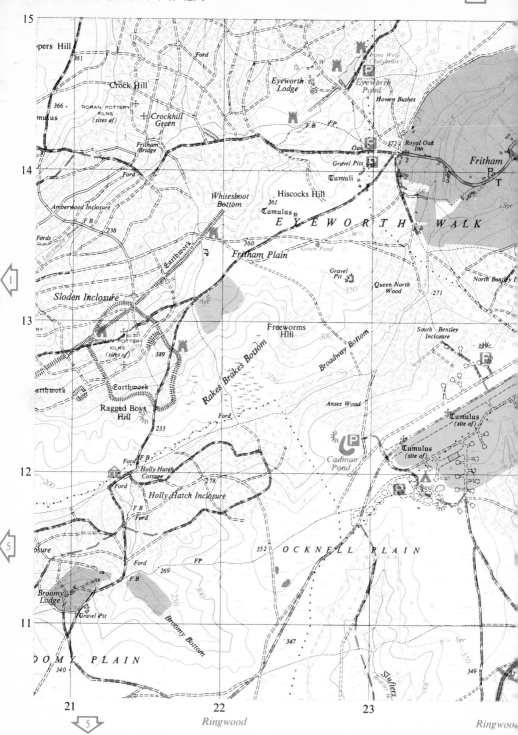

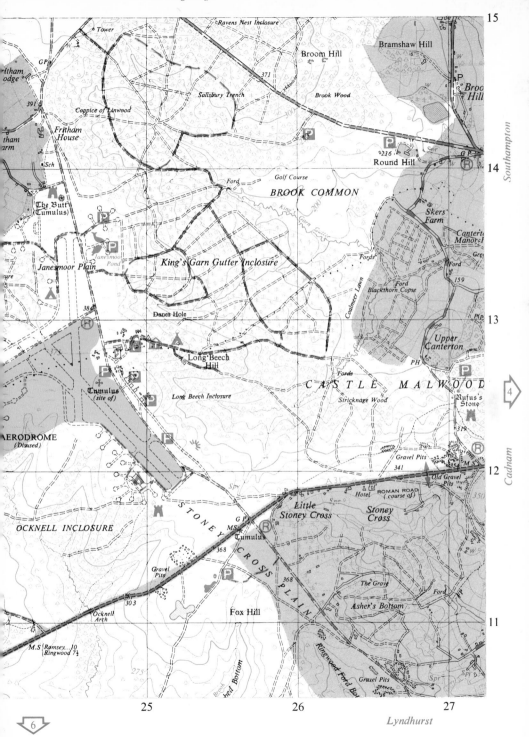

15

Tower

Ravens Nest Inclosure

Broom Hill

Bramshaw Hill

GP

Fritham
Lodge

371

Salisbury Trench

Brook Wood

Broo
Hill

P

391

Coppice of Linwood

300

P

Fritham
House

236

GP

R

tham
arm

Sch

Round Hill

14

Ford

Golf Course

BROOK COMMON

Southampton

The Butt
(Tumulus)

P

Skers
Farm

P

Janesmoor
Pond

Janesmoor Plain

King's Garn Gutter Inclosure

Fords

Cantert
Manor

159

Ford

Ford
Blackthorn Copse

384

Coulmeer Lawn

13

Danes Hole

Upper
Canterton

R

PH

Long Beech
Hill

Fords

P

P

CASTLE MALWOOD

4

Cadnam

Tumulus
(site of)

P

Long Beech Inclosure

Stricknage Wood

Rufus's
Stone

319

P

R

M.S

Gravel Pits

AERODROME
(Disused)

341

12

Old Gravel
Pits

A31

Hotel

ROMAN ROAD
(course of)

350

OCKNELL INCLOSURE

GP
M.S
Tumulus

Little
Stoney Cross

Stoney
Cross

R

STONEY CROSS PLAIN

368

Gravel
Pits

368

The Grove

Ford

303

Fox Hill

Asher's Bottom

11

Ocknell
Arch

Gravel Pits

Spr

4

CASTLE MALWOOD WALK

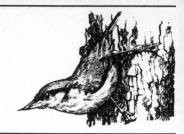

Overlapping with Eyeworth and Bramblehill Walk, this Walk was created for the large Master Keeper's lodge at Castle Malwood, where it is alleged William Rufus spent the night before his death. Castle Malwood and Bramblehill Walks combine to form the northern Bailiwick. Today the Lodge, rebuilt, is divided into private residential flats close to the great iron-age fort at Running Hill.

Through this Walk runs the London–Plymouth trunk road, soon to have the M27 motorway added to its traffic volume. Thus the Walk is divided by this trunk road and to its north is the most visited place in the Forest – Rufus Stone. Access to remnants of woodland is from the Brook road into a beautiful ancient and ornamental wood, Bignell. From the Cadnam inter-change the main artery to the capital of the Forest, Lyndhurst, is the A337 which passes through some lovely heathland and woodland. Car parks at Shave Green offer access to the Shave Green Inclosures and the minor road to Minstead offers occasional stopping places to Hazel and Brockishill Woods.

Provision is being made for car park access to Busketts Lawn and Ironshill Inclosures and the beautiful enclosed forest lawns of Busketts Wood. Limited access is possible from the Ashurst Forest Office on the A35 and from woodlands to the north of Ashurst.

Visitors may be interested in the details of the original Rufus Stone compared to the iron casing of today. The Rufus Stone was a three-sided stone pillar erected in 1745 by John, Lord Delaware, when he was Master Keeper at Bolderwood Lodge, to perpetuate the memory of the death of William Rufus (King William II) which by legend occurred at Canterton Glen, although recent doubts about this location are discussed in Chapter 6. The inscription placed on the Stone, which is given below, embroiders the plain facts which have come down to us.

The Anglo Saxon Chronicle does not mention an oak nor Tirel nor that the King was struck on the breast. The spelling of Tirel is also different from that accepted today, but standard spellings are a comparatively recent development.

The inscription read:

"Here stood the Oak Tree on which an arrow shot by Sir Walter Tyrrell at a stag glanced and struck King William II surnamed Rufus on the breast of which stroke he instantly died on the second day of August anno 1100.
King William II being thus slain was laid on a cart belonging to one Purkess and drawn from hence to Winchester, and buried in the Cathedral Church of that City. That the spot where an event so memorable happened might not hereafter be unknown this Stone was set up by John, Lord Delaware, who has seen the tree growing in this space."

Later the following inscriptions were added to the Stone but were lost when the present iron casing was added:

"This spot was visited by King George III and Queen Charlotte on the twenty-seventh of June, MDCCLXXXIX."
"This Stone was repaired by John Richard Earl Delaware anno 1789."

The Stone was attacked by relic-hunting vandals, and it was found necessary to place the present iron casing over it bearing the original inscriptions slightly amended as well as the following one:

"This Stone having been much mutilated and the inscriptions on each of the three sides been defaced, this more durable memorial with the original inscription was erected, in the year 1841 by William Sturges Bourne, Warden."

1 *Stricknage Wood.* [RF]
2 *New Forest cicada.* [RF]
3 *Ocknell Clump – first planting of Scots pine in the New Forest in 1775.* [RF]
4 *Rufus Stone.* [DS]
5 *Purple loosestrife.* [HA]

1

4

5

2

3

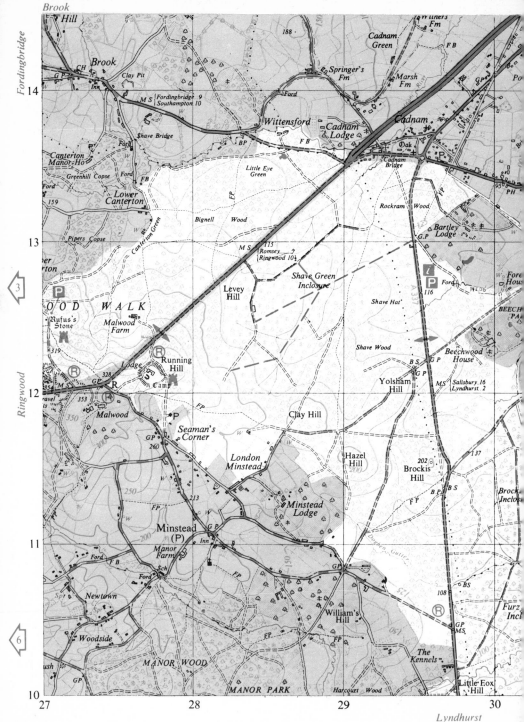

Fordingbridge

Ringwood

Lyndhurst

5
BROOMY
WALK

Forming part of the west boundary, believed to have been named after the birch and broom thickets in the oak heath, this Walk has some very diverse woodlands both unenclosed and enclosed.

The main stream courses of Dockens Water and Linford Brook flow from the northeast to the southwest bound for the River Avon through Forest lawns. They provide good wet pastures on the open forest and shaded woody corridors especially in Milkham and Roe Inclosures where stream life abounds.

One of the notable historic features of this Walk is the infamous smugglers' road along which illicit goods were conveyed from Christchurch and Mudeford to Winchester. A good description of these activities will be found in Chapter 7. A traditional historic royal bee-hive garden will be seen at King's Garden now a reseeded lawn on the east side of Roewood Inclosure and still valued by today's beekeepers. Extensive earthworks can be traced amidst the trees in the centre of Roe Inclosure.

Car parks will be found at Linford Bottom with access to picnic places on the stream banks and paddling in gravel-bottomed streams Appleslade Inclosure offers extensive varied walks and scenery; Milkham Inclosure has a great diversity of natural wildlife within the Inclosure, which can be witnessed when following the forest rides. Using the map many long and varied walks can be undertaken particularly to Pinnick and Red Shoot Woods where a variety of plant life can be seen during the seasons.

1 *Broad-bordered Bee Hawk moth.* [RF]
2 *Foxgloves.* [RF]
3 *Amberwood Inclosure in autumn.* [RF]
4 *Linford Bottom.* [RF]
5 *Dockens Water.* [HA]
6 *Slufters Pond.* [RF]
7 *Broomy Inclosure oak – planted 1829.* [HA]

1

2

3
4
6
5
7

5 BROOMY WALK

Fritham

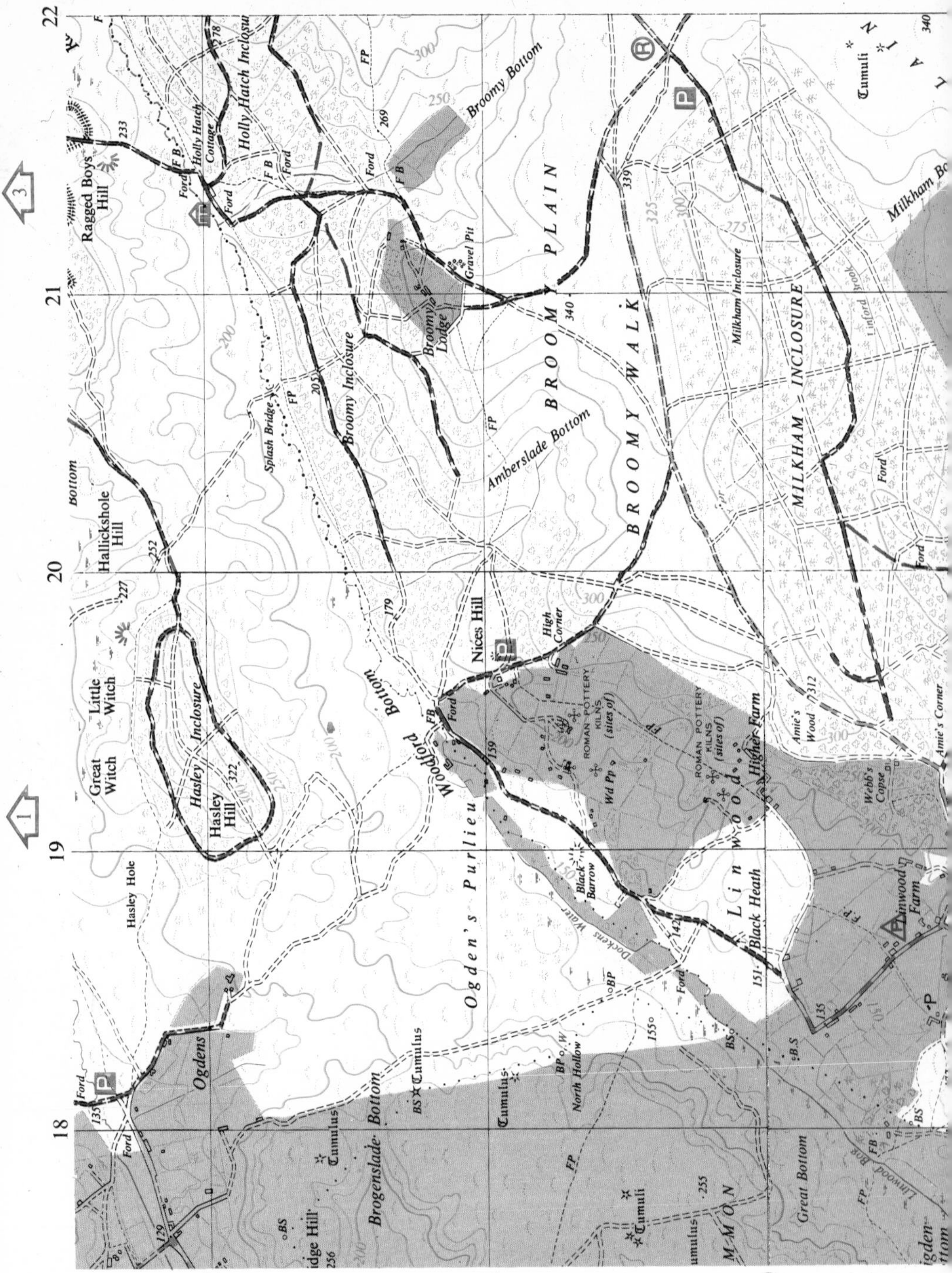

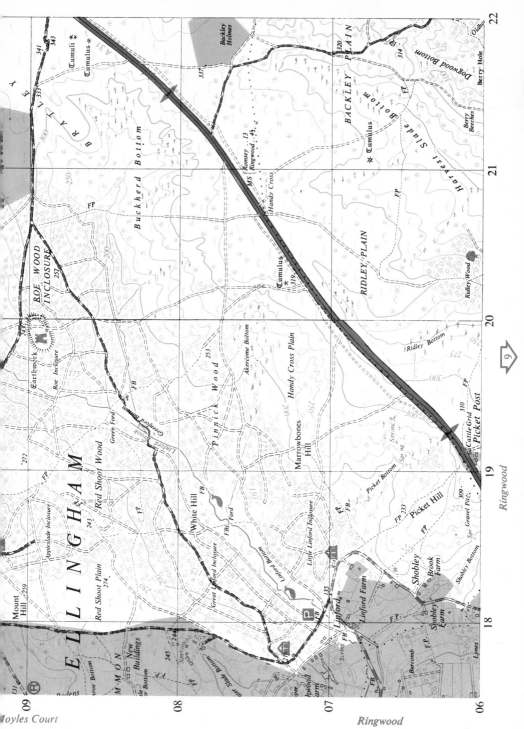

6

BOLDERWOOD WALK

This Walk situated in the central highland south of the A31 takes its name from the Master Keeper's Lodge pulled down in 1833 near to the present Keeper's Cottage. "Bolder" is an old English word for house. One of the main features of this Walk is the stand of giant Douglas Fir planted in the old Lodge grounds in 1859, and the adjoining arboretum and deer sanctuary. Other equally attractive features are the extensive woodlands, through which the energetic walker may step back into the past and see the oldest pollarded tree in the Forest, the Knightwood Oak.

Ancient scenic woodlands will be found at Bratley, Backley and Mark Ash Wood with the intervening valleys of Bushy Bratley, Blackensford Bottom and Highland Water, all of which are accessible by forest tracks.

Near Millersford Bridge will be seen the recently restored Portuguese Fireplace, a relic of 1914–1918 war buildings occupied by Portuguese troops. The Eagle Oak, a very mature oak, is where the last white-tailed eagle was shot in 1810. Backley Holms is a wartime reseeded lawn where wildlife and ponies often share early morning grazing. Access from the A31 has now been restricted for safety reasons.

Car parks are situated at Mogshade, where a simple oak cross erected on 14 April 1946 commemorates the presence of 3rd Canadian Division of RCASC in the Forest. From here access to an extensive forest road system within Highland Water Inclosure can be made. Bolderwood Green is well situated for the Forestry Commission's waymarked walks, including the Earl of Radnor's Memorial Stone, Moorsbarrow, Knightwood Oak and No Man's Walk, all associated with scenic woodlands and the historic old pollarded trees.

Near the small car park at Holidays Hill Cottage is a collection of forest reptiles which can be seen and studied in safety. On the Bolderwood–Emery Down road will be found the Highland Water viewpoint car park and a delightful series of small woodland car parks in settings offering a variety of scenery and walks into unenclosed woodlands. Small car parks at Acres Down give access to the north part of Highland Water Inclosure and the energetic will be rewarded by reaching Puckpits Inclosure, the home of some very tall mature conifer trees.

Camping is confined to a small informal site at Holidays Hill.

1 *Mark Ash forest walk.* [RF]
2 *Detail from Radnor Stone.* [FC]
3 *Fallow deer.* [HA]
4 *Bolderwood Douglas firs and natural regeneration.* [HA]
5 *Roman bridge, Holidays Hill.* [RF]
6 *Rose Chafer.* [RF]
7 *Mark Ash wood.* [RF]

1

2

3

5
6

4

7

6 BOLDERWOOD WALK

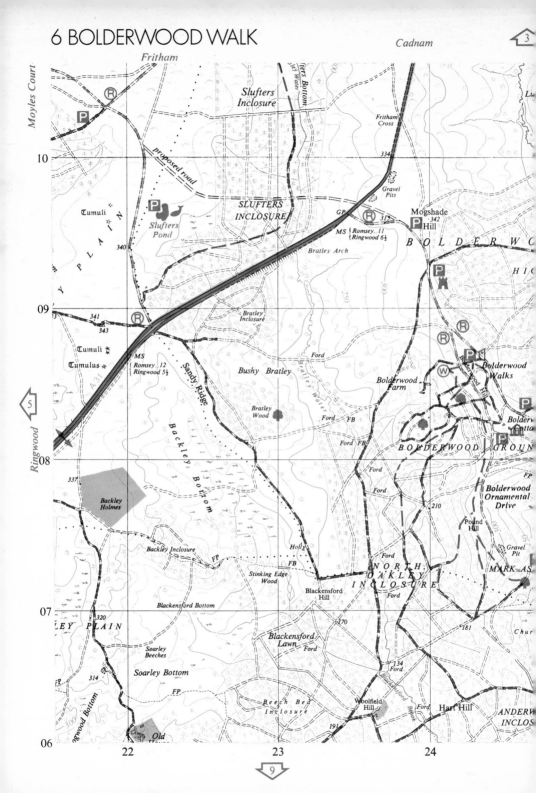

Cadnam

Fritham

Moyles Court

Slufters
Inclosure

Fritham
Cross

proposed road

10

334

Gravel
Pits

Tumuli

SLUFTERS
INCLOSURE

Mogshade
Hill · 342

GP

MS Romsey..11
Ringwood 6¼

BOLDERWO

PLAIN

340

Slufters
Pond

Bratley Arch

HIG

09

341

Bratley
Inclosure

343

Bolderwood
Walks

Tumuli

MS

Ford

Sandy Ridge

Bushy Bratley

Bolderwood
Farm

W

Tumulus

Romsey..12
Ringwood 5¼

Bolderw

Bratley
Wood

Ford

FB

Bolder

Ringwood

Backley Bottom

Ford FB

BOLDERWOOD GROUN

08

337

Ford

Bolderwood
Ornamental
Drive

Backley
Holmes

Ford

210

FP

Pound
Hill

Backley Inclosure

FP

Holly

Ford

Gravel
Pit

FB

NORTH

MARK·AS

Stinking Edge
Wood

OAKLEY

INCLOSURE

Blackensford
Hill

Ford

07

320

LEY PLAIN

Blackensford Bottom

270

Blackensford
Lawn

181

Chur

Ford

Soarley
Beeches

Soarley Bottom

314

134
Ford

FP

Beech Bed
Inclosure

Woolfield
Hill

Ford

Hart Hill

ANDERW

wood Bottom

Old

191

INCLOS

06

22

23

24

5

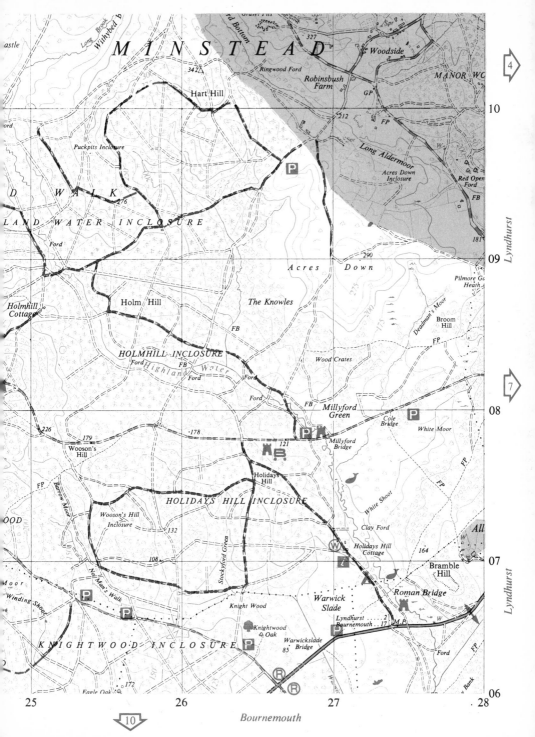

7

IRONSHILL WALK

The centrepiece of this Walk is the ancient Royal Manor of Lyndhurst, the capital of the Forest (the name being derived from the old English "Limetree Hill"). The Queen's House is the manor house, the present building dating from 1509 and the Verderers' Hall, dating in part from 1388, adjoins it. Further information is available at the Information Centre and the Hall. Surrounding Lyndhurst are delightful open spaces such as Whitemoor; Bolton's Bench, named after Lord Bolton, a Lord Warden of the Forest in 1688; and Matley Heath, interspersed with woodland of all ages, including Rushpole, Bramble Hill, Janeshill and Matley Woods.

The most notable of the Inclosures are Pondhead and Park Ground which were early fields sown with oak in 1810, Ironshill where it is believed ironstone was worked, and Denny Inclosure which contains some early relics of mature beechwoods.

Interesting early earthworks can be seen at the Park Pale, or The Ridge, which encircled in 1291 an early, two hundred acre royal deer park south-east of Lyndhurst, later to be replaced in 1670 by Charles II by creation of "New Park" near Brockenhurst.

This walk is well served by county roads radiating from Lyndhurst, off which are forest car parks offering walks of all lengths and varied scenery, from heathland at Bolton's Bench and Matley Bridge to old woodland at Janeshill, Whitemoor and Denny Wood. There are some buildings around Lyndhurst worthy of mention: delightful thatched cottages at Swan Green, small forest dwellings at Gritnam Village and mellow Stuart symmetry of Queen's House, viewed from Shrubbs Hill Road. The Queen's House is now the headquarters of the Forestry Commission in the South East region, which includes the New Forest.

Camping is confined to Matley and Denny Woods, good centres for exploring on foot the great mass of Inclosure woodland to the west and south. The Girl Guide Centre is at Foxlease south of Lyndhurst off the A337.

1

2

1 *Giant lacewing.* [RF]
2 *Lyndhurst – Bolton's Bench from the air, 1971.* [FC]
3 *Park Hill, Lyndhurst.* [HA]
4 *Walkers track, Rushpole Wood.* [RF]
5 *Pondhead Inclosure oak – planted 1810.* [RF]

4

3

5

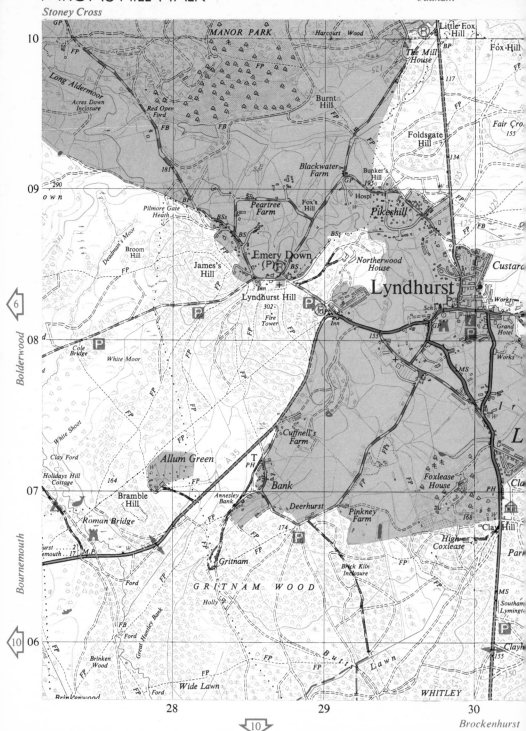

Long Aldermoor

MANOR PARK

Harcourt Wood

Little Fox Hill

Fox·Hill

The Mill House

Acres Down Inclosure

Red Open Ford

Burnt Hill

Foldsgate Hill

Fair Cro

Blackwater Farm

Bunker's Hill

Pilmore Gate Heath

Peartree Farm

Fox's Hill

Pikeshill

Hospl

Deadman's Moor

Broom Hill

James's Hill

Emery Down (P)

Northerwood House

Lyndhurst

Custard

Inn

Lyndhurst Hill

Fire Tower

Cole Bridge

White Moor

Grand Hotel

Works

Bolderwood

White Shoot

Clay Ford

Holidays Hill Cottage

Cuffnell's Farm

Allum Green

Bank

Foxlease House

Bramble Hill

Roman Bridge

Annesley Bank

Deerhurst

Pinkney Farm

Clay Hill

High Coxlease

Bournemouth

Gritnam

Brick Kiln Inclosure

GRITNAM WOOD

Holly

Southam Lymingt

Brinken Wood

Great Huntley Bank

Ford

Butts Lawn

Clayh

Wide Lawn

WHITLEY

10

Irons Hill
Irons Hill
Ironshill Lodge

Rushpole Wood

Redbridge Hill

Ironshill Inclosure

Lodgehill Inclosure

Ashurst Wood

53

Whitebridge Hill

94

M.S. Southampton 8 Lymington...10

Lodgehill Cottage

09

Ford

Mallard Wood

Mallard Mead

As. Lo

84

Foxhill Moor

B.S

FP

Dunces Arch

CH

BSs

Works

Longwater Lawn

Earthwork

A

Fox Hill

Row Hill

White Moor

Cemy

Pol Sta

M.S. Southampton 9 Lymington...9

Tumulus

92

FP

P

Bolton's Bench

Tumulus (site of)

161

White   Moor

08

8

The Bench

MATLEY

Matley Wood

ns Hill Walk

The Ridge

B 3056

98

134

143

Gravel Pit

70

A

P

LYNDHURST

Matley Ridge

Matley Bog

Pondhead Inclosure

Parkhill Hotel

FP

Pondhead

Matley Passage

FP

07

Church Place

114

Beaulieu

Parkhill Lawn

Little Holmhill Inclosure

Thorn Hill

Denny Wait

Tumuli

Ground Inclosure

Denny Inclosure

n 11

148

Park Hill

96

06

Heath

150

Denny Wood

132

31

32

33

8
ASHURST WALK

This Walk was part of the East Bailiwick, with the Groom Keeper's residence at Ashurst Lodge which is now a private residence. Even today will be found natural regeneration of ash in this walk continuing its long association with its name.

Early resistance to aligning the railway line in 1847 directed it southwards bypassing Lyndhurst and dividing the Walk into east and west halves. Crossing on foot can be made at seven bridges which provide strategic links for walks over the scenic heath, bogland and the Inclosures of Church Place and Deer Leap, the latter deriving its name from a legendary jump by a deer of over eighteen yards which was originally marked by two posts.

At Beaulieu Road Station there is the sale yard where on six occasions during the year New Forest ponies are auctioned to the highest bidder. Ample car park space is available to assist the visitor witness this traditional mart in the Forest.

Provision is being made for a car park in the vicinity of Deer Leap providing access onto open heath walks and into Church Place and Longdown Inclosures. It is also hoped that a small car park adjacent to Yew Tree Heath will afford the walker some walks across this beautiful heathland, specially towards Round-eye Hill. One of the accesses on foot to the Bishop's Dyke may be found from Shatterford car park. A car park is located at Ipley Bridge and is part of the northern Beaulieu River walking complex. Camping is confined to the Ashurst site with access off the A35 just south of Ashurst Village.

1

2

3

1 *Sundew.* [HA]
2 *Petty Whin.* [RF]
3 *Ashurst camp site from the air, 1971.* [FC]
4 *High Brown fritillary.* [RF]
5 *Denny Wood camp site.* [FC]
6 *Mallard Wood.* [RF]

4

5

6

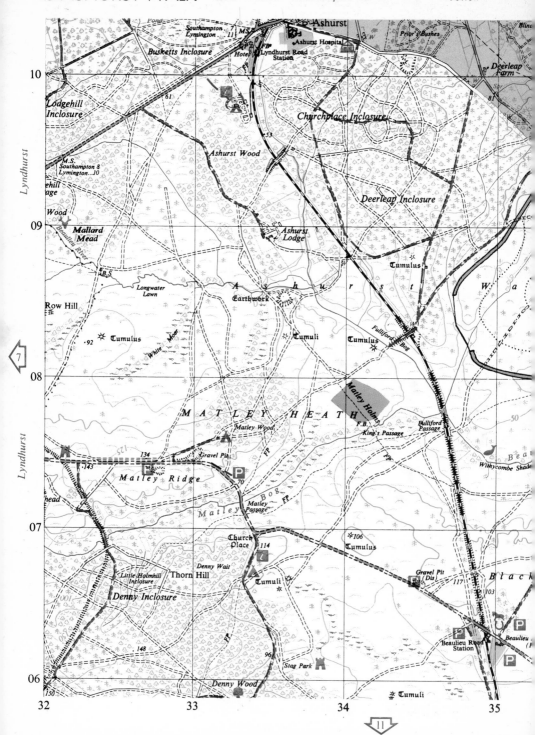

Ashurst

Prior's Bushes

Ashurst Hospital

Southampton-
Lymington

Busketts Inclosure

Deerleap Farm

Hotel

Lyndhurst Road
Station

Churchplace Inclosure

10

Lodgehill
Inclosure

Ashurst Wood

M.S.
Southampton 8
Lymington...10

Deerleap Inclosure

ehill
age

Wood

09

Mallard
Mead

Ashurst
Lodge

Cumulus

Longwater
Lawn

A s h u r s t   W   a

Earthwork

Row Hill

Cumulus

Tumuli

Cumulus

Fulliford Bog

08

White Moor

MATLEY HEATH

Matley Holm

F.B.

Fulliford
Passage

King's Passage

Matley Wood

Bea

Withycombe Shade

Gravel Pit

MATLEY RIDGE

Matley
Passage

Matley Bog

07

Church
Place

Cumulus

Little Holmhill
Inclosure

Thorn Hill

Denny Wait

Cumuli

Black

Gravel Pit
(Dis)

Denny Inclosure

Stag Park

Beaulieu Road
Station

Beaulieu

06

Denny Wood

Cumuli

32   33   34   35

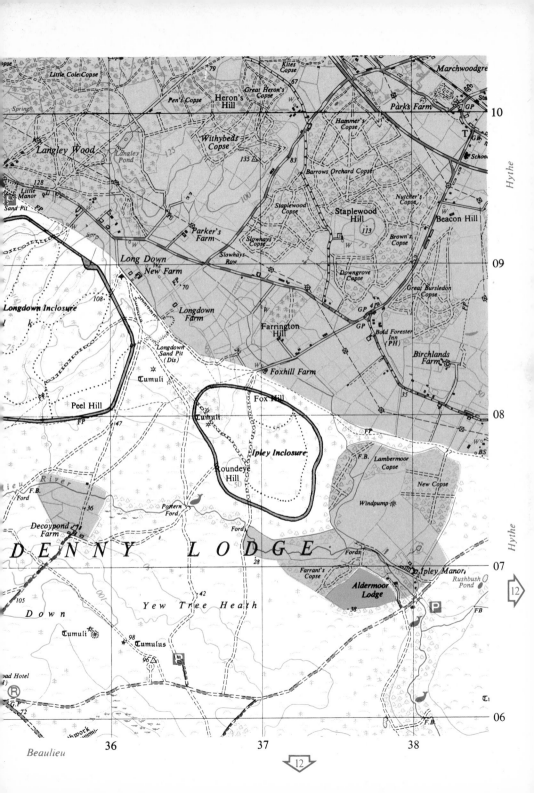

9

BURLEY WALK

Mostly occupied by the Manor of Burley, once the Bailiwick of Burley, under the Dukes of Bolton who between 1680 to 1786 ruled this bailiwick as if it were not Crown property, it is now a large settlement of residences and small holdings, surrounded nevertheless by some of the most contrasting scenery to be found in the Forest.

The western rolling heath and bogland are reminiscent of northern latitudes and in the heath north east of Burley will be found sylvan relics of early fifteenth and sixteenth century encoppicement banks inside which ancient pollarded beech abound. These are ancient relics of the method of feeding deer and supplying fuel wood where the tree in its prime had its head cut off, ie pollard – "to behead" – and the resulting growth of branches was used as coppice supplying fodder and fuelwood. This practice was made illegal in 1698 by William III and today the very heavy branched trees, whose longevity of life is said to be extended by this treatment, are now reaching senility, and, helped by severe winds in the winter, are beginning to disintegrate. In Berry and Ridley Woods are excellent examples for the walker to ponder their true age.

There is an interesting extract from "Book of Survey of Royal Forests" by Roger Taverner, Queen's Surveyor, in 1563 where a reference is made to Ridley Wood where twenty acres of old oak had been topped. This gives an interesting insight as to the possible ages of some of our pollards.

Car parks will be found at Vereley from where an interesting and refreshing walk southwards along Smugglers' Road will remind the walker of another age or northwards along high forest tracks to Ridley Wood across Ridley Green and thence to Berry Wood, where remnants of the pollarding system can be seen, with a return via Turf Croft to Vereley.

Car parks at Undersley Wood and Lucy Hill will lead the walker to interesting Inclosure walks showing a diversity of tree species and the ranges of ages with some fascinating insights to natural wildlife.

For the less energetic, car parks at Burley Lawn, Clay Hill and Burley Cricket Pitch may provide, on certain occasions, a more restful form of entertainment. Concentrations of grazing ponies will often be seen at Spy Holms Lawn, south of which lies an old highway which conveyed the early vehicles from Lymington across the present A35 at Wilverley Post.

1

2

3

1 *Cranes Moor from Castle Hill.* [RF]
2 *Sand lizard.* [RF]
3 *Burley village cricket from the air, 1971.* [FC]
4 *Pollarded beech.* [HA]
5 *White fork moss cushions.* [HA]
6 *Stinkhorn fungus.* [HA]

4

5

6

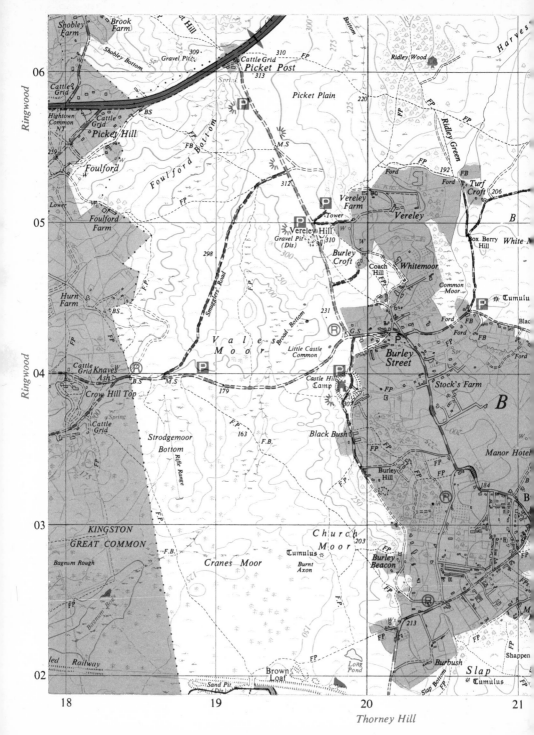

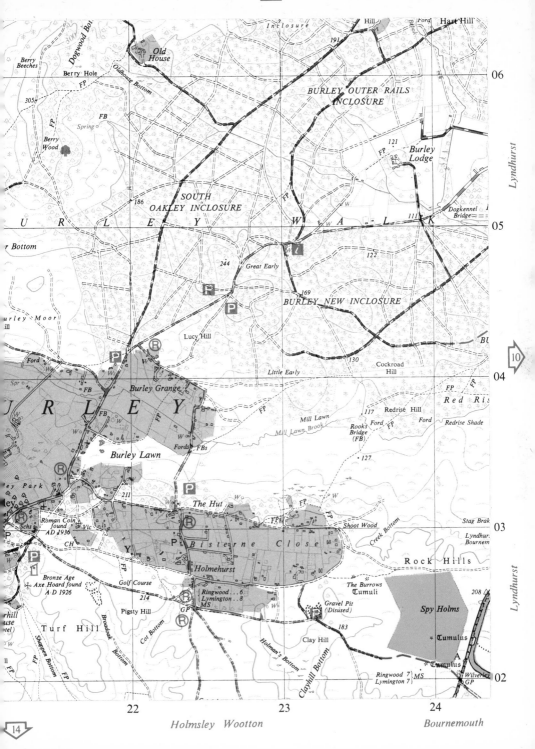

10

RHINEFIELD WALK

The name of this Walk is said to originate from the word "rhine" or "rhyne" meaning the removal of oak bark or else improvement by drains of fields surrounding the present Lodge. This Walk is undoubtedly one of the most popular, lying north west of Brockenhurst. It offers not only open heathland and bogs, but a large tract of enclosed woodland where long and short walks are possible on the network of forest roads and rides.

The Lymington River is swollen by tributaries such as the Ober Water, Black Water and Highland Water, all joining the main river above Balmer Lawn Bridge.

The Groom Keeper's Lodge was said to be originally close to the present Rhinefield House which is now a private residence, built by Lt Munro-Walker after 1877. The name New Park is a distinction from the Old Park at Lyndhurst. The first statutory Inclosure created to grow timber was at Vinney Ridge in 1700 and a small reconstruction of the original bank and pale fence will be seen on the Tall Trees Walk. The favourite walk of Queen Eleanor, wife of Edward I, was said to be to Queen's Bower, which is an area alongside the stream clothed in elderly beech. Markway is alleged to be the site where Hessian troops encamped during the Jacobite Rebellion. It was at Black Knowl that Theodore Roosevelt completed his famous walk in

the New Forest from Stoney Cross on 9 June 1910.

The first flying bomb in the 1939–45 war to reach the Forest fell to the west of Puttles Bridge and many incendiary bombs rained down on the forest north of Rhinefield Lodge, causing extensive forest fires.

This Walk is well provided with car parks of all sizes offering special way-marked walks from Blackwater and Brock Hill car parks, where the Tall Trees Walk offers a view of a double avenue of giant conifers. At Puttles Bridge, Aldridge Hill, and Blackwater there is stream-side paddling, picnicking and walking. Whitefield and Whitemoor car parks offer extensive grass lawns on which children can play in safety. Seclusion is also offered at Clumbers with occasional walks into the wilderness to the west.

Extensive exploratory walks into Anderwood and Knightwood Inclosures are available from the Anderwood and Vinney Ridge car parks. From Bolderford Bridge car park charming riverside walks are possible northwards into Highland Water Inclosure.

On the east boundary of this Walk is New Park where equestrian and other recreational activities are organised by arrangement with the Forestry Commission within a 240 acre field system. Camping is available at Aldridge Hill.

1

2

4

1 *Ober Water, Markway.* [RF]
2 *Tall Trees Walk car park and picnic place.* [RF]
3 *Rhinefield Ornamental Drive.* [DS]
4 *Knightwood oak.* [HA]
5 *Tall Trees forest walk.* [RF]
6 *Recreation at Puttles Bridge.* [RF]

3

5

6

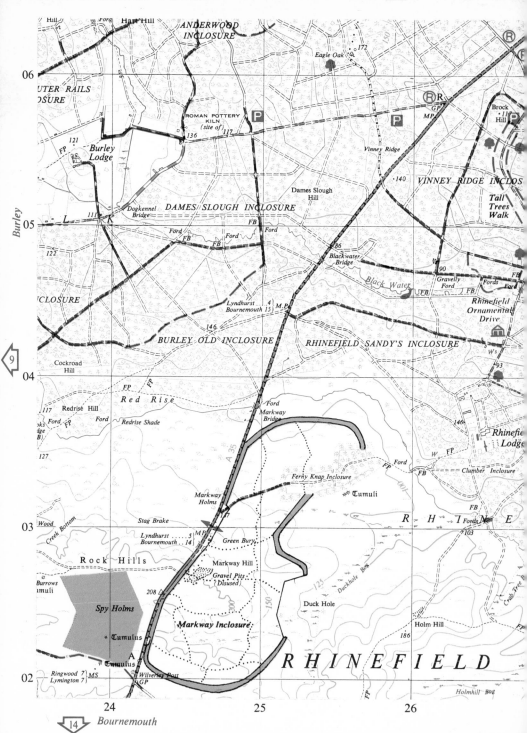

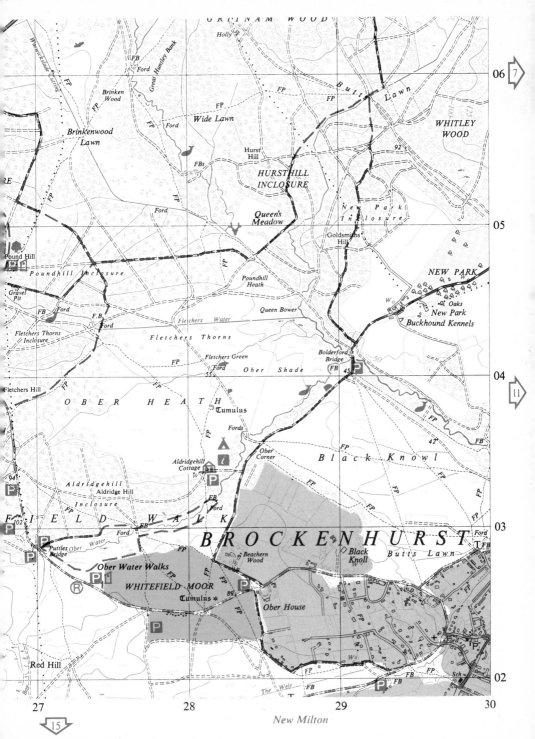

GRINAM WOOD

Holly

FB
Ford

Great Huntley Bank

Brinken
Wood

Brinkenwood
Lawn

Wide Lawn

Ford

FP

FP

FP

Butts Lawn

WHITLEY
WOOD

06

92

RE

FP

Hurst
Hill

FBs

HURSTHILL
INCLOSURE

New Park
Inclosure

FP

Ford

Pound Hill

Poundhill Inclosure

Queen's
Meadow

Goldsmiths
Hill

NEW PARK

05

Poundhill
Heath

FP

Gravel
Pit

FB Ford

F.B.
Ford

Fletchers Thorns
Inclosure

Fletchers Water

Fletchers Thorns

Queen Bower

Fletchers Green
Ford

Ober Shade

Bolderford
Bridge

FB 45

New Park
Buckhound Kennels

Oaks

W

50

04

Fletchers Hill

FP

OBER HEATH

Tumulus

Fords

Ober
Corner

Black Knowl

FP

FP

47

FB

FP

Aldridgehill
Cottage

94

Aldridgehill

Aldridge Hill

Inclosure

FB
Ford

FP

Ober
House

Black
Knoll

FIELD WALK

02

FB

BROCKENHURST

Ford

T FB

Ford

Puttles
Bridge

Ober Water

Beachern
Wood

Black
Knoll

Butts Lawn

Ober Water Walks

WHITEFIELD MOOR

Tumulus

89

Ober House

Red Hill

03

FP

The Weir

FB

Sch

02

11
WHITLEY RIDGE WALK

This Walk originally went southwards to include the now privately-owned Brockenhurst Park and for convenience in the presentation in this Guide it now takes in part of the westerly Denny Lodge Walk. It embraces one of the largest continuous tracts of woodland in the Forest, severed only by the main railway line. Balmer Lawn is a large forest lawn kept well grazed by ponies and cattle, a one-time race course for New Forest ponies, and is now surrounded by self regenerating woodlands such as Hollands and Whitley Woods and in the north east by a unique area of bog surrounded by a medieval earthwork said to have been the boundary of church land resulting from a famous crawl by the Bishop of Winchester. On the east lies Frame Wood, which is a fine example of woodland regenerating naturally since 1860 in spite of intense grazing both by ponies and deer.

An historic link with the past will be found on the track leading through Hollands Wood camp site northwards to Ashurst – an ancient saltway where the salt obtained from the salterns on the coast was transported from Lymington to Ashurst.

During the assembly of troops for the invasion of France in the 1939–45 war, Balmer Lawn Hotel was the operational headquarters, used by General Eisenhower and General Montgomery.

The Inclosures are numerous and are well linked by gravel forest roads essential for strategic management and emergencies but made available for pedestrian use. Extensive walks are possible linked from the few car parks north and south of the railway line. South of this railway line will be found the main home of the Japanese Sika deer and on the north side will be found Roe and Fallow, which will often be seen on the grass rides in the early or late part of the day.

Car parks are situated at Balmer Lawn riverside, Standing Hat, Ivy Wood, Ladycross, Stockley and Hawkhill.

Camping is available at Hollands Wood and Roundhill, with emergency overflow areas at Beaulieu Heath.

1 *Balmer Lawn riverside.* [RF]
2 *Cotton grass.* [RF]
3 *Hollands Wood open forest.* [HA]
4 *Bog myrtle.* [HA]
5 *Hollands Wood camp site.* [RF]
6 *Sika stag with hinds.* [RF]
7 *Forest donkeys.* [RF]

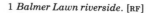

3
4

6
7

5

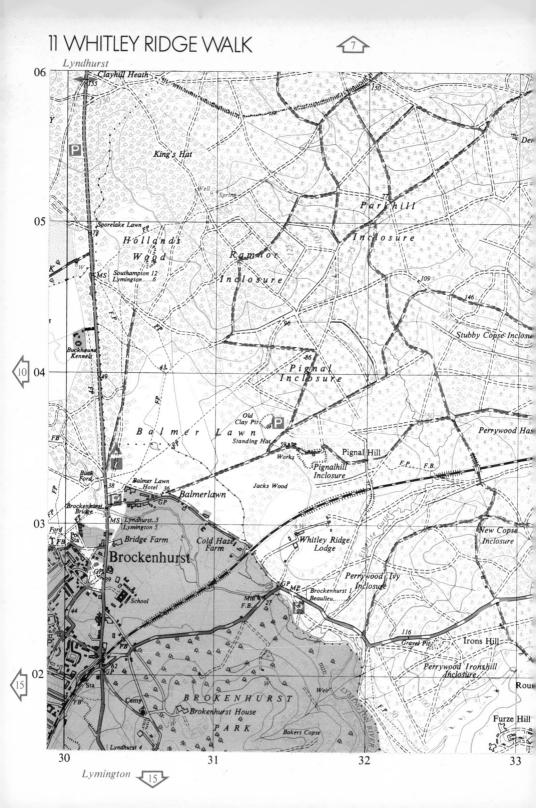

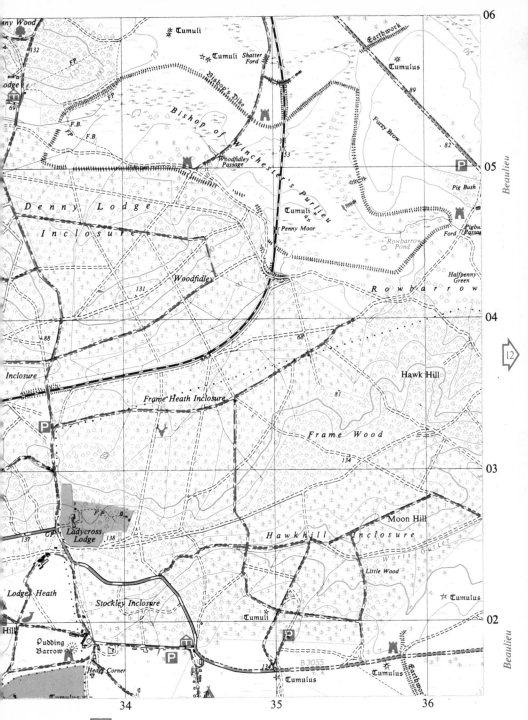

06

ny Wood

132

odge

69

FP

FP

F.B.

FP

F.B.

Cumuli

Cumuli Shatter
Ford

Bishop's Dike

Bishop of Winchester's Purlieu

*Woodfidley
Passage*

53

Cumulus

Earthwork

Cumulus

Fury Brow

89

82

P 05

Beaulieu

Pig Bush

*Pigbush
Passage*

Ford

*Halfpenny
Green*

Rowbarrow

Cumuli

Penny Moor

*Rowbarrow
Pond*

D e n n y   L o d g e
I n c l o s u r e

131

Woodfidley

88

04

68

81

Hawk Hill

Inclosure

P

Frame Heath Inclosure

Frame Wood

134

03

Moon Hill

137

F P

*Ladycross
Lodge*

138

H a w k h i l l   I n c l o s u r e

Worts *Gutter*

Little Wood

Tumulus

Lodge Heath

Stockley Inclosure

Cumuli

02

Beaulieu

Hill

*Pudding
Barrow*

P

P

Hedge Corner

134

B 3055

Cumulus

Earthwork

Cumulus

Tumulus

Cumulus

34

35

36

12
16

12 & 13
DENNY LODGE
WALK

This Walk embraces the largest parish by area in the United Kingdom, with a total population of 470 in 1973, and is depicted on two maps with parts still included in the Ashurst Walk. It extends from Matley Heath (Ashurst) to King's Copse Inclosure near Fawley in the south. The original Groom Keeper's Lodge is situated in the centre and is now a Head Forester's residence.

It is chiefly heath and bogland, with new Inclosures planted on the eastern boundary between 1963 and 1965 in an attempt to screen the waterside industrial landscape. These Inclosures are growing well and will one day offer the visitor a welcome respite from the industrial scenery. The well-wooded and efficiently farmed Beaulieu Estate abuts on to the southern boundary of this Walk and offers the visitor to the Forest a variety of interests including the National Motor Museum.

There is an abundance of ancient bronze age burial barrows scattered over the heathland but tragically all have been destroyed by early incompetent excavations.

There are few remnants of Roman occupation in the Forest other than occasional pottery kilns in the north; however, a Roman Road with a prominent agger (camber) can still be seen in Fawley Inclosure.

Car parks at Culverley offer walks westwards into the delightful Tantany, Stubbs and Hawkhill Ancient and Ornamental Woodlands of great maturity. Access is also possible from this car park, for those who are careful to Bishop's Dyke earthworks. Car parks at North Gate, King's Hat, and Ipley Bridge make available to the walker the Beaulieu riverside and the fine open lawns of Brick Hill.

King's Copse Inclosure is the most easterly island of woodland in the Forest and offers the walker short walks on the forest ride system, possibly unaware of how close are the Refinery and Power Station of Fawley.

In complete contrast a lakeside car park will be found at Hatchet Pond, overlooking this artificial pond where bird life abounds. A narrow causeway path has been constructed to enable the walker safely to proceed southwards without having to regain access on to the highway.

1

2

3

5

1 *Natural oak, Stubbs Wood.* [DS]
2 *Kings Copse Inclosure.* [DS]
3 *Orange peel peziza.* [RF]
4 *Bog pimpernel.* [HA]
5 *Culverley car park and picnic place.* [RF]
6 *Sphagnum bog, Bishop's Dyke.* [HA]

4

6

12 DENNY LODGE WALK *Calshot*

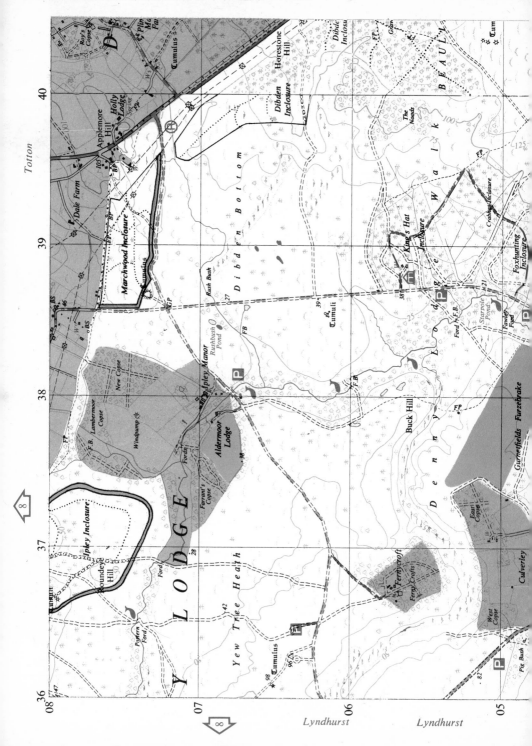

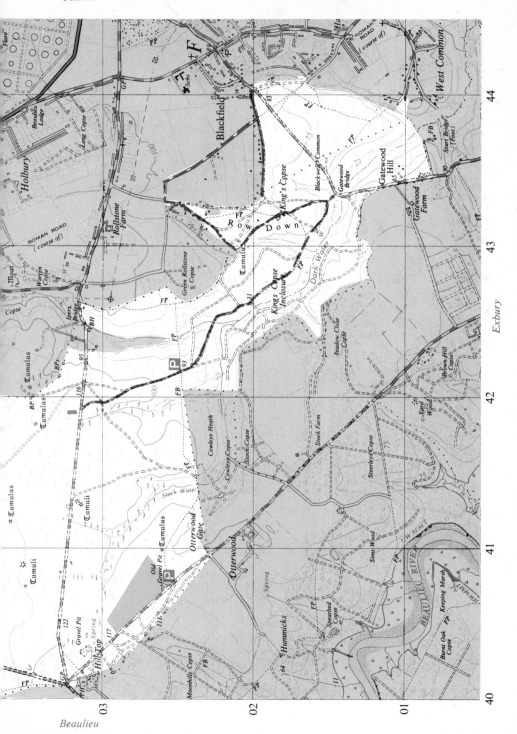

Exbury

14

HOLMSLEY
WALK

Deriving its name from "holm" (holly), extensive copses called "Hats" existed prior to the construction of the airfield in 1942. Relics of these can still be seen to the north of the camp site, as it exists today, with such delightful names as Great Hat, Bell's Hat and Thorney Hill Holms. The Groom Keeper's Lodge is today a private residence. Records show that this airfield, opened in September 1942, was used extensively by many different types of aircraft and latterly made a major contribution to the invasion of Europe in 1944. It was closed in 1946. In May 1940 the first German high explosive bomb fell at Wilverley Post, killing a pony.

This Walk is comparatively speaking a small one but still offers some scenic gems to the adventurous walker as he traverses the great expanse of natural heath at Dur Hill Down overlooking Bisterne Common and Whitten Bottom. The Inclosures are well served by streams and are rich with insect life. Holmsley, Brownhill and Wootton Coppice are worthy of exploring with their neat small plantations of all ages and species.

Car parks are available at Dur Hill, Burbush, Holmsley Ridge, Goats Pen, Ossemsley Ford, Wilverley Post and Pigsty Hill, each offering a change of scenery and walks of varied length and interest.

Camping is confined to the Holmsley Airfield and the woodlands behind, where modern facilities will be found.

1

2

4

1 *Roe kid.* [RF]
2 *Dur Hill heath.* [RF]
3 *Silver-washed fritillary.* [RF]
4 *Bog asphodel.* [HA]
5 *Holmsley camp site.* [RF]
6 *Beech stump "garden".* [RF]

3

5

6

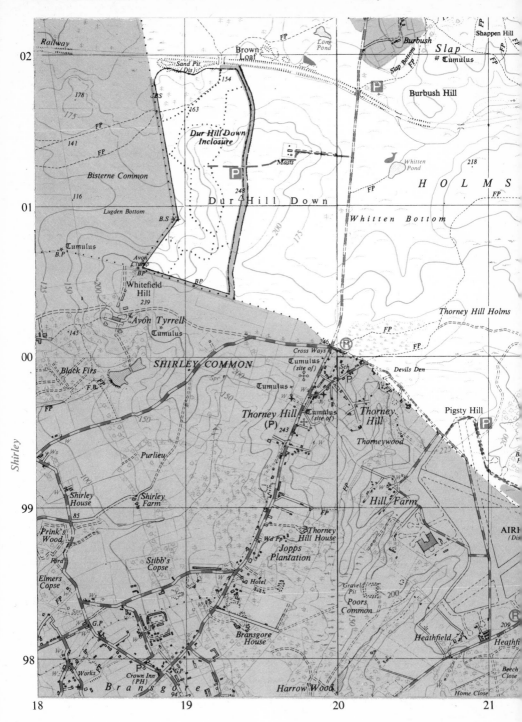

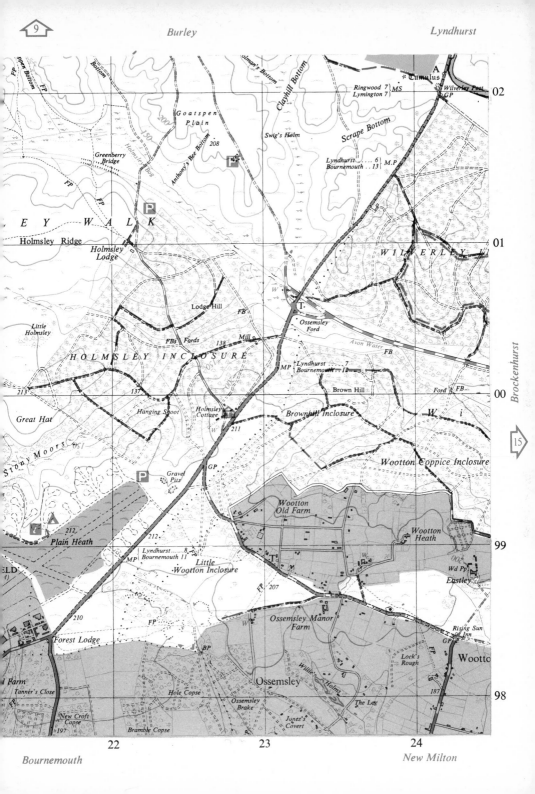

Brockenhurst

15

WILVERLEY WALK

Believed to be named after the natural willows of the Avon Water which traverses this southern part on its way eastwards to the sea, this Walk offers a wide variety of open heath, artificially reseeded lawns, mature Inclosures, fascinating bogs and associated natural lawns. There are some fine views of Rhinefield Walk, particularly from Hincheslea Plain in the late evening, when a panoramic landscape can be viewed with the sun in the west. Grazing ponies and cattle are often concentrated at Wilverley Plain and Longslade Bottom.

The names of Inclosures and woodland, if studied with the assistance of the Oxford Dictionary of English Place Names by Ekwall, will often confirm how the original tree crops were established. For example, Setthorns owes its name to acorns being sown with thorn as hawes, to aid their survival against grazing.

The "Naked Man" is a relic of a gibbet tree referred to in Chapter 7.

Car parks afford a wide variety of peaceful pastimes, notably at Wootton Bridge, Broadley, Boundway Hill, Setthorns, Longslade Bottom, Horseshoe Bottom, Wilverley Plain, Wilverley Pit, Hincheslea Viewpoint, Hincheslea Moor, Hincheslea Bog and Setley Pond.

Camping is confined to within Setthorns Inclosure where gravel pitches for caravans are separated by trees and undergrowth.

The main London–Bournemouth railway passes through the southern section of this Walk, stopping at Sway and Brockenhurst.

1 *Bastard balm.* [RF]
2 *Pine male flowers.* [HA]
3 *Wootton Bridge car park at Avon Water.* [RF]
4 *Longslade Bottom.* [HA]
5 *Stag beetle.* [RF]
6 *Larch female flowers.* [HA]
7 *Wilverley Inclosure from the air, 1971.* [FC]
8 *Wilverley Plain from the air, 1971.* [FC]

1

2

3

4

5

6

7

8

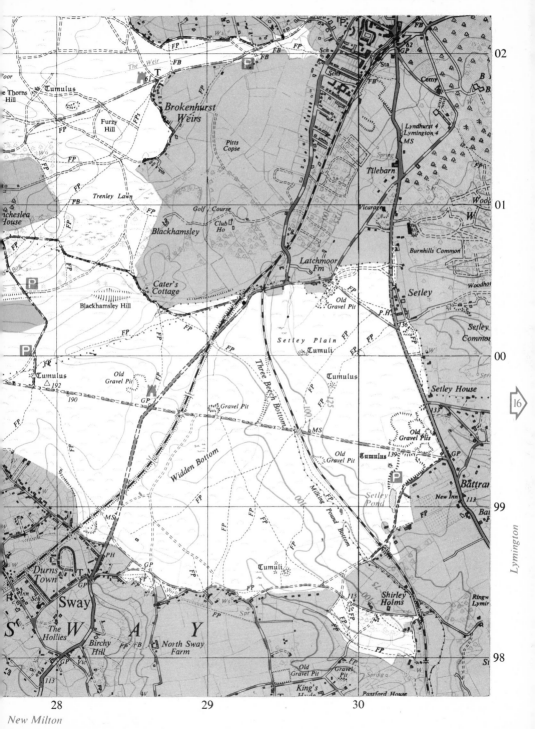

02

01

00

99

98

28   29   30

16
LADY CROSS WALK

This Walk is fairly flat with magnificent skyscapes to be seen in changeable weather. The Isle of Wight can be seen from the open places made more exposed by the construction of Beaulieu Airfield in 1942, from where in 1944 major attacks on flying bombs and invasion targets were made. The use of this airfield continued right up until November 1959. Some of the old runways have been removed but the remainder are being maintained to afford the visitor a complete contrast to the enclosed landscapes of the central walks. One of the major attractions is Hatchet Pond which has been stocked with coarse fish offering fishing on permits from the Forestry Commission. It is believed it was originally the water storage supply for a mill in East Boldre.

There are many Bronze Age barrows throughout this area, alas no longer retaining their original profile. In the south is the only Inclosure to be found, Norley, which is a southern outlier offering sheltered walks amidst the plantations of tomorrow.

Car parks are available at Beaulieu Old Airfield; Hatchet Moor; Crockford; Crockford Clump – where the early field system can be seen on the ground as referred to in Chapter 2, Bull Hill and Norley, each offering a contrast and in some cases shelter from whichever way the wind blows.

The numerous rectangular water-filled hollows alongside the road from Lymington to Beaulieu have naturally evolved into miniature pond habitats. They owe their origin to the anti-aircraft gun positions used in the Second World War to defend Beaulieu airfield.

1

2

3

4

1 *Crossleaved heather.* [RF]
2 *Purple heather.* [HA]
3 *Ling.* [HA]
4 *Beaulieu Heath with the Isle of Wight in the distance from the air, 1971.* [FC]
5 *Hatchet Pond.* [HA]
6 *Hatchet Pond car park.* [FC]
7 *Crockford Clump car park.* [RF]

6

5

7

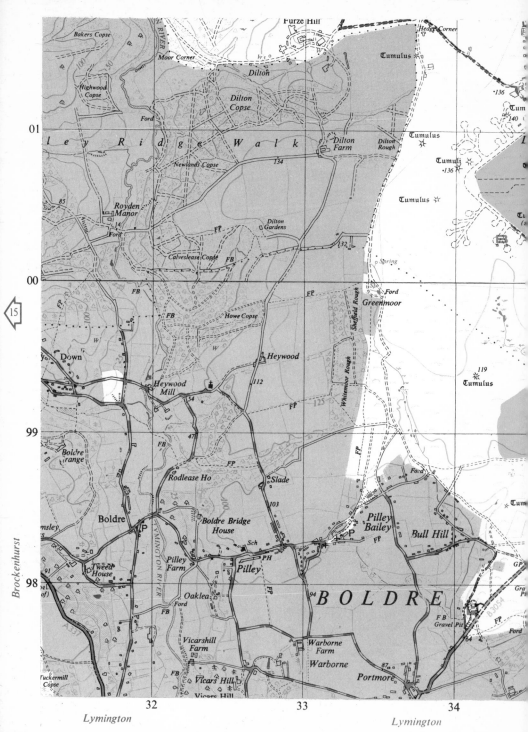

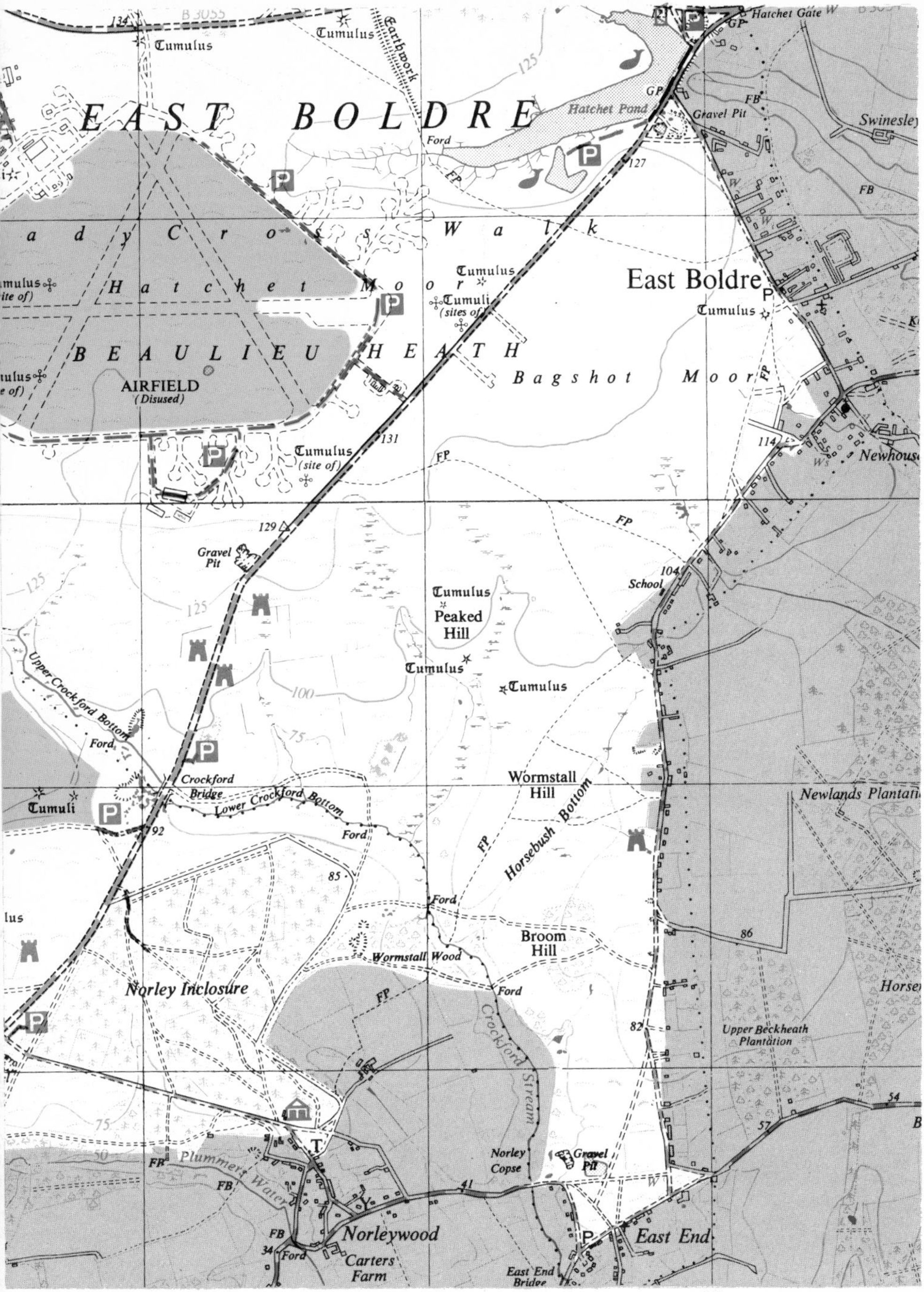

EAST BOLDRE

Hatchet Gate W

Swinesley

Hatchet Pond

Gravel Pit

East Boldre

Tumulus

Newhouse

BEAULIEU HEATH

Bagshot Moor

AIRFIELD
(Disused)

Tumulus
(site of)

Tumulus
Peaked
Hill

Tumulus

Tumulus

School

Gravel
Pit

Upper Crockford Bottom

Ford

Crockford
Bridge

Tumuli

Lower Crockford Bottom

Wormstall
Hill

Newlands Plantation

Ford

Ford

Horsebush Bottom

Norley Inclosure

Wormstall Wood

Broom
Hill

Ford

Horse

Upper Beckheath
Plantation

Plummert Water

FB

Norley
Copse

Gravel
Pit

Norleywood

Carters
Farm

East End
Bridge

East End

01

00

99

98

35   36   37

Fifteen

General information

How to reach the Forest

By train: the main station and motorail terminal for the Forest is Brockenhurst, and most Waterloo–Bournemouth trains stop there. Local trains stop at Lyndhurst Road, Beaulieu Road and Sway. Southampton and Bournemouth are the nearest major stations. British Rail enquiries: Southampton 29393.

By coach: Royal Blue Express Services from London (Victoria Coach Station, SW1).

By bus: local services are operated by Hants & Dorset Motor Services Ltd, The Square, Bournemouth (23371).

By road: via M3 (London), M27 (south-east coast), A34 (north and midlands). Overnight parking in the Forest (except as permitted for camping) is against the Byelaws.

By air: Hurn Airport, Bournemouth.

By ferry: from Southampton across the Solent to Hythe (pedestrians and cyclists only). Car ferries to Lymington from the Isle of Wight.

Camping

Forestry Commission camp sites open from the Thursday before Good Friday or 1 April, whichever is the earlier, to the last weekend before or including 1 October. Holmsley Camp only remains open until the end of October. Full details from the Forestry Commission, the Queen's House, Lyndhurst, Hampshire or from the Information Centre at Lyndhurst public car park. Camping without a permit or elsewhere than on a designated site is against the Byelaws.

Holiday accommodation

The Forest is well supplied with hotels, the majority being in Lyndhurst and Brockenhurst: list from New Forest Hotels & Restaurants' Association, David Bell's Forest Lodge, Lyndhurst. There are Youth Hostels at Norleywood, Burley and Southampton – for details write to the Youth Hostels Association, 8 St Stephen's Hill, St Albans, Herts.

Riding and Sports

There are many riding schools and livery stables in and around the Forest, see address

1 *Camping.* [HI]
2 *Riding.* [RF]
3 *Fishing.* [HI]

1

2

below. The district has its own packs of fox-hounds, buckhounds and beagles.

Permits for fishing (coarse and trout) may be had from the Queen's House, Lyndhurst, or from camping offices during the season.

There are golf courses at Lyndhurst, Burley, Brockenhurst and Bramshaw.

Wildlife conservation

All wild life in the Forest is protected by the Byelaws. Permission to study or collect specimens for scientific purposes must be sought in writing from the Deputy Surveyor.

Useful addresses

The Official Verderer, Emery Down, Lyndhurst (2052).

New Forest District Council, Appletree Court, Lyndhurst (2891).

Hampshire County Police (New Forest Division), The Police Station, Lyndhurst (2813).

New Forest Association – Hon Sec Mrs L K Errington, Rockford End, Ringwood, Hampshire.

New Forest Pony Breeding & Cattle Society – Hon Sec Miss D M Macnair, Beacon Corner, Burley, Ringwood, Hampshire.

Hampshire Field Club (New Forest Section) – Hon Sec Mrs J Irvine, 4 Clarence Road, Lyndhurst, Hampshire.

Association of New Forest Riding Establishments. Warren Stables, Balmer Lawn Road, Brockenhurst (3351).

Nature Conservancy Council (Area Office), Shrubbs Hill Road, Lyndhurst (2840).

Hampshire County Council, The Castle, Winchester (4411).

3

Land area

Distribution of Land Ownership within the Perambulation

Figures show total area in hectares. 1 hectare=2.47 acres

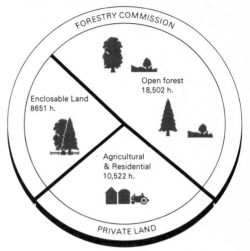

Total Area 37,675 h. (93,082 acres)

Distribution of Vegetation within Forestry Commission Areas

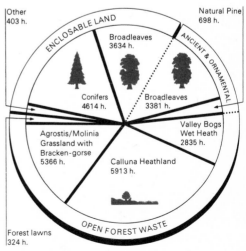

Total Area 27,157 h. (67,082 acres)

1

2

A note on books

The most valuable modern scientific work is *The New Forest: An Ecological Study* by Colin R Tubbs, published by David and Charles, Newton Abbot, in 1969, priced £2.50. Well illustrated, it embraces all aspects of field natural history and agricultural economy.

The classic work on the New Forest is that entitled *The New Forest, its History and Scenery*, by John R Wise (Gibbings, London). first published in 1863. Although long out of print, it ran through several editions and second-hand copies are fairly easy to find. The main text deals with the history, topography, scenery and customs of the Forest, whilst the appendices include lists of plants, birds and insects, and an interesting glossary of the local dialect.

There are many more recent works that describe and illustrate the Forest's attractions in a more popular style, including the following:

The New Forest by G E Briscoe Eyre, 1883
The New Forest by C J Cornish, 1894
The New Forest by De Crespigny & Hutchinson, 1895
The New Forest by Mrs Rawnsley, 1904
The New Forest by Horace Hutchinson, 1904
The New Forest by E Godfrey, 1912
Hampshire's Glorious Wilderness by G R Tweedie, 1925
The New Forest Beautiful by F E Stevens, 1925
Walking in the New Forest by Joan Begbie, 1934
The New Forest by John C Moore, 1934
The New Forest published by Messrs Dent, 1960

Remarks on Forest Scenery (2 vols, 1791) is a well-known work by the Rev William Gilpin, sometime Vicar of Boldre, who had much to say on the beauties of trees in the Forest landscape. An interesting record of sporting life in the Forest is to be found in *Thirty-five Years in the New Forest* (1915) by the Hon Gerald Lascelles, a former Deputy Surveyor. The great authority on the Forest's archaeology was Heywood Sumner, whose published works include:

Ancient Earthworks of the New Forest, 1917, *A Map of Ancient Sites in the New Forest*, 1923, *Guide to the New Forest*, 1924, *Excavations in New Forest Roman Pottery Sites*, 1927, *Local Papers, Archaeological and Topographical, Hants, Dorset and Wilts*, 1931.

Dr F E Kenchington has described the history and customs of the Commoners, and the war-time schemes for the improvement of the Forest grazing, very fully in *The Commoners New Forest* (Hutchinson, London, 1943). Very full accounts of the Forest's history and topography appear in the *Victoria County History of Hampshire* (1900, 6 vols), which includes an informative article on forestry by Lascelles and Nisbet.

The best known work of fiction having a New Forest background is probably *The Children of the New Forest* (1853) by F Maryatt, a story of Civil War days. R D Blackmore was the author of *Cradock Nowell; a Tale of the New Forest*, a three-volume work published in 1866. Mrs Gaskell featured the New Forest in her *North and South*, 1855, as did Conan Doyle in his *The White Company*, 1891. Children of all ages will enjoy two more modern and well-illustrated stories by Allen W Seaby, entitled *Skewbald, the New Forest Pony*, and *The White Hart*, the latter story being based on the life of a white deer which actually roamed the Rhinefield woods a few years ago.

A useful modern guide, giving details of some thirty walking routes, is *Russell's Graphic Guide to the New Forest*, published at 25p by Russell & Co. Ltd., Southampton. Another up-to-date guide to the neighbourhood, entitled *The New Forest*, is published in Messrs Ward, Lock & Co's series.

The Killing of William Rufus, by Duncan Grinnell-Milne (David & Charles, Newton Abbot, 1968, £1.75) is a thrilling investigation into the Forest's best-known historical event.

Wilverley Plain and Inclosure with Spy Holms in the background from the air, 1971, looking north-west [FC], *and the Ordnance Survey map of the same area.*

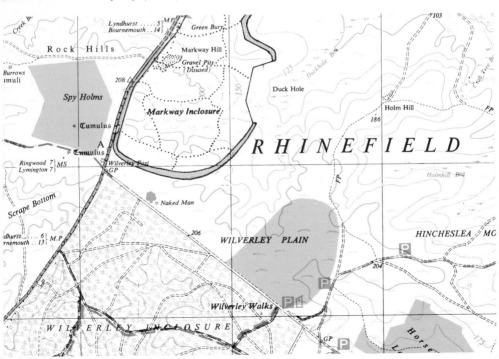

Legend to the maps

Motorway. Trunk and Main Road (Dual Carriageway)	M 4 *or* A 6(M)	A 123 *or* A 123(T)
Trunk & Main Road	A 123 *or* A 123(T)	
Secondary Road	*Fenced* B 2314	*Unfenced*
Road Under Construction		
Other Roads	*Good, metalled*	*Poor, or unmetalled*
Footpaths	FP	FP

Railways, Multiple Track   Station   Road over   *Fenced*   *Unfenced*   FB

    Sidings   Cutting   Tunnel   (*Footbridge*)

,,   Single Track   Viaduct   Level Crossing   Embankment   Road under

,,   Narrow Gauge

Aerial Ropeway   *Aerial Ropeway*

Boundaries { County or County Borough
       ,,   ,,   County of City (in Scotland)

   ,,   ,,   ,,   ,,   ,,   with Parish

   ,,   Parish

Pipe Line (Oil, Water)   *Pipe Line*

Electricity Transmission Lines (*Pylons shown at bends and spaced conventionally*) – ⊠ – – – – – ⊠ –

Post Offices (In Villages & Rural Areas only)   P   Town Hall......TH   Public House......PH

Church or Chapel with Tower... **╪**   Church or Chapel with Spire... **╪**   Church or Chapel without either... ■

Triangulation Station.........△   on Church with Tower........   without Tower.......▲

Intersected Point on Chy...○   on Church with Spire....○̇   without Spire.... ■   on Building....▬

Guide Post   GP.   Mile Post   MP.   Mile Stone....MS.   Boundary Stone...BS ○   Boundary Post...BP○

Youth Hostel...Y   Telephone Call Box (Public)....T   (AA)...A   (RAC)...R   Antiquity (site of)....✛

Public Buildings		Glasshouses
Quarry & Gravel Pit		Orchard
National Trust Area	*Sheen Common NT*	Furze
,, ,, ,, Scotland	NTS	Rough Pasture Heath & Moor
Osier Bed		Marsh
Reeds		Well W ○
Park, Fenced		Spring Spr ○
Wood, Coniferous, Fenced		Wind Pump.......Wd Pp.
Wood, Non-Coniferous Unfenced		*The grid lines on this sheet are at 1 kilometre interval.*
Brushwood, Fenced & Unfenced		*Contours are at 25 feet vertical interval.*
		Spot Height.......123·

Ferries — Foot, Vehicle
Sand Hills
LWMMT
Mud
Flat Rock
Slopes
HWMMT
Highest point to which Medium Tides flow
△ Beacon
Sand
Lightship
Lake
Canal
Bridge
Lock
Weir
Sand & Shingle
Towing Path
Aqueduct
Ford
FB (Footbridge)
Cliff
Dam
Lighthouse

© Crown copyright 1975

FOOTPATHS (NEW FOREST CROWN LAND ONLY)
The representation of any road, track or path is no evidence of the existence of a public right of way. There are no public rights of way over the New Forest (other than the metalled surface of any highway maintained by the Highway authority) but the public are permitted to use existing paths on foot for air and exercise.

Forestry Commission tourist information added to Ordnance Survey maps.

The reproduction of a boundary is approximate and is not intended to depict the limits of land title.

Private land

Forest Information

Forest car parks and picnic places

Forest viewpoints

Forest toilets

Forest barbecue sites reserved by application to Queen's House

Forestry Commission camp sites: tents and caravans

Forestry Commission camp sites: caravans only

Private camp sites: tents and caravans

Forest Keepers' houses

Forest access road, official vehicle access only except for access to car parks and camp sites

Forest underpass, horse-drawn vehicles, animals and pedestrians only

Width restriction on County roads not exceeding 6' 6"

Forest waymarked walks

Forest lawns or grazing strips

Wildlife Centres

Deer observation towers reserved by application to Queen's House

Forest fishing by permit only

Ornamental and historic trees

Selected historic locations

Pony sales

117

Acknowledgements and contributors

DESIGN HMSO/Dennis Greeno.

GRAPHIC ILLUSTRATION Gary Hincks.

PHOTOGRAPHS Heather Angel, F.R.P.S., Robin Fletcher, Hugh Insley, Norman Orr, A.R.P.S., Donn Small, and Forestry Commission photographic staff, led by I A Anderson, F.I.I.P.

SOURCE MATERIAL FOR ILLUSTRATION The British Museum and the Hampshire Record Office, Winchester.

MAPS The Ordnance Survey, by kind permission of the Controller of Her Majesty's Stationery Office.

MRS K MERLE CHACKSFIELD has made a special study of smuggling; she is the author of "Smuggling Days" and has lectured and written numerous articles on the subject. She is an artist and has written a book on research in modern educational methods. She is Headmistress of a school and lives at Romsey.

JOHN CHAPMAN is on the staff of the Forestry Commission at Lyndhurst.

MICHAEL CLARKE is a Head Keeper of the New Forest; he has an enthusiastic and practical knowledge of deer management and is a knowledgeable naturalist.

DAVID COBB is a professional marine artist who lives locally and has made a special study of the architectural history of the wooden ship.

MALDWIN DRUMMOND is an elected Verderer of the New Forest and a Hampshire County Councillor. He went to the Royal Agricultural College, Cirencester before taking up farming and forestry on the south eastern fringe of the Forest, on the Solent shore. He is a Justice of the Peace for Hampshire and holds a Certificate in Environmental Science from Southampton University.

HUGH INSLEY is a professional Forest Officer on the staff of the Deputy Surveyor. He is an enthusiastic and knowledgeable naturalist.

ARTHUR T LLOYD is a history teacher, has made a study in depth of derivations of local names and is renowned for his new contributions to the interpretation of historical records.

MISS DIONIS MACNAIR was born at Burley in the New Forest. She has had ponies in the Forest since she was a child and teaches all branches of riding. She is an elected Verderer, a member of the Council of the Commoners' Defence Association and has been Honorary Secretary of the New Forest Pony Breeding and Cattle Society since 1967.

ANTHONY PASMORE is an elected Verderer, Vice Chairman of the New Forest Section of the Hampshire Field Club, a member of the Councils of the Commoners' Defence Association and the New Forest Association, and of the Hale Purlieu Advisory Committee. He is an amateur local historian and archaeologist, and a Chartered Surveyor.

HUGH C PASMORE came to live at Fritham in the New Forest in 1933 and apart from war service has remained in the Forest ever since. He practised as a Chartered Surveyor until 1965 and remains as a Consultant. For the past twenty years he has bred New Forest ponies. He was appointed a Verderer by the Minister of Agriculture in 1968. He is a member of the Councils of the New Forest Association, the Pony Breeding and Cattle Society and the Commoners' Defence Association. For ten years he has contributed to local newspapers a monthly article entitled: The New Forest Commoners' Notebook.

DONN SMALL is a professional forest officer who has served in the Colonial Forest Service in Sierra Leone, West Africa, and in the Forestry Commission in East Anglia and the Chilterns. He was appointed Deputy Surveyor of the New Forest in 1971. He is the Chief Officer responsible for the management of the New Forest and the implementation of the Conservation proposals for the New Forest published in 1971.

MRS MARJORIE TRIGGS has lived in or near the Forest all her life. She is an experienced researcher into ancient documents and records.

DAVID J STAGG is a local historian and archaeologist, and takes an active part in Forest affairs.

COLIN TUBBS is an Assistant Regional Officer for the Nature Conservancy Council, a naturalist and expert on the New Forest, with the conservation of which he has had a great deal to do.

118

Index

Index to place names, within crown property as printed on Ordnance Survey Maps 1:25000 scale in this guide.

To locate name two references are given.
a. First figure refers to map number.
b. Second four figures locate the lower left hand grid reference of the kilometre square eg 2016.

A

Abbott's Well 1/1712
Acres Down 6/2608
Akercome Bottom 5/1907
Alder Hill 1/2013
Alder Hill Bottom 1/2013
Alder Hill Incl 1/2013
Aldermoor Lodge 8/3706
Aldridge Hill 10/2703
Aldridge Hill Cottage 10/2803
Aldridge Hill Incl 10/2703
Alum Green 7/2707
Amberslade Bottom 5/2010
Amberwood Incl 3/2113
Amies Corner 5/1909
Amies Wood 5/1909
Anderwood Incl 10/2406
Annesley Bank 7/2806
Anses Wood 3/2212
Anthony's Bee Bottom 14/2201
Applemore Hill 12/3907
Appleslade Bottom 5/1809
Appleslade Incl 5/1808
Ashley Bottom 1/2014
Ashley Cross 1/2014
Ashleycross Hill 1/2014
Ashley Hole 1/2015
Ashurst 7/3300
Ashurst Lodge 7/3308
Ashurst Wood 7/3309
Avon Clump 14/1800
Avon River 1/1616
Avon Water 14/2300
Avon Water 15/2599

B

Backley Bottom 5/2208
Backley Holms 5/2107
Backley Incl 6/2207
Backley Plain 5/2106
Balmer Lawn 11/3003
Bagnum Bog 9/1802
Bagnum Rough 9/1802
Bagshot Moor 16/3600
Bank 7/2807
Barrow Moor 6/2507
Bartley Water 4/3116
Battramsley 15/3099
Beaulieu Airfield 16/3500
Beaulieu Heath 13/4005 & 16/3500
Beaulieu Road Pony Sales 8/3406
Beaulieu Road Station 8/3406
Beaulieu River 8/3208
Beech Bed Incl 6/2306
Beechern Wood 10/2802
Beeches Bottom 2/2516
Bell's Hat 14/2199
Berry Beeches 5/2106
Berry Hole 5/2106
Berry Wood 9/2105
Bignell Wood 4/2813
Bishop of Winchester's Purlieu 11/3405
Bishop's Dyke 11/3405
Bisterne Common 14/1801
Black Barrow 5/1810
Blackbush 9/1903
Blackbush 2/2515
Blackbush Plain 2/2415
Blackdown 8/3506

119

Blackensford Bottom 6/2207
Blackensford Hill 6/2307
Blackensford Lawn 6/2306
Blackfield 13/4302
Black Gutter 1/2016
Black Gutter Bottom 1/2016
Blackhamsley Hill 15/2800
Black Heath 5/1810
Black Hill 9/2104
Black Knowl 10/2903
Black Water 10/2504
Blackwater Bridge 10/2504
Blackwell Common 13/4301
Blissford Hill 1/1713
Bolderford Bridge 10/2804
Bolderwood Cottage 6/2408
Bolderwood Farm 6/2308
Bolderwood Green 6/2408
Bolderwood Grounds 6/2308
Bolderwood Hill 6/2408
Bolderwood Walks 6/2408
Bolton's Bench 7/3008
Boundway Hill 15/2698
Box Berry Hill 9/2004
Bramble Hill 2/2515
Bramble Hill 7/2706
Bramshaw 2/2615
Bramshaw Hill 3/2614
Bramshaw Incl 2/2516
Bramshaw Telegraph 2/2216
Bramshaw Wood 2/2516
Bratley Arch 6/2309
Bratley Incl 5/2208
Bratley Water 6/2310
Bratley Wood 5/2208
Brick Kiln Incl 7/2906
Brinkenwood Lawn 10/2705
Brinkenwood 10/2705
Broad Bottom 9/1904
Broadley Incl 15/2599
Broadoak Bottom 9/2102
Broadway Bottom 3/2213
Brockenhurst 11/3002
Brockenhurst Weirs 15/2801
Brock Hill 10/2605
Brockis Hill 4/2911
Brockis Hill Incl 7/7011
Brogenslade Bottom 5/1811
Brook Common 3/2613
Brook Hill 3/2614
Broom Hill 3/2614
Broom Hill 16/3698
Broom Hill 6/2708
Broomy Bottom 3/2111
Broomy Incl 5/2011
Broomy Lodge 5/2011
Broomy Plain 5/2010
Brown Hill 14/2300
Brownhill Incl 14/2399
Brown Loaf 14/1902
Buckherd Bottom 5/2008
Buck Ford 11/3003
Buck Hill 12/3705
Bull Hill 16/3398
Bunkers Hill 7/2909
Burbush 9/2002
Bur Bushes 2/2116
Burbush Hill 14/2001
Burley 9/2103

Burley Beacon 9/2202
Burley Croft 9/1904
Burley Lawn 9/2103
Burley Lodge 9/2305
Burley Moor 9/2104
Burley New Incl 9/2304
Burley Old Incl 10/2404
Burley Outer Rails Incl 9/2305
Burley Park 9/2103
Burley Street 9/2004
Burnford Bridge 2/2615
Burnshill Common 11/3000
Burnt Axon 9/1902
Burnt Balls 1/1814
Bushy Bratley 5/2208
Busketts Incl 8/3210
Busketts Lawn Incl 7/3110
Busketts Wood 4/3111
Butcher's Corner 2/2615
Butts Lawn 10/2902
Butts Lawn 10/2905

C

Cadman's Pool 3/2212
Cadnam 4/2913
Cadnam Bridge 4/2913
Canterton Green 4/2713
Castle Hill 1/1616
Castle Hill Camp 9/1903
Chilly Hill 1/1713
Church Moor 9/1902
Church Moor 6/2406
Church Place 7/3306
Church Place Incl 8/3309
Clay Ford 7/2707
Clay Hill 9/2302
Clay Hill 4/2811
Clay Hill 7/3007
Clay Hill Bottom 9/2302
Clayhill Heath 7/3005
Clay Pits Bottom 2/2216
Clumber Incl 10/2603
Cockley Hill 1/1915
Cockroad Hill 9/2304
Cole Bridge 6/2707
Coalmeer Lawn 3/2613
Cole's Hole 13/4205
Common Moor 9/2004
Coopers Hill 1/2014
Coppice of Linwood 3/2414
Costicles Incl 7/3210
Costicles Pond 7/3210
Cot Bottom 9/2202
Crab Hat Incl 12/3905
Crabtree Bog 10/2602
Cranes Moor 9/1902
Creek Bottom 9/2302
Crockford Bridge 16/3599
Crockford Green 16/3499
Crockford Stream 16/3698
Crock Hill 3/2114
Crock Hill Green 3/2114
Crow Hill Top 9/1803

Crows Nest Bottom 2/2416
Culverley 12/3604
Cunninger Bottom 1/1916
Custards 7/3008

D

Dames Slough Hill 10/2505
Dames Slough Incl 10/2405
Danes Hole 3/2513
Dark Water 13/4204
Dark Water 13/4201
Dead Buck Hill 1/2012
Dead Man Bottom 1/2017
Dead Man Hill 1/2016
Dead Man Moor 7/2708
Deer Leap Incl 8/3409
Deer Leap Sand Pit 8/3509
Denny Inclosure 7/3206
Denny Lodge Incl 11/3304
Denny Wait 7/3306
Denny Wood 11/3305
Devil's Den 14/2099
Dibden Bottom 12/3806
Dibden Inclosure 12/3906
Dilton 16/3201
Ditch End Bottom 1/1815
Ditch End Brook 1/1815
Dockens Water 5/1800
Dogkennel Bridge 10/2305
Dogsben Gutter 4/2911
Dogwood Bottom 5/2106
Duck Hole 10/2502
Duck Hole Bog 10/2502
Dunces Arch 7/3108
Dur Hill Down 14/1901
Dur Hill Down Incl 14/1901

E

Eagle Oak 6/2506
East Boldre 16/3700
East Copse 12/3705
East End 16/3697
Eastley 14/2498
Eaves Hill 7/3011
Elkham's Grave 15/2598
Emery Down 7/2808
Eyeworth Lodge 3/2214
Eyeworth Pond 3/2214
Eyeworth Wood 2/2215

F

Fair Cross 7/3009

Fawley Ford 12/3804
Fawley Incl 13/4105
Fernycroft 12/3605
Ferny Knap Incl 10/2505
Five Thorns Hill 15/2701
Flash Pond 13/4105
Fletcher's Green 10/2804
Fletcher's Hill 10/2603
Fletcher's Thorn Incl 10/2704
Fletcher's Thorns 10/2804
Fletcher's Water 10/2804
Foldsgate Hill 7/2909
Forest Lodge 14/2198
Foulford 9/1805
Foulford Bottom 9/1805
Foxhill 3/2511
Foxhill 7/3108
Foxhill 8/3608
Fox Hill 7/3009
Foxhill Moor 7/3108
Foxholes 15/2699
Foxhunting Incl 12/3804
Foxlease House 7/2907
Frame Heath Incl 11/3403
Frame Wood 11/3503
Freeworms Hill 3/2212
Fritham 3/2314
Fritham Bridge 3/2114
Fritham Cross 6/2310
Fulliford Bog 8/3408
Fulliford Passage 8/3407
Furzy Brow 11/3505
Furze Hill 11/3201
Furzey Lawn Incl 4/3010
Furzey Lodge 12/3602

G

Gatewood Bridge 13/4301
Gatewood Hill 13/4301
Gaze Hill 1/2013
Goatspen Plain 14/2201
Godshill Inclosure 1/1716
Godshill Ridge 1/1815
Godshill Wood 1/1616
Goldsmith's Hill 10/2904
Gravelly Ford 10/2604
Gravel Pit Hill 1/1816
Great Ashen Bank 15/2699
Great Earley 9/2204
Great Hat 14/2199
Great Huntley Bank 10/2705
Great Linford Incl 5/1807
Great Witch 1/1912
Great Wood 2/2515
Greenberry Bridge 14/2101
Green Bury 10/2402
Greenford 5/1908
Greenford Bottom 5/1908
Green Pond 3/2213
Gritnam 7/2806
Gritnam Holly 7/2806
Gritnam Wood 7/2806
Gurnetfields Furzebrake 12/3704

Gutter Heath 4/3010

Hursthill Incl 10/2805
Hyde Common 1/1712

H

Hag Hill 15/2500
Halfpenny Green 12/3604
Hallickshole Hill 1/2012
Hampton Ridge 1/1813
Handy Cross 5/2007
Handy Cross Plain 5/1907
Hanging Shoot 14/2299
Hardley Roman Road 13/4204
Hart Hill 6/2610
Hart Hill 1/1714
Hart Hill 6/2406
Harvest Slade Bottom 5/2006
Hasley Hill 5/1911
Hasley Hole 1/1812
Hasley Incl 1/1912
Hatchet Gate 16/3701
Hatchet Moor 16/3500
Hatchet Pond 16/3601
Hawk Hill 11/3503
Hawkhill 12/3603
Hawkhill Incl 11/3502
Hazel Hill 4/2911
Hedge Corner 11/3301
High Corner 5/1900
High Coxlease 7/2906
Highland Water 6/2508
Highland Water Incl 6/2409
Hill Top 13/4003
Hincheslea Bog 15/2700
Hincheslea Holms 15/2600
Hincheslea Moor 15/2601
Hiscocks Hill 3/2213
Holidays Hill 6/2607
Holidays Hill Cottage 7/2707
Holidays Hill Incl 6/2607
Holland Bottom 1/1712
Hollands Wood 11/3004
Holly Hatch Cottage 3/2112
Holly Hatch Incl 3/2111
Holmans Bottom 9/2202
Holm Hill 10/2602
Holmhill Bog 15/2601
Holmhill Cottage 6/2408
Holmhill Ford 6/2608
Holmhill Incl 6/2508
Holmsley Airfield 14/2198
Holmsley Bog 14/2201
Holmsley Cottage 14/2299
Holmsley Inclosure 14/2200
Holmsley Lodge 14/2100
Holmsley Ridge 14/2101
Homy Ridge 2/2316
Honey Hill 12/3604
Horsebush Bottom 16/3698
Horseshoe Bottom 15/2600
Horstone Hill 12/4006
Howen Bottom 2/2315
Howen Bushes 3/2314
Hungerford 1/1712
Hurst Hill 10/2805

I

Ipers Bridge 13/4203
Ipley Inclosure 12/3707
Irons Hill 11/3202
Irons Hill 7/3109
Irons Hill Incl 7/3109
Ironshill Lodge 4/3110
Irons Well 3/2214
Islands Thorns Incl 2/2115

J

Jack's Wood 11/3103
James's Hill 7/2808
Janesmoor Plain 3/2413
Janesmoor Pond 3/2413
Judds Hill 2/2616

K

King's Copse 13/4301
King's Copse Incl 13/4201
King's Garden 5/2009
King's Garn Gutter 3/2513
King's Garn Gutter Incl 3/2513
King's Hat 11/3005
King's Hat Incl 12/3805
King's Passage 8/3407
Kingston Great Common 9/1802
Knaves Ash 9/1804
Knightwood 6/2606
Knightwood Incl 10/2506
Knightwood Oak 6/2606

L

Latchmore Bottom 1/1812
Latchmore Brook 3/2013
Latchmore Shade 1/1812
Lay Gutter Valley 1/1813
Leaden Hall 1/2015
Levey Hill 4/2812
Linford Bottom 5/1807
Linford Brook 5/1908
Linford Brook 5/2009
Linwood 5/1810
Little Castle Common 9/1904

Little Cockley Plain 1/1911
Little Early 9/2204
Little Eye Green 4/2813
Little Fox Hill 4/2900
Little Holbury 13/4204
Little Holmhill Incl 7/3206
Little Holmsley 14/2100
Little Honey Hill Wood 12/3603
Little Linford Incl 5/1807
Little Witch 1/1912
Little Wood 11/3502
Little Wootton Incl 14/2298
Lodge Heath 11/3302
Lodge Hill 14/2200
Lodge Hill 1/1915
Lodgehill Cottage 7/3109
Lodgehill Incl 7/3209
Longbeech Hill 3/2512
Longbeech Incl 3/2512
Longbottom 1/1813
Long Brook 6/2510
Longcross 2/2515
Longcross Plain 2/2415
Longcross Pond 2/2415
Longdown Incl 8/3508
Longdown Sandpit 8/3608
Longpond 9/1902
Longslade Bottom 15/2600
Longwater Lawn 7/3208
Lord's Oak 2/2617
Lower Canterton 4/2713
Lower Crockford Bottom 16/3598
Lucas Castle 6/2410
Lucy Hill 9/2204
Lugden Bottom 14/1800
Lyndhurst 7/2908
Lyndhurst Hill 7/2808
Lyndhurst Rd Station 8/3310

M

Mallard Wood 7/3109
Mallard Mead 7/3209
Malwood Farm 4/2712
Malwood Lodge 4/2712
Marchwood Incl 12/3807
Margaret's Bottom 2/2615
Mark Ash Wood 6/2407
Markway Bridge 10/2503
Markway Incl 10/2402
Markway Hill 10/2402
Markway Holms 10/2403
Marrowbone Hill 5/1907
Matley Bog 8/3307
Matley Heath 8/3307
Matley Holms 8/3407
Matley Passage 8/3307
Matley Ridge 7/3207
Matley Wood 8/3307
Milkham Bottom 5/2009
Milkham Incl 5/2009
Milking Pound Bottom 15/2998
Millers Ford 1/1816
Millersford Copse 1/1917

Millersford Plantation 1/1917
Mill Lawn 9/2303
Mill Lawn Brook 9/2303
Millyford Bridge 6/2607
Millyford Green 6/2708
Mogshade Hill 6/2309
Moor Corner 16/3201
Moorhill 11/3502
Mount Hill 5/1809
Must Thorns Bottom 1/1914

N

Naked Man 15/2401
National Motor Museum 12/3802
New Copse Incl 11/3202
New Park 10/2904
New Park Incl 10/2905
Nices Hill 5/1911
Nomansland 2/2517
No Man's Walk 6/2506
Norley Incl 16/3498
Norley Wood 16/3597
North Bentley Incl 3/2313
Northerwood Incl 7/2908
Northgate 12/3804
North Oakley Incl 6/2307

O

Oaken Brow 15/2699
Ober Corner 10/2803
Ober Heath 10/2703
Ober Shade 10/2804
Ober Water 10/2702
Ober Water Walks 10/2702
Ocknell Arch 3/2411
Ocknell Incl 3/2411
Ocknell Plain 3/2211
Ocknell Pond 3/2311
Ogden's Purlieu 5/1811
Old House Bottom 9/2205
Old Racecourse Lyndhurst 7/3008
Ossemsley Ford 14/2300
Otterwood Gate 13/4102

P

Park Ground Incl 7/3006
Park Hill 7/3106
Park Hill Incl 11/3205
Park Hill Lawn 7/3106
Park Pale 7/3107
Peaked Hill 16/3699

Peel Hill 8/3508
Penerley Gate 12/3603
Penerley Wood 12/3704
Penny Moor 11/3504
Perrywood Haseley Incl 11/3203
Perrywood Incl 11/3102
Perrywood Ironshill Incl 11/3202
Perrywood Ivy Incl 11/3202
Picket Corner 2/2216
Picket Hill 5/1806
Picket Plain 9/1906
Picket Post 9/1906
Pickets Bury 1/1914
Pig Bush 12/3604
Pigbush Passage 12/3604
Pignal Hill 7/3103
Pignal Hill Incl 11/3103
Pignal Incl 11/3104
Pigsty Hill 9/2102
Pigsty Hill 14/2099
Pilmore Gate 7/2708
Pilley Bailey 16/3398
Pinnick Wood 5/1907
Pipers Copse 4/2713
Pipers Wait 2/2416
Pitchers Knowle 1/2013
Pitts Wood Incl 1/1914
Plummers Water 16/3597
Plain Green 4/3010
Plain Heath 14/2199
Pond Head Incl 7/3001
Pottern Ford 12/3607
Poternsford Bridge 4/3210
Pound Hill 6/2407 & 10/2604
Pound Hill Heath 10/2804
Poundhill Incl 10/2704
Puck Pits Incl 6/2509
Pudding Barrow 11/3301
Puttles Bridge 10/2703

Q

Queen Bower 10/2804
Queen North Wood 3/2313
Queen's Meadow 10/2805

R

Ragged Boys Hill 3/2112
Rakes Brake Bottom 3/2112
Ramnor Incl 11/3104
Ravens Nest Incl 3/2514
Redbridge Hill 7/3109
Red Hill 10/2702
Red Hill Bog 15/2601
Red Open Ford 7/2709
Red Rise 10/2403
Redrise Hill 9/2303
Redrise Shade 10/2403

Red Shoot Plain 5/1808
Red Shoot Wood 5/1808
Rhinefield Lodge 10/2603
Rhinefield Sandys Incl 10/2504
Ridley Green 9/2005
Ridley Plain 5/2006
Ridley Wood 9/2006
Rock Hills 9/2302
Rockram Wood 4/2913
Roe Inclosure 5/1908
Roe Wood Incl 5/2008
Roman Bridge 6/2706
Rookham Bottom 1/1714
Rooks Bridge 9/2303
Round Hill 16/3301
Round Hill 3/2614
Roundeye Hill 12/3607
Rowbarrow 11/3504
Rowbarrow Pond 11/3504
Row Down 13/4302
Row Hill 1/2013
Row Hill 7/3208
Rufus Stone 3/2712
Running Hill 4/2712
Rush Bush 12/3806
Rushbush Pond 12/3806
Rushpole Wood 7/3009
Rushy Flat 2/2117
Rushy Slab 2/2616

S

Salisbury Trench 3/2514
Sandy Ridge 5/2208
Scrape Bottom 14/2301
Seamans Corner 4/2811
Setley Plain 15/2900
Setley Pond 15/3099
Setthorns 15/2600
Setthorns Incl 15/2699
Shappen Bottom 9/2102
Shappen Hill 9/2102
Shatter Ford 11/3405
Shave Green Incl 4/2812
Shave Hat 4/2912
Shave Wood 4/2912
Sheepwash Lawn 15/2599
Shepherds Gutter 2/2615
Shepton Bridge 12/3704
Shepton Water 12/3604
Shirley Holms 15/3098
Shobley Bottom 5/1806
Shoot Wood 9/2303
Slap 9/2002
Slap Bottom 9/2002
Sloden Incl 3/2013
Slufters Bottom 6/2310
Slufters Incl 6/2209
Slufters Pond 6/2209
Soarley Beeches 6/2206
Soarley Bottom 6/2206
South Bentley Incl 3/2312
South Oakley Incl 9/2205
Splash Bridge 5/2011

Sporelake Lawn 11/3004
Spy Holms 9/2302
Stag Brake 10/2403
Stag Park 7/3306
Standing Hat 11/3103
Starpole Pond 12/3805
Stinking Edge Wood 6/2207
Stockley Incl 11/3302
Stockyford Green 6/2606
Stone Quarry Bottom 1/1916
Stoney Cross 3/2611
Stoney Cross Plain 3/2511
Stonyford Pond 13/4103
Stony Moor 14/2199
Stricknage Wood 3/2612
Strodgemoor Bottom 9/1803
Stubby Copse Incl 11/3204
Studley Castle 2/2215
Studley Head 2/2216
Studley Wood 2/2216
Stubbs Wood 12/3603
Sway 15/2898
Swigs Holm 14/2301

T

Tall Trees Walk 10/2605
Tantany Wood 12/3604
The Burrows 9/2302
The Butt 3/2413
The Butts 2/2115
The Hut 9/2203
The Knowles 6/2608
The Noads 12/3905
The Reptillary 6/2607
The Ridge 7/3107
The Weir 15/2801
Thompson's Castle 1/1813
Thorney Hill Holms 14/2000
Thorn Hill 7/3206
Three Beech Bottom 15/2999
Trenley Lawn 15/2801
Turf Croft 9/2005
Turf Hill 9/2102
Turf Hill 1/2017
Turf Hill Incl 1/2017

U

Upper Crockford Bottom 16/3499

V

Vales Moor 9/1904

Vereley Hill 9/1904
Vinney Ridge 10/2505
Vinney Ridge Incl 10/2605

W

Warwick Slade 6/2606
Warwickslade Bridge 6/2606
Warwickslade Cutting 10/2606
Watergreen Bottom 1/2012
Whitebridge Hill 7/3109
Whitefield Hill 14/1800
Whitefield Moor 10/2702
White Hill 5/1807
White Moor 6/2707
White Moor 7/3108
White Moor 7/3208
White Moor 15/2701
White Moor Bottom 9/2104
White Shoot 15/2600
White Shoot 6/2707
White Shoot Bottom 3/2213
Whitley Ridge Lodge 11/3102
Whitley Wood 10/2905
Whitten Bottom 14/2000
Whitten Pond 14/2001
Widden Bottom 15/2899
Wide Lawn 10/2805
Wilverley Incl 14/2401
Wilverley Plain 15/2501
Wilverley Post 10/2402
Wilverley Walks 15/2501
Winding Shoot 6/2406
Windmill Hill 1/1812
Withybed Bottom 6/2510
Withycombe Shade 8/3407
Wood Crates 6/2608
Woodfidley 11/3404
Woodford Bottom 5/1912
Woodgreen 1/1717
Woodside Bottom 2/2517
Woolfield Hill 6/2306
Woolmer Post 2/2117
Wooson's Hill 6/2507
Wooson's Hill Incl 6/2507
Wootton Bridge 15/2499
Wootton Coppice Incl 14/2499
Wormstall Hill 16/3699
Wormstall Wood 16/3498
Wort's Gutter 11/3502

Y

Yew Tree Bottom 15/2500
Yew Tree Heath 8/3606
Yewtree Hill 4/3010
Yolsham Hill 4/2912

Category	Type	Activity
Butterflies		Emergence
Snakes & Lizards		Emergence / Hibernation
Frogs & Toads		Emergence / Hibernation
Fungi		Bracket / Toadstool
Badger	Boar / Sow	Mating / Cubs born
Fox	Dog / Vixen	Mating / Cubs born
Foxhounds		Fox hunt
Beagles		Hare, buck & doe hunt
Buckhounds		Fallow buck hunt
Fallow Deer	Buck	Cull Antlers cast
Fallow Deer	Doe	Cull Fawns born
Roe Deer	Buck	Cull Antlers cast
Roe Deer	Doe	Cull Kids born
Sika & Red Deer	Stag	Cull Antlers cast
Sika & Red Deer	Hind	Cull Calves born

Most periods are approximate. Fishing and shooting on the first day of the month unless otherwise shown. Camping starts at end of March or Easter whichever is earlier. Verderers Court dates announced each year.